The Origin of the Jesuits

THE ORIGIN

of the

JESUITS

JAMES BRODRICK, S.J.

FOREWORD BY JOSEPH N. TYLENDA, S.J.

an imprint of
LOYOLA PRESS
Chicago

an imprint of

LOYOLA PRESS
3441 N. Ashland Ave.
Chicago, Illinois 60657

Cover Design: Shawn Biner

Library of Congress Cataloging-in-Publication Data
Brodrick, James, 1891–1973
    The origin of the Jesuits / James Brodrick.—[New paper ed.]
       p.   cm.
    Originally published: London : Longmans, Green, 1940.
    Includes bibliographical references and index.
    ISBN 0-8294-0930-0
    1. Jesuits—History—16th century. 2. Ignatius, of Loyola, Saint,
1491–1556.   I. Title.
BX3706.B7   1996
271' .53'09—dc20
[271' .53'009031]   96-31317
                                            CIP

1 2 3 4 5 / 01 00 99 98 97

CONTENTS

FOREWORD

The Origin of the Jesuits first appeared in 1940. Europe was then engulfed in war. Father James Brodrick, the author, had intended a work describing the role that the early generations of Jesuits played in the period we now call the Counter Reformation. But because of the circumstances of the time and the restrictions placed on a nation in wartime, only the first part could appear. The sequel, *The Progress of the Jesuits (1556–1579)*, did not follow until seven years later.

The present volume covers the life span of St. Ignatius of Loyola (1491–1554) and treats his background, conversion, studies in Paris, early companions, settling down in Rome, and the founding of the Society of Jesus. The reader meets the founder's companions and acquaintances and is introduced to the principal apostolic works that the Society undertook in those years. Father Brodrick also writes of the missionary endeavors of St. Francis Xavier, one of Ignatius' first associates, and describes Xavier's labors in two chapters, one dealing with his work in China and the other about his work in Japan. Nor is the Society's early commitment to education in Italy, Spain, and elsewhere forgotten. These pages, thus, serve as an introduction to the Society of Jesus and its members as well as to its works.

Father Brodrick's career as a writer was almost exclusively dedicated to writing Jesuit history. He was born in County Galway, Ireland, in 1891, and was educated in Dublin. He went to London with the hope of becoming a journalist, but instead he entered the English Province of the Society of Jesus in 1910. He earned his degree at the University of London in 1923, and two years later joined the staff of *The Month*, a Jesuit periodical published in London. He remained on the staff's roster for two years, but, on his own admission, he did not enjoy writing book reviews and articles on ephemeral topics.

His primary interest was the early history of the Society of Jesus, which he strove to make better known. With the exception of a few general biographies of its founder, there was nothing available to the English-reading public in those days on the Society's early endeavors. Thus Father Brodrick devoted his talents, time, study, and research to this end. The first work to come from his pen was his two-volume biography of the Jesuit Cardinal Robert Bellarmine (1542–1621) in 1928. He had been interested in the cardinal and his writings since his days as a theological student. In 1935 there followed his biography of St. Peter Canisius (1521–97). Both works were acclaimed as major achievements. Father Brodrick's success resides in the fact that his hagiographical writing is not merely adulation or hero worship. He certainly has his heroes, but unlike earlier hagiographers, he sees his subjects as human beings, who are dynamically alive. While recognizing their strengths, at the same time he acknowledges their weaknesses.

After the publication of *The Origin of the Jesuits*, war came to London itself, and Father Brodrick was asked to be Spiritual Father to the seminarians from Rome's Venerable English College, then housed at Stonyhurst in Lancashire. After peace returned to the country, the sequel to the present volume appeared in 1947. Immersed in the history of the Society's early years, Father Brodrick next wrote a biography of St. Francis Xavier (1506–52), published in 1952. He then turned to the Society's founder in *Saint Ignatius Loyola: The Pilgrim Years 1491–1538*, which appeared in 1956. This is a detailed study of Ignatius' life from his conversion to the year when he and his first companions arrived in Rome to offer their services to Pope Paul III. Father Brodrick did intend a second volume that would cover Ignatius' years as general of the Society, but circumstances, primarily health problems, prevented him from realizing his goal.

Father Brodrick's health was precarious since his first coronary, suffered in Chicago in 1948, while on an American tour. There was also the insistence of his publisher to revise and reduce his two volumes on Bellarmine into one. This revised version was published in 1961, and as an offshoot there came Father Brodrick's work on Galileo in 1964. In 1968 he suffered another heart attack and in the following year was transferred to a nursing home, where he died on August 26, 1973, at age eighty-two.

In writing his books Father Brodrick did not have fellow historians in mind but the educated general reader. His books, nevertheless, are fine history, for he brings original historical insights and judgments to bear on others' research, and his readers are fascinated by the author's native talent as a storyteller. Father Brodrick's footnotes are read with the same eagerness as the text, for it is in these that he permits his dry humor to express itself.

At his funeral in London, Father Brodrick's lifetime friend, Father Philip Caraman, referred to the present volume as "his most perfectly finished work. . . . I find it difficult to think of any other work of Catholic history in which so many brief and brilliant portraits are drawn with such perfect balance and precision."

This is the book you now hold in your hands. Do enjoy it.

Joseph N. Tylenda, S.J., Director
Woodstock Theological Center Library
Georgetown University, Washington, D.C.

PREFACE

This little book is only the first instalment of a much more extensive history of the Jesuits which the War and other contingencies have at least temporarily frustrated. It is published separately now because not even Bellona herself, that grim dame with bombs in her hair, would begrudge so tiny a tribute to the Society of Jesus on the attainment of its fourth centenary. Besides, some of the people in the book, especially St. Ignatius and St. Francis Xavier, are peculiarly fortifying company in times of danger. They here speak very largely in their own voices, sometimes even in their native tongues, as does Our Lord in the Gospels. If the book has any merit at all, it is in allowing them that rather unusual liberty. A strenuous effort was made to keep the spelling of names uniform, but, owing to the diversity of sources, that could not always be attained. At any rate, the reader will always recognize his man, which is the main thing. If the same reader shows any disposition to welcome further instalments of the story, progressively more exciting instalments, then in God's good time they will be gladly provided.

CHAPTER I

A GOOD SOLDIER OF JESUS CHRIST

THE early history of the Society of Jesus is very largely the history of two Basque gentlemen, Ignatius
Loyola and Francis Xavier. It was Xavier's good
fortune to labour far away from the contentions of
Europe, and to die young, so the world, Protestant and
Catholic alike, has agreed to overlook the fact of his
having been a Jesuit and to love him as a man. Loyola,
on the other hand, whose very name has come to sound
like a challenge, lived out his days and often a good part
of his nights at the G.H.Q. of the Catholic crusade for
the soul of Europe. In a sense, he personified the crusade,
and the other side, whose attempts at expansion he was
largely the means of thwarting, have never forgiven him.
Even now, a measure of cold respect, tempered with
polite suspicion, is all that he can look for in history books.
People who do not much believe in God have discovered
a new formula for him: they compare him to Lenin and
leave it at that. But it is only necessary to study the
many extant letters of Ignatius and Francis to see that in
the broad essentials of character they were wonderfully
alike, Basque to the bone, intense, practical, steadfast, un-
effusive, completely self-forgetful. Their passionate orthodoxy and their clear-cut vision of human life as a battle-
ground of God and the devil were inheritances from the

age-long struggle of Spain against the Moslems. Francis as much as Ignatius bears the stamp of his proud country and tumultuous age, and Ignatius as much as Francis is a star in the eternal where there are no countries and no ages. To find the poetry of saintliness in the one and only its cold prose in the other is to misread the evidence.

The background of the two men's lives was Spain of the last Moslem wars and the first great discoveries, Spain of Isabella, Columbus and Cortez. But in the fore-ground rode a Basque edition of the gaunt Knight of La Mancha. The grandfather of Ignatius might have served for a model of the immortal Don, so much did he make a habit of charging windmills and of challenging his peace-able neighbours. To cool these feudal ardours, the King of Castile demolished the old swashbuckler's stronghold of Oñaz and demilitarized the Castle of Loyola. At Loyola near Azpeitia in the province of Guipúzcoa, Ignatius was born, the last of thirteen children, including three who fell in the foreign wars of Spain. The year was most probably 1491. Of his youth very little is known, except that he learned the "Exercises of a Gentleman," and not much else, in the household of Queen Isabella's chief treasurer. To judge by a minute of the correctional court of Guipúzcoa before which he was cited in 1515 for brawling, he was the true grandson of the Quixote of Oñaz. He claimed benefit of clergy on the ground that he had received the tonsure, but the lay court appealed to two bulls of Alexander VI, *de gloriosa recordaçion*, in proof that his claim must be called and considered *nullum, cassum, irritum, subrecticium et obrecticium*. The bulls laid down that a cleric who, for four months before the commission of a crime, had not gone about in the dress and tonsure becoming to his state, thereby forfeited his privilege. Now this Enecus de Layolla had so offended, not for four months, but for many years, wearing, against all the regulations "long locks down to his shoulders, and parti-coloured hose and a coloured cap." Moreover, he was not registered as a cleric with the Vicar-General of Pamplona, and "usually appeared in public in a leather cuirass and breastplate, carrying sword, dagger, musket, and all other sorts and descriptions of weapons."[1] That is plainly the portrait of a gentleman looking for trouble. And he found it readily. Four years after his death, one of his spiritual sons pronounced his final vows at Salamanca. Suddenly, in the midst of the simple ceremony, the guest of honour, Salamanca's bishop, astonished all present by bursting into tears. Later, at the festive dinner, the good old man explained to the Fathers that he could not forbear to weep when he beheld their rector taking his vows in a religious order founded by a man whom he had seen with his own eyes charging, sword in hand, a gang of armed roughs in Pamplona. They had jostled him as they passed, whereupon his sword was out in a flash, and had somebody not seized him from behind and restrained him, concluded the bishop, "either he would have killed some of them or they would have killed him."[2] In an oral account of his life from the time of his conversion to the date, thirteen years later, when he founded his Society, Ignatius avowed by way of preface that up to the age of

[1] *Monumenta Historica Societatis Jesu. Monumenta Ignatiana, Scripta de Sancto Ignatio*, vol. I, pp. 588–92. The *Monumenta* which have now reached their sixty-fourth volume will be referred to henceforth by the initials, M.H.S.J.
[2] M.H.S.J., *Scripta de Sancto Ignatio*, vol. I, p. 566.

thirty[1] "he was a man given to the vanities of the world, whose chief delight consisted in martial exercises, with a great and vain desire to win renown."[2] Polanco, afterwards for many years his secretary and intimate friend, adds a more sombre detail to that laconic bulletin, namely that in his youth he had been "*satis liber in mulierum amore*." It was the bad way of his world, and he had, at any rate, the reputation of being a chivalrous and very generous foe who bore no malice against his enemies and always fought like a gentleman.[3]

Meantime, in a grim castle on the confines of Navarre, Francis Xavier had come into the world while priests retained by his parents chanted the Vespers for Good

---

[1] The age mentioned by the Saint was twenty-six but that seems to have been a mistake. Perhaps he thought that the year of his birth was 1495 rather than 1491, as did his closest associate, Polanco.

[2] It was only with the greatest difficulty and after years of earnest pleading that the Fathers of the Society of Jesus in Rome persuaded Ignatius in the last year or two of his life to relate the story of God's dealings with his soul. Even when begun, the story was interrupted constantly, sometimes for months on end, because Ignatius gladly seized any excuse to stop talking about himself. That we possess it at all is due to the almost heroic persistence of Father Luis Gonzales de Camara, a man of portentous memory who listened to the story and then, in spare moments, wrote it down or dictated it to amanuenses word for word. The original manuscript is in the Vatican Library. It is written in Spanish or Italian, according to the nationality of the amanuenses available to Father Gonzales. A transcription and an early Latin translation of it are given in the M.H.S.J., *Scripta de Sancto Ignatio*, Vol. I. A very good English version of the Latin text was made forty years ago by E. M. Rix and published under the title, *The Testament of Ignatius Loyola*. Most of the Spanish and Italian text is translated in Professor Paul van Dyke's sympathetic and scholarly biography of St. Ignatius, published in 1926. The Testament or Autobiography or Confessions, as we choose to call it, is written throughout in the third person. All quotations relative to St. Ignatius in the following pages for which no reference is given are from this source.

[3] M.H.S.J., Polanco, *Chronicon*, vol. I, pp. 10, 13.

Friday of the year 1506 in the family chapel. It was rumoured of him and also of Ignatius that at the time of their birth their respective mothers had retired to a stable out of devotion to the mystery of Bethlehem. But, to quote the dry comment of a modern writer, neither of them began his imitation of Christ as early as all that, and the stories are mere legend. The Xaviers were noble people of trifling political but tremendous personal importance. In spirit they exactly resembled the Loyolas. Juan Xavier, the favourite brother of Francis, would never attend a bull-fight, because, as he put it, "there a man learns the habit, not of attacking the foe nor even of waiting for him, but of dodging him altogether."[1] It was a great spirit, though it had only a very tiny stage at first for its deployment. Nowhere more markedly than in Navarre is to be found that "splendid smallness which is the soul of local patriotism." In 1478, the King of the country, desiring to recompense the father of Francis for services rendered, granted by royal patent "to him and his heirs for all time the civil jurisdiction of Ydocin which is situated in the valley of Ybargoiti, with all the homicides, demi-homicides, sixantenas, calonyas, and civil rights which obtain in the said district of Ydocin, . . together

[1] Cros, *Saint François de Xavier, sa vie et ses lettres*, Paris, 1900, vol. I, p. 54. Père Cros, S.J., the son of a notary and cradled among archives, pursued for twenty years what a friendly critic called *enquêtes acharnées* into the history of the Xavier family. He would have loved, if able, to trace St. Francis back to Noah's Ark. His prefaces are full of delightful grumbling against the obduracy of publishers who would not allow him space for all the bits and pieces which he had unearthed about the aunts and uncles and cousins of St. Francis. Unless we believe in a rigid determinism of the blood, we must side with the publishers. It was this same indefatigable Père Cros who collected the invaluable three volumes of documents entitled, *Histoire de Notre-Dame de Lourdes*.

with the right to create mayors, judges, bailiffs, and other officials in the said jurisdiction."[1] Very grand it reads, but the fact is that Ydocin was merely a Spanish Stoke Poges. Whatever else a man might cultivate in Navarre, he always grew a family tree. Pride of family and pride of orthodoxy went hand in hand. When some local genealogist twitted an uncle of Francis on his pretensions to nobility he answered with spirit that he came from two castles which were standing before Charlemagne's day, and that he belonged to two families which "thanks be to God were never in their existence tainted with heresy."[2]

To the disgust of their peasantry, but to Père Cros' great content, the Xaviers insisted very rigidly and proudly on their demi-homicides and other seignorial rights. A mere dispute about a tax for grazing sheep led to the following declaration in court by Juan de Jaso y Atondo, Francis's father, who was a doctor of laws of Bologna: "The House of Xavier is one of the most ancient and privileged of the Kingdom of Navarre. Its Lord enjoys sovereign seignorial rights, without being held to any duty of recognition or feudal homage to the King or Crown of Navarre, save only the obligation of making war or peace at his command. The House of Xavier has had at divers times Lords of great distinction, several of whom were governors of the Kingdom or in other eminent posts at the Court of the King."[3] Francis himself

[1] Cros, *Saint François de Xavier, son pays, sa famille, sa vie. Documents nouveaux*, 1ʳᵉ série, Toulouse, 1894, p. 50. Homicides were tributes paid by a locality for the privilege of shielding a murderer, and calonyas were fines for libel.

[2] Cros, *S.F.X., sa vie et ses lettres*, I, p. 20.

[3] Cros, *S.F.X., sa vie et ses lettres*, I, p. 54. "Quel bruit d'armures," remarks the French Academician, André Bellessort, in his charming sketch

first enters the pages of history with a rush, in the guise of a hot, indignant little boy chasing and helping to round up a flock of sheep which their crafty owner had tried to smuggle across the estate without paying toll. A time was to come when he would not stop rushing, and chasing another sort of sheep, right across the world, until he fell with his dying gaze upon China.

Navarre straddled the Pyrenees and had one foot in France, from which fair land it drew most of its princes. From 1234 to 1512 the country on both sides of the mountains was either united to the Crown of France or ruled independently, except for one Spanish king, by sovereigns of French extraction. This naturally did not please Ferdinand and Isabella who dreamed of a united Spain and only bided their opportunity to annex Navarre. It came in 1512 when Pope Julius II, the Emperor, the Venetian Republic and Henry VIII of England combined in what they were pleased to call the Holy League against France. Ferdinand then promptly sent his troops into Navarre and three years later formally joined the country to Spain, with the Duke of Najera for its first viceroy. This nobleman, one of the richest and most powerful grandees in Spain, was a friend of the Loyola family, so to his court at Pamplona Ignatius betook himself, bestriding a charger and in full martial array. It was his glorious hour, but the day of doom for the Xaviers who, unflinchingly loyal to the lost cause of Navarre, had their castle half pulled down about their heads and all their treasured seignorial rights abolished. The father of Francis

---

of St. Francis, "et quel froissement de parchemins à propos de brébis paissantes!" Bellessort's book, which appeared originally in the *Revue des Deux Mondes* in 1916, is easily the best popular account of St. Francis.

went into exile with his king but did not long survive his little country's disasters. However, Ferdinand died too, and that was Navarre's opportunity. While the new king, Charles, tarried in his native Flanders and the proud communes of Castille organized revolt, a French army streamed through the pass in the Pyrenees where Roland had blown the last undying notes on his horn. Among those who marched and sang that day were Juan and Miguel Xavier, the two brothers of Francis. Soon they were in Pamplona and had driven the small garrison of Spain there into the citadel. One soldier raged at the ignominy, remembering how a short while before it was he, Ignatius, the ever-undefeated, who had charged through the breach at Najera. And he had scorned the prizes of victory, for it was booty enough in his eyes to be a victor.[1] Now, at Pamplona, when the commandant and senior captains debated surrender, he cried out to them to remember their honour, that word of magic power for the chivalry of Spain. It was enough to rally them. No priest being available, Ignatius confessed his sins to one of his companions-in-arms in token of true repentance, and then made ready to die on the last redoubt with his honour untarnished. On May 20th, 1521, at the climax of the bijou battle which was yet one of the most decisive in the history of Christendom, a cannon ball, fired perhaps by Juan or Miguel Xavier, shattered his right leg that had been wont to step so proudly in its coloured hose. He was badly wounded in the left leg too, and with his fall all the heart went out of the forlorn little band in the citadel. When the French marched in they found him in his blood and honoured him as a gallant foe. After some surgery that was not the

[1] M.H.S.J., Polanco, *Chronicon*, vol. I, p. 13.

equal of their courtesy, they sent him home on a litter, the long *via dolorosa* to the castle of his ancestors.

The doctors summoned in haste by his brother shook their heads over him, and, no doubt, passed acid judgment on the handiwork of their French confrères. The leg must be reset, they declared, or the bones would never knit. Then began again what Ignatius, the least exaggerative of men, called "that butchery." More than thirty years later, when he had long shed the last vestiges of his hidalgo pride, he could not forbear to tell how "in all those operations which he suffered before and after this, he never spoke a word, nor showed any sign of pain except to clench his fists tightly." But his fortitude did not save him from physical collapse. He must rally, said the doctors, by midnight of June 28th, when St. Peter's feast-day began, or else surely die. Now, he had always felt a special devotion to St. Peter, perhaps because he recognized in him a brother soul, impetuous and quick to strike with the sword, "so it pleased God that by midnight he had taken a turn for the better." Soon he was out of danger but that only meant into greater pain. As the leg mended, it became obvious that the Spanish surgeons had bungled almost as badly as the French ones, for a piece of bone protruded below his knee and the damaged limb threatened to be shorter than its fellow, on which only a flesh wound had been inflicted. To a man proud of his appearance and bent on military glory, such disfigurements were more intolerable than any suffering. The doctors warned him that the treatment necessary to remedy them would involve prolonged and terrible pain, but he bade them proceed and endured his fresh "butchery" with the same silent, stoical courage as before.

The species of rack attached to his leg in order to
lengthen it obliged him to remain in bed, which bored
him unutterably. To relieve the tedium and to help him
forget the pain he asked for some tales of knight-errantry
wherein distressed and lovely ladies were rescued by
gallant gentlemen like himself with infinite daring. Sur-
prising to tell, that castle of Quixotes was bare of such
literature, and the invalid had to content himself with
lives of Our Lord and the Saints, mere women's reading.
As he idly turned the pages of the big, uncouth volumes,
his mind used to wander for hours at a time, building
much finer castles than the one he lay in. He imagined
himself the squire of a great lady, and planned the sallies
of wit, the gallant speeches he would make to her and the
yet more gallant deeds that he would do in her service.
He was as sentimental as any Orlando. However, he
began in time to take a certain speculative interest in the
stories of the saints. He thought, talking with himself:
"How would it be if I did this thing that St. Francis did,
or what St. Dominic did?" Already, the ambition of his
generous heart, its delight in difficult and heroic feats, was
moving on to a higher plane, though for a while longer
his Dulcinea would by no means capitulate to St. Francis
or St. Dominic. Remembrance of her and sweet plotting
for the favour of her eyes alternated in his mind with
grim projects of fasting and faring barefooted to Jerusalem.
Only he began to notice a curious difference in the way
those competing day-dreams affected him. While the
image of his Dulcinea was present to him it made him
happy, but when through weariness or pain it receded, he
felt himself dry and discontented, like a man who after
a glorious sunset finds the sky grey and a chill in his

bones. On the other hand, musings about the saints and plans to emulate their austerities rendered him contented and joyful, not only while he dwelt upon such thoughts, but afterwards, when weariness had eclipsed them. The uniformity of the experience gradually arrested his attention and made him seek for its cause, which little by little, and not quite clearly until a later stage in his pilgrim's progress,[1] he discerned to be the working of God or the devil in his soul. "This," he said, "was his first reasoning about the things of God." The facts, as simple as the fall of an apple, led eventually to a theory of history on its own level no less far-reaching and profound in consequences than the law of gravitation. Two flags unfurled before his eyes, the flag of God and the flag of the enemy of God, planted in every soul, waving over the nations, disputing and deciding all human destinies. Whatever in other times people may have thought of this conception, they will not be disposed to question its stark symbolic appropriateness in 1940.

His reading of the saints and a vision which he had one night of Our Lady and the Holy Child filled Ignatius with loathing of his past life and its carnal indulgences. Soon his thoughts of penance turned to resolutions, and he made up his mind to go to Jerusalem in the true spirit of a pilgrim, which from then on he accounted himself. When able to move about the house again, he set himself with great diligence to copying into a large, lined note-book excerpts from the lives of Our Lord and the saints which

[1] There is a remarkable parallelism between the early religious development of Ignatius and of John Bunyan, though, as has been pointed out, had they met, they would have shrunk from one another in horror, unconscious of their deep kinship.

had done his soul such service, "putting the words of Christ in red ink and those of Our Lady in blue." He was proud of his beautiful handwriting, and carried with him wherever he went that treasured note-book, three hundred quarto pages in size. Much of his time he spent in prayer, "and the greatest consolation he had was in looking at the heavens and the stars, which he did very often for a long time, because when so engaged he felt in himself a very great power to serve Our Lord."[1]

That last conviction of God's raw recruit shows him full of goodwill but still very remote from any true understanding of Christian holiness. Before he attained to it, he had a pilgrimage to make far longer and more full of heart-break than the journey to the earthly Jerusalem. "It seemed to him then," he told the Fathers in Rome the year before his death, "that holiness was entirely measured by exterior austerity of life and that he who did the most severe penances would be held in the divine estimation for the most holy, which idea made him determine to lead a very harsh life."[2] Of any interior virtue, he said, of humility, of charity, of patience, of discretion, he knew nothing, "but all his purpose was to do those great outward works because the saints had done them for the glory of God." He was still Ignatius the *caballero*, dreaming of renown, even if he now sought it in a nobler form than the smiles of fair ladies.

His brother, who greatly desired him to resume his promising military career after convalescence and so to

[1] Like the Psalmist, Dante, Kant, Gladstone, and other great men, Ignatius was an inveterate star-gazer. "How mean earth seems when I look up to the heavens!" is one of his exclamations.
[2] M.H.S.J., *Scripta de Sancto Ignatio*, vol. I, p. 101.

bring glory to Loyola, was much perturbed by the change in his conduct. It was not like him to be so long on his knees or to talk so much about God, and some violent break with the past appeared imminent. Ignatius himself contemplated joining the Carthusians in Seville as a lay-brother after his return from Jerusalem, allured to the life, it seems, by the strange bait that "he could there live on herbs and nothing else." His brother's persuasions he put aside very gently and without detriment to the truth, which "even then was one of his strongest principles," by saying that he was going to Najera to rejoin the Viceroy of Navarre. This he did, and, as only a slight limp was left to remind him of Pamplona, he might have been a dashing cavalier again in a little time, because the Duke offered him a handsome commission. But his face was set steadfastly towards Jerusalem. With some arrears of his soldier's pay which he collected, he settled a few debts, restored and adorned a neglected shrine of the Blessed Virgin and rode off alone on a mule to the famous sanc-tuary of Montserrat in Catalonia, "still blind, but all on fire with longing to serve God to the best of his know-ledge." How poor that best was became apparent in his encounter with a Moor, a civil and companionable man, who, having the topic forced on him, professed a willing-ness to believe that Our Lady was a virgin before Our Lord's birth, but not afterwards. For a Moslem it was no mean concession to admit half of the Catholic truth, but Ignatius chose to imagine that Our Lady had been insulted and perhaps also felt a need to vindicate his own honour after failing to convince a mere Moor in argument. Long and earnestly he debated with himself whether he had not a duty to kill the unsuspecting infidel who had ridden on ahead to a certain town beyond a fork in the road. "Wearied with debate and unable to come to any conclusion, he decided to give the mule her head and if, when they came to the parting of the ways, the beast turned towards the place where the Saracen was, then he would seek him out and stab him; if she kept to the highway, he would let him be." The mule, a near relative of Balaam's ass, kept to the highway.

At the first big village on his route, Ignatius, dreaming always of "the great things he meant to do for the love of God," bought a piece of cloth such as was used for making sacks, "which is very prickly," and had a garment tailored for himself reaching down to his feet. He also bought a pilgrim's staff or *bordon*, a calabash for holding water, and hempen sandals, of which he retained only one for his bad leg that was still bandaged and swollen. Arrived at Montserrat, he made a general confession of his sins in such detail that it took three days to write down. Then he hung his sword and dagger, the emblems of his abandoned dreams, beside the Lady-statue in the church of Montserrat, and surely Mary, the Mother of pity and understanding, smiled as her Quixote deposited the weapon lately intended for a perfectly innocent Mussulman. With great secrecy he bestowed all his fine raiment, blue mantle, yellow hose, and gaily coloured cap, on an astonished tramp, and, clothed in the sackcloth, went to spend the entire night of March 24th, 1522, in vigil before Our Lady's altar. That inspiration had come from Amadis de Gaul and other manuals of chivalry, but Ignatius meant desperately well by God, for all that he still knew so little of His ways. To avoid any danger of recognition, he set out at daybreak for Barcelona and his ship by a circuitous route which took him through "a town called Manresa." Little did he guess that his detour would fill the whole world with Manresas, or that there he would be recognized down to the last concealment of his subtle and complicated pride by no less a person than Ignatius Loyola.

He had not intended to delay more than a few days in the town, "to write down a few matters in his book, which he had brought with him carefully and much to his consolation." But the new Pope, Adrian VI, from whom permission for the pilgrimage had to be obtained, delayed his entrance into Rome, and afterwards the plague descended on Barcelona, so the few days grew into ten months, grew for significance into an eternity. He who was to gain the title of "the world's novice-master" was himself now to be a novice, to be treated by God, as he expressed it, "like a boy at school." It is fascinating to watch the process of his education, which God carried out by a curriculum of trial and error as hazardous and heart-breaking as any Desert Father ever became involved in. He lived by turns in a hospice for the poor and in a cell put at his disposal by the kindly Dominican Fathers. Daily, like any vagrant, he, the proudest of the proud, begged his bread in the streets. He ate no meat at all, but on Sundays, observing a tiny ritual in his austerities, would drink a little wine if anybody gave it to him. From the time of his convalescence he had been wont to scourge himself once a day; now he scourged himself mercilessly three times a day. "As he had been somewhat nice about the arrangement of his hair,[1] as was the fashion of those

---

[1] A fellow-Spaniard, Pedro Ribadeneira, who knew Ignatius intimately, says that his hair was of "a reddish tint and very beautiful." He did not have much of it in his later years.

days and became him not ill, he decided that he would allow it to grow naturally, and neither combed it nor trimmed it nor wore any head-covering by day or night. For the same reason he did not pare his finger- or toe-nails, because in his care of them he had been extremely fastidious." Daily he was present at the High Mass and at Vespers and Compline in the Dominican church, and during Mass "it was his custom to read the story of the Passion, always possessing his soul in tranquillity."

But the tranquillity did not last, though he spent seven hours a day in faithful prayer and at midnight always broke his scanty sleep for the same purpose. A great deal of his time was passed communing with God in a cave of the hills outside Manresa which became his Sinai, his Valley of Achor, his Gethsemane. There he went through the dread, mysterious Dark Night of the Soul known to the great mystics, and there too he was caught up into Paradise and heard secret words which it is not granted to man to utter.

Utterance was never one of Ignatius's strong points. Basques are famous for their taciturnity and when they speak they do so right on, as plain, blunt men, unaddicted to rhetoric. Azpeitia and Avila might have been in different hemispheres for any resemblance in power of self-expression between Ignatius and Teresa, though as mystics they were brother and sister. Using music as an illustration we might say that Teresa was a master composer, developing her themes and conveying by sheer genius all the rich harmonies of her experience. The most that Ignatius could do, or indeed wanted to do, was to hum the bare melody of his. "One day," he says, "while he knelt on the steps of the monastery reciting the Hours of the Blessed Virgin, the eyes of his mind were opened and he saw the Most Holy Trinity as it were under the likeness of a triple plectrum or of three keys on an organ." No doubt whatever, that is what he did see, but would such a simple vision have caused him to weep uncontrollably out of sheer joy for the rest of the day, or have left so profound an impression that throughout his subsequent life "he was filled with warm devotion whenever he prayed to the Most Holy Trinity," unless it had been accompanied by a marvellous divine illumination of which he says nothing? It is the same with his visions of Our Lord's Humanity, of Our Lady, of how the world was created, of the manner in which Our Lord is present in the Blessed Sacrament. So vivid and penetrating was his apprehension of these mysteries of faith that he said "even if Scripture had not taught them, he would have been resolved to die for them after what he himself had seen," and that was all he could tell. Put beside St. John of the Cross or St. Teresa or Mother Mary of the Incarnation, he seems at first sight like a sparrow among nightingales, but deeper understanding reveals him as belonging absolutely to their company.

There is a charming naiveté in his account of his education. "He began," he says, "to experience great changes in his soul; sometimes he was destitute of all taste for spiritual things, and found no sweetness in saying prayers, nor in hearing Mass, nor in the practice of any other devotion; sometimes, on the contrary, the very opposite feelings would arise within him, and that so suddenly that all heaviness and sorrow were taken away, like as when one snatches a cloak from a man's shoulders. When he became aware of these changes hitherto unknown, he grew astonished and said within himself, 'What new kind of life is this on which we are entering?'" Among the vicissitudes was an attack of scruples caused by his newly awakened but still uninstructed conscience. It brought him to the very brink of despair, so much so that he felt violently tempted to end the misery by jumping out of a window. For months the agony persisted in spite of the remedies recommended to him by priests whom he consulted. "Greatly distressed, he gave himself to prayer, and as he prayed his heart became hot within him until he broke out and cried with a loud voice to God, saying: 'Make haste to help me, Lord, for there is no help in man, neither in any creature do I find relief! Ah, if I knew where I might find it, no labour would seem great nor hard. Lord show me where it is hid. As for me, had I to go after a dog's whelp and take my cure from him, I would do it.'" Overwhelming indeed must have been the anguish that wrung such a cry from Ignatius who had borne the butchery of his leg without a moan.

So the stern education went on. Daily the pupil learned to know better the real Ignatius, long masked from him by the tawdry shibboleths of Spanish knight-errantry, and daily he learned to see more clearly Jesus Christ, long hidden in the mists of conventional devotion. A holy old lady of the town said to him on one occasion: "Oh, would that my Lord Jesus Christ might appear to thee some day!" Taking the words literally, he was shocked, and answered, exactly in the vein of his friend, St. Peter: "How could Christ appear to me?" Christ did indeed appear to him, appeared to his mind and heart, and awakened in him a passion of personal love and loyalty that may be measured only by the burning paradoxes of St. Paul. Our Lord's sufferings were his constant meditation and from them he learned the unimportance of everything, long hair, long nails, long fasts, long prayers even, compared with the long love that bears out the will of God even to the edge of doom. More and more, his meditations kindled in him a great eagerness to bring others to the knowledge and love of Christ. In his soul Martha and Mary kissed, for, while remaining all his life a profound contemplative, he became also a most ardent apostle. Indeed, the apostleship had begun at Loyola as soon as he was out of bed, and he continued it, in the spirit of the Sons of Thunder, on the road to Montserrat. In Manresa, his zeal, kindled to a bright, illuminating flame by the Gospels, led to the first big surrender of his own spiritual notions. "Seeing," he says, "the fruit reaped from helping other souls, he ceased from this time from the extreme severities which he had been wont to practise, and also he began to cut his nails and his hair." Thus were means and ends steadily falling into their right relation. Ignatius became spiritually by one impulsion of grace after another the most tidy-minded of saints. He had always been neat in his dress and habits; now he acquired a splendid supernatural neatness, an instinct for decorum in God's business, the fruit of that Divine Wisdom which ordereth all things sweetly. His dialectic of the matter is charming in its simplicity. "When it was time for him to go to bed," he told his blessedly persistent Roman sons, "often great spiritual consolation came to him and intimations of divine things which made him lose a large part of the time destined for sleep—and that was not much. Considering this, he reflected that he was giving all the rest of the day, besides the fixed

19

hours set aside, to communion with God. And so he came to doubt whether these enlightenments were really from the Good Spirit, and arrived at the conclusion that it was better to ignore them and sleep the hours allotted to sleep. And so he did." By similar tactics he won his long battle with the demon of scruples, and even took to eating meat again in spite of the hint of his confessor that the impulse to do so might be a temptation.

It is now an established historical fact that Ignatius at Manresa sketched out roughly the main lines of his famous little book, the *Spiritual Exercises*, which, unemotional almost as a treatise of geometry, has yet set so many loving hearts on fire and filled the history of the Church with heroes. During the years between Manresa and the final redaction of the book in Rome about 1540, Ignatius constantly retouched and added to his notes as he himself progressed in his knowledge of God and his understanding of human nature. The originality of the *Exercises* lies in the fact that, though completely traditional in its ascetical teaching and based to some extent on the work of other spiritual writers, the book is not so much a book as the condensed, the suffered experience of a most noble heart that had wrestled with God and won emancipation at tremendous cost. Could we get behind the letter to the history of its many rules and annotations and additions, all to appearance so like the dreary paraphernalia of a Latin grammar, we would see how each of them is, as it were, the survivor of a grim battlefield, a war-worn veteran, stiff-jointed indeed, but wise beyond the fashion of many more graceful counsellors.

One thing more must be added. The "sublime vagabond" who limped into Manresa from Montserrat could never of his own unaided powers have achieved the little divinely simple masterpiece. It is a manual, and the best ever written, of Christian prudence, whereas he had in the beginning no prudence; it concentrates, codifies, systematizes the entire ascetical tradition of Christianity with a marvellous taut energy and utter *kenosis* of literary embellishment, whereas he was ever one for the appearances, a deviser of high-flown gallantries, who had to have his leg blown to bits in order to discover that there existed such a thing as Christian asceticism. That such a one who hardly knew the alphabet of Christian humility, who thought a dagger might be a theological argument pleasing to God, who found his highest inspirations in the rubbish of Amadis de Gaul, should in ten short months have become one of the supreme masters of the spiritual life is not explicable except by the clue which he himself provides. Once, on his way to a little chapel a short distance from Manresa, he sat down near a wayside crucifix, facing the swiftly flowing Cordoner, a tributary of the River Llobregat. Thus sitting and praying his mind was suddenly, in an instant, illuminated with so deep an understanding of spiritual things that not all he learned in after years, to the end of his life, seemed to him its equivalent. "By it his understanding was as much enlightened as if he had been made another man and another mind had been given to him." Another mind indeed, the "mind which was also in Christ Jesus."

The central aim and purpose of the *Spiritual Exercises* is to bring the mind and heart of the person who makes a retreat into ever closer conformity with the mind and heart of Christ, so that out of love of Christ and a desire to be more like Him, he may learn to prefer and embrace

21

poverty with Jesus Christ poor, rather than riches; shame and insults with Jesus Christ reproached and insulted, rather than honours; the reputation of a fool with Jesus Christ mocked and scorned, rather than a great name for wisdom among men.[1] It is a terrifying programme to flesh and blood, but no more than an explication, an inexorably logical unfolding of Our Lord's own words: "If any man will come after Me and be My disciple, let him deny himself and take up his cross daily and follow Me." Let him deny himself, that is the insistent, ever-recurring theme of the *Exercises*, for, vigorous realist that he was, Ignatius saw in self-conquest and self-denial the indispensable preconditions of an active, enduring love of Our Lord. The detachment which he so mercilessly harps on is entirely for the sake of that grand attachment. From beginning to end Christ presides over the *Exercises*. The first page of the book bears the *Anima Christi*, and the spirit of that prayer, which is the formulated sigh of the loving Christian heart to Christ, permeates all the meditations and considerations that follow. The first "week" of the four into which the book is divided, is preliminary, a clearing of the ground, a digging up of old roots and weeds for the sowing that is to be done later, yet the first meditation of that "week" ends with the following colloquy between the soul and Christ: "Representing to myself Our Lord Jesus Christ on His cross before me, I shall ask Him how, being Creator of all things, He could stoop so low as to become a man; how, possessing eternal life, He could deign to accept a temporal death and to undergo it in very truth for my sins. Then,

---

[1] This disposition St. Ignatius calls the "Third Degree of Humility." It is the culminating point of the *Spiritual Exercises*.

turning to myself, I shall inquire what I have so far done for Jesus Christ, what I am now doing for Jesus Christ, what I ought to do for Jesus Christ." Similarly the meditations on the solemn themes of Hell, Judgment, Death, bring the chastened soul through its valley of troubling, to Christ, its door of hope. After the first "week" and its drive for repentance, Christ becomes the entire content of the *Exercises*, for the subsequent three "weeks" are devoted almost exclusively to meditations and contemplations on every aspect of His earthly life in its lowliness, its labours, its sufferings, its glory. Ignatius, to adapt a famous phrase, was a "Christ-intoxicated" man.[1]

His austerities, chosen deprivations and long hours of prayer brought Ignatius twice to the gates of death at

[1] About the so-called "Ignatian method" of prayer there is this to be said, that the Saint proposed, not one method, but at least five, all of them means rather than ends, and in substance merely an application to supernatural truths of ordinary human habits of thinking. There is nothing in the least mysterious or recondite in the methods, nothing even original. Like the famous character who was astonished to learn that he had been speaking prose all his life without knowing it, people who never heard of St. Ignatius make meditations according to his "method" every time they apply their minds seriously to reflect on the past or to plan for the future. Remembering his various Sions, his old school, his childhood's home, his favourite holiday haunt, a man spontaneously makes a "composition of place," applies the powers of his soul to consideration of persons, places and things, and very often finds himself communing in spirit with some old friend of long ago. In his delightful book, *Don Fernando*, Somerset Maugham tells an amusing story of how he first made the acquaintance of St. Ignatius, and of the dire consequences of his valiant effort to make an hour's meditation in the Ignatian manner. But he missed the whole point of the matter by mistaking the meditation for an academic exercise, possible even to unbelievers like himself. It was like trying to play the flute, not by ear or by note, but by sheer force, and naturally the effort produced a headache instead of music.

Manresa. Gladly would he have passed through those gates, for the *cupio dissolvi et esse cum Christo* of St. Paul became so much the mood of his soul that in after years he dared not think of death at all because the prospect of it invariably threw him into an ecstasy. Frail and exhausted from his second grave illness, with his stomach permanently weakened, he yet held to his resolution of labouring for Christ his master on the sacred ground where Christ had laboured for him. Towards the end of February, 1523, he parted for Barcelona, lived there a few weeks as a mendicant, at last found a kindly ship's captain to take him for nothing, landed in plague-stricken Italy, made his way through many tribulations to Rome, obtained the Pope's blessing, walked half the length of Italy to Venice, faced the Doge in his grand palace, and obtained a free passage on a government ship to Cyprus. By then he had been two months on his travels, two months of almost fantastic hardships. When he was about to embark at Barcelona, he found himself in possession of five or six silver pieces which he had begged in the city. Desiring "to place all his trust and hope and affection in God alone, . . . he left them on a bench close by the landing-stage." In Rome, people persuaded him that he could not possibly hope to reach Palestine without some funds, so·out of fear of not being able to proceed he accepted six or seven gold coins to pay his passage. "By the time that he was three days' journey from Rome, he recognized that this fear had sprung from distrust, and was grieved to the heart that he had taken the moneys. . . . He resolved to bestow them liberally on all whom he should meet, and by so doing only as many farthings remained to him when he reached Venice as would pay for a night's lodging." On the journey he had no lodging, but was obliged to sleep out of doors under hedges or sheds because the prevalence of the plague had chilled the hospitable instincts of the Italian villagers. In Venice, he begged his bread as usual, and at night lay down under the stars in the Piazza of St. Mark's. This went on for another two months, and when at last the ship stood ready to sail, he was so wasted by fever that a doctor told him cheerfully to go on board by all means, if he wanted to be buried at sea. "He nevertheless embarked and set off that day, and was so sea-sick that he began to feel easier and altogether to recover his strength." From Cyprus the voyage was made in a special pilgrim's galley, built by the looks of it as an instrument of penance, which, he says he "boarded with the same provision as before, his hope in God." At last, six months after leaving Barcelona, he beheld with a thrill of "more than mortal joy" the goal of his desire, Jerusalem. There he had planned to remain for the rest of his days, haunting the Holy Places and striving might and main to make his Divine Master better known and loved in His native land. It was an ingenuous dream, which the guardians of the Holy Places, the Franciscans, with their long and grim experience of Turkish rule, could not possibly have countenanced. For a fortnight Ignatius was ideally happy, following with loving eagerness the footsteps of Jesus. Then he received a polite but very firm dismissal, to which he bowed with infinite reluctance, indeed only under a gently insinuated threat of excommunication. On the day before his departure "an overpowering longing possessed him to ascend the Mount of Olives once again." He slipped away alone, prudence forgotten, everything forgotten, except that he must venerate for the last time "the stone from which Our Lord went up into Heaven . . . wherein His footprints may yet be discerned." Turkish guards barred his way but he bribed them with a treasured penknife. "Having made his prayer and been comforted, he conceived the desire of going to Bethphage, where it occurred to him that he had not sufficiently noted on Mount Olivet the precise position of the right foot and the left." Back again he went, this time parting with his scissors to the guards for the consolation of making sure which way Our Lord faced when He ascended into Heaven. Somehow one feels that few evidences of love could be greater than that little anxiety of Ignatius.[1]

Belated crusader, his voyage home, which took over a hundred days, was almost as full of alarms and excursions as the return of the medieval warriors. At Cyprus his fellow-travellers spoke warmly in praise of him to the captain of "a very magnificent and powerful ship," but when this proud person learned that he had no money he refused him a berth, saying scornfully: "Let him get across as Blessed James did, if he is so holy a man." However, he was readily given a free passage on a little ship which landed him safely on the coast of Apulia after battling through a storm that sent the very magnificent and powerful ship to the bottom of the sea. "It was

[1] The stone on Olivet with the imprints of feet, much blurred by the kisses of generations of pilgrims, is still to be seen. Guides tend to be facetious about the imprints, but, as the present writer made bold to point out to one of them, we ought to reverence the reverence of other people, even if we cannot accept the genuineness of the object that inspires it. In any case, such objects acquire, like photographs, a representative authenticity. A Jesuit could hardly forbear to weep at the sight of the stone and its half obliterated footprints, remembering his Father.

winter, and exceeding cold, with snow falling, and the pilgrim was clothed only in breeches of a coarse material down to his knees, his legs being quite bare. He had an open doublet of rough cloth, torn to rags at the shoulders, and a threadbare coat." In Venice, a kindly man gave him fifteen or sixteen gold pieces and a length of cloth, "which he folded and placed on his stomach as a defence against the cold." Then was taken one of the most fateful resolutions of his life. "It seemed best and grew more clear to him that he should spend some time in study as a means of helping him to work for souls." To work for souls, to suffer for them, to die, if need be, that they might learn to love his Master, such was now the pinnacle of his ambition. On the journey home to carry it out, he gave away all his gold pieces, was twice arrested as a spy, and barely escaped capture by the French while crossing the sea to Spain. Manresa drew him like a magnet, but the holy Cistercian of the town whom he hoped might be his tutor had died, so Barcelona claimed him. There, aged thirty-one, he went to school for two years, taking his place on the bench with children, and trying, at first less successfully than they, to memorize Latin declensions and paradigms. It was a new sight in history for the angels. Out of school hours, he begged his bread as before, only bread, for he subsisted on bread and water. Did anyone give him richer fare, he took it joyfully to his daily rendezvous with the hungry vagrants of Barcelona. By night he used to seek out poor people who were ashamed to ask for help and press on them sweetly and humbly the coins he had collected in the streets.

In 1526, Ignatius carried his small, laboriously acquired stock of Latin to Alcalá to trade with it in the open markets of scholasticism. He was getting on, turned thirty-four, so he must hurry with his education, which he innocently imagined could best be done by taking all knowledge for his province at one swoop. The lectures in Cardinal Ximenes' great new university were free, so, unattached and unadvised, he roamed from one hall to another, attending courses on dialectics, Aristotelian physics and Peter Lombard's theology, all at the same time. Apart from his heterogeneous studies, he employed himself, he says, "in giving the Spiritual Exercises and instructions on Christian doctrine." In Paris just then, Francis Xavier was also entering the labyrinths of scholasticism, but more methodically and without the slightest intention of giving anybody instructions on Christian doctrine. Whatever shape his young dreams may have been taking, they certainly bore no resemblance to those that agitated the heart of Ignatius. The will o' the wisp which Ignatius calls "the credit of a great name upon earth" would seem by many tokens to have been the chief light on the morning horizon of Francis. Poor but debonair, he held his head high, remembering his castles in Spain, and let the streets of Paris know that he was a hidalgo. The streets of Alcalá witnessed a different sight, a man of aristocratic mien in a shabby grey pilgrim's robe limping along very contented with a great bundle on his back containing "bed-hangings of various colours, some candle-sticks, and other things of the kind," all the fruits of his begging "wherewith he might provide for some people in want." Or again he is being followed down the street by a man of wealth and position who thinks that the non-descript student bears an extraordinary resemblance to the long-vanished cadet of Castle Loyola. He disappears into a miserable little hovel, soon re-emerges, and limps away. His watcher enters the mean house too, and finds its occupant to be a poor widow from whom he eagerly inquires the name of her recent visitor. "I do not know who he is nor from where he comes," she answered, "but only that each day he brings me an alms."[1]

Three men whom he had known in Barcelona, even less learned than himself but of the same devout, apostolic mind, joined Ignatius in Alcalá, adopted his pilgrim's dress, and assisted him in his labours to help souls. At the hospital where he lodged Ignatius was often to be seen in the midst of a group of ten or twelve persons, mostly women, whom he taught how to examine their consciences and to make a meditation. Such activities, carried on by men who were not priests, quickly roused the suspicions of the vigilant Spanish inquisitors. The Protestant movement, then in the enthusiasm of its youth, was full of missionary ardour, cleverly organized, and bent on capturing the European seats of learning. Besides this menace, Spain had its own indigenous brands of heresy to be afraid of, types of Judaic Christianity, Moslem perversions of the faith, illuminism and other queer, persistent cults. What if Ignatius and his three grey-robed disciples were the vanguard of a new assault on Spain's Catholicism? Inquisitors from Toledo arrived to hold an elaborate inquiry into the activities of the four men,[2] but could find nothing whatever to censure except the uniform colour of their garments. Ignatius willingly dyed his robe black and also, according to orders, ceased

[1] M.H.S.J., *Scripta de Sancto Ignatio*, vol. II, p. 193.

[2] The minutes of the investigation occupy twenty-six pages as reproduced in the *Scripta de Sancto Ignatio*, vol. I, pp. 598–624.

going about barefooted, but thereby his troubles were not
ended. On April 21st, 1526, he was thrown into prison
and kept in durance for six weeks until the authorities,
at their leisure, discovered him to be perfectly innocent
of the silly charge alleged against him. It was a mild form
of captivity, very similar to that of St. Paul in Rome.
For Ignatius too the Word of God was not bound, and
he was able, he says "to teach the Christian religion and
give the Exercises, as well as if he had been free." One
of the many visitors to the fascinating prisoner was a
distinguished professor of the university who became so
absorbed by his conversation that he arrived back late
for his lecture. As an apology to his pupils he said with
emotion: *Vidi Paulum in vinculis.*

This time, though pronounced innocent of any fault
whatever, Ignatius was forbidden under pain of excommunication and banishment from the Kingdom to wear
other than ordinary scholar's attire, or to teach at all,
whether in public or private, for the space of three years.[1]
No sentence could have borne more heavily on him, for
by it he saw, in his own words, "the way barred to
helping souls." Hoping for better fortune elsewhere, he
migrated with his companions to Salamanca.

Salamanca, grandest of the Spanish universities, offered
him a chilly welcome. Less than a fortnight after their
arrival, he and his faithful disciple Calisto were prisoners
again, without reason assigned, "in a little cell very
dirty with age and long disuse." This time the careful
ministers of the Inquisition had them bound foot to foot
by a short chain fastened to a stake in the middle of the
cell, and, like Paul and Silas at Philippi, they lay awake

[1] M.H.S.J., *Scripta de Sancto Ignatio*, vol. I, pp. 621-2.

the whole night, hot and hungry, praising God. Tedious examinations followed, that of Ignatius by four judges who had all previously scrutinized his manuscript of the *Spiritual Exercises*. Good but wooden men, it occurs to one that they badly needed instruction in the "discernment of spirits" as set forth in the book of which they were so suspicious. In recollecting one point of the interrogation, Ignatius must have smiled as he described to Father Gonzales how he had answered: "Told to give his usual explanation of the first commandment of the Decalogue, he had, once launched, so many things to say, and was so long in saying them, that he made them loth to ask him anything else." Against the *Exercises* the only objection they could find was that he, a man untrained in theology, had there ventured to show how mortal and venial sins are to be distinguished. They did not question his doctrine, but his credentials, which was perhaps narrow minded of them, though reasonable enough, considering the dangers of the time.

Visitors had free access to the prison, and these, between the interrogations, Ignatius continued to advise and instruct with his usual holy alacrity. One sympathetic visitor, the future Cardinal Archbishop of Burgos, asked him in a kindly way whether he was suffering from his imprisonment. "I give you my word," he replied, "that there are not so many fetters, handcuffs and chains in Salamanca, but I should wish to wear still more for the love of God." Very much as happened to Paul and Silas, one morning the doors of the prison were found wide open and all the convicts gone, except the four victims of the Inquisition. Pauline too was the reaction of Ignatius when, after three weeks in chains, he learned that he and

his companions might continue teaching Christian doctrine
and talking with others on sacred subjects as they had
always done, on the strict condition of leaving the difference between mortal and venial sins to theologians until
they had studied for four more years. "The pilgrim's
answer was that he would do exactly those things mentioned in his sentence, but could not acknowledge its
fairness, since they had closed his mouth which had
spoken no evil, and so prevented him from giving as much
help as he might to his neighbour. Doctor Frias might
enlarge to his heart's content on the kindly affection he
bore him, yet not for that would the pilgrim be drawn
on to say more than that he would obey orders as long
as he remained in the diocese of Salamanca."

Not for Doctor Frias nor for all the doctors of Salamanca
put together would Ignatius abandon his project "of
helping souls and of directing his studies to that end."
Rather would he abandon their city and seek in Paris
the small liberty of doing good which they denied him.
All his friends cried out against the project, bidding him
remember "the great and fearful wars" then raging in
France, and recounting stories of atrocities, such as im-
paling, which had been perpetrated on captured Spaniards.
It was waste of breath, for "no sort of fear of these
things could gain possession of his soul." A few weeks
after being released from prison he set out alone on foot,
driving before him a little donkey with his few books on
its back. By Segovia, Siguenza, Saragossa and Lerida he
pursued his way to Barcelona where he comforted his
staunchest friend, Iñes Pascual, a shopkeeper like St. Paul's
Lydia, and then passed on amid the tears of those who
loved him into the unknown. Ten years ago two English-

men emulated the walking exploit of Ignatius in the reverse direction, and wrote a large and interesting book about their experiences entitled, *Journey into Spain*. The most that Ignatius chose to reveal of his ups and downs on his winter journey, a penniless enemy alien traversing a country at war, is contained in the following lines of a letter to Iñes Pascual: "By the grace and goodness of God Our Lord, in favourable weather and safe and sound, I arrived in this city of Paris on February 2nd, resolved to study there until such time as the Lord shall otherwise ordain."[1] It is the sublimity of reticence, but tells one secret clearly, that to know and do the will of God was now the only interest of Ignatius.

[1] M.H.S.J., *Epistolæ et instructiones*, vol. I, p. 74. There are twelve volumes in this sub-series of the *Monumenta*, containing the letters and instructions of Ignatius from 1536 to the time of his death.

CHAPTER II

BRETHREN BY THE NAME OF
OUR LORD

T HE college of the University to which Ignatius attached himself on arrival in Paris in February 1528 was Montaigu, from which Spartan establishment John Calvin had shortly before retired. By all accounts it was a place of terror, even if we take with a grain of salt the lurid description of the regime given by its most famous victim, Erasmus. Ignatius joined Montaigu as a "martinet," or external student, who was left to find whatever nest he could outside, and to provide for his own entertainment. From his experiences in Spain he had come to the conclusion that to live by begging was too great a handicap for a student, and he therefore brought with him to Paris a bill of exchange for twenty-five gold crowns, given him by his friends in Barcelona. As he never liked to have money about him, he entrusted the cash which he received for his bill to a fellow-countryman lodging at the same inn as himself. Now this fellow was a thief and dissipated the entire sum on his private pleasures, with the result that by Easter Ignatius had to resort to a poor-house a long way from his College for a lodging, and to the streets again for a livelihood. It was a cruel disappointment because it involved the loss of two lectures a day, one before dawn and one after dark, times at which he was not permitted to leave the poor-house. Conscious that he still lacked a proper foundation of Latin, he had joined Montaigu as a place where a man might sit with boys, incidentally on the ground, and start once more from the beginning. A few other men in history have started Latin at thirty-seven but none for quite the same reasons as Ignatius. No flame of a humanist made paradigms glow like poems for this student. They were never more to him than paradigms, dusty means to the only end, "the greater glory of God and the help of souls." Who knew but that an ablative absolute might not some day have a bearing on the Kingdom of God? He therefore felt the loss of his two lectures bitterly, and tried to find a position as a college servant, on observing that these people were given time enough for their studies. Going the rounds on this thankless and fruitless quest, he used to say to himself: "I will imagine the Master to be Christ, and I will name the professors, one Peter, another John, and in like manner call the others by the names of the other Apostles. So then if the Master order me anything, I will imagine him to be Christ commanding me; or if another bid me do a thing, I will think it is Blessed Peter bids me."

As no one would hire him, his limp and his years being doubtless the hindrance, he soon became completely destitute. At that crisis he fell in with a Spanish friar who charitably advised him that his best plan would be to go to Flanders, where in two months he could obtain enough alms from the rich and open-handed Spanish merchants to keep him for the rest of the year. He followed this good counsel, but of his annual expeditions to the Low Countries nothing is known except that he visited Antwerp and Bruges, and in the latter town had an amicable little controversy one evening over supper with that *enfant terrible* of the Renaissance, Luis Vivès.[1] Vivès was just back from England, his temper honourably inflamed against Henry VIII, and it may well have been he who gave Ignatius the idea of crossing the Channel. Ignatius, all the same, was quite capable of conceiving the idea for himself, as never a man lived, not even Francis Xavier, less frightened of adventuring into unknown places. What he says of the journey is not greatly informative, but extremely pleasing: "He crossed over to England once, and there received more alms than in all the former years." These strenuous and successful exertions as a quæstor were not principally for the purpose of keeping his own body and soul together. Rather did he constitute himself "a sort of student-relief agent," obtaining bills of exchange from charitable people in Spain, Flanders and England, which he deposited with a banker in Paris as a fund to be drawn on for the benefit of all struggling scholars.[2]

On returning from his first visit to Flanders, Ignatius heard that the Spaniard who had squandered his twenty-five gold crowns lay sick and friendless at Rouen. "He felt constrained," he says, "to visit and succour him," and, to obtain grace for the poor fellow's soul, thought it would be well to cover the distance between Paris and Rouen barefooted and fasting. Until he had journeyed beyond Argenteuil, "where the coat of Our Blessed Lord is said to be," he suffered agonies of fear that by his

[1] M.H.S.J., Polanco, *Chronicon*, vol. I, p. 43.
[2] M.H.S.J., *Scripta de Sancto Ignatio*, vol. I, p. 735; Polanco, *Chronicon*, vol. I, p. 40.

action he might be tempting God, but then "great comfort and spiritual energy filled his soul, and he became so joyful that he began to shout and to talk with God on his way through the fields." That day he walked fourteen leagues and spent the night in a poor-house with "a certain beggar"—a lucky beggar! "He reached Rouen the third day, on foot, and without having taken food or drink, according to his resolution. He brought comfort and help to the sick man, and had him taken on board a ship bound for Spain, with letters of recommendation to his companions who were at Salamanca."

Those companions of Salamanca proved a disappointment to Ignatius. They were not of his quality. Three others who joined him with enthusiasm at Paris also quickly fell out of the race, after getting him into trouble by their indiscretions, but both groups of disciples helped on the education of their master in the great art of estimating men. Few of the world's famous ones have been more adept than Ignatius at learning from their own or other people's mistakes. The whole system of instruction at Montaigu was a mistake, a painful, pitiful mistake, and as his understandng Protestant biographer, Professor Van Dyke, suggests, the old student may very well have learned in class with underfed, overworked, mercilessly bullied children, a better thing than appreciation of Cicero, "the tender, paternal care for the health of all his spiritual children from the professed to the youngest novice, which was so marked in his later life."[1] Having

[1] *Ignatius Loyola, the Founder of the Jesuits*, p. 80. The more one studies this book of the Vine Professor of History at Princeton University, the deeper becomes one's admiration for the mind of the good and faithful servant of true learning who wrote it.

acquired as much of the dry bones of Latin as Montaigu could give him, Ignatius, with his fund at the bank to help, joined the rival and more humane college of Sainte-Barbe as an internal student, to brave for a second time the frowns of Aristotle. He could not pay much and so was obliged to share a room with two other poor men, much younger than himself but far more advanced in their studies.

The first of these was Pierre Favre[1] who as a shepherd lad in Savoy used to weep with longing for an education. By that autumn of 1529 when he first met Ignatius, the education was nearly achieved, and Pierre, disillusioned, felt more tempted to weep for his lost pastoral solitude, undisturbed by the Yeas and Nays of the philosophers. He was born a quiet soul, all of whose drama was within. Later, at the end of his short life, he wrote a kind of spiritual diary of one year of it, a *Memoriale* of his gratitude to God, which has been described by a good judge as "une des plus tendres confessions de lyrisme intérieur que possède la littérature mystique."[2] Tenderness was the keynote of his character, a brooding pity that found room under its wing even for such as Luther and the King of England. Also, he had a genius for friendship and for winning souls, as Simon Rodriguez, another disciple of Ignatius, noticed. "In his dealings with others," writes this witness, "there flowered in particular a rare and delightful sweetness and grace such as, I confess, I have never hitherto seen in anyone else. By I know not what means he so much

[1] This is the correct form of his name, employed by himself in the only letter of his in French which is extant. The form Faber is merely a Latin adaptation of the name.
[2] André Bellessort, *Saint Francois Xavier*, p. 30

38

became their friend, so imperceptibly stole into their souls, that by his example and his slow pleasant speech he kindled in them all a vehement love of God."[1] Ignatius, looking upon this young man of twenty-three, loved him and marked him for his own. He was the first Jesuit.

The other sharer of the room, last seen chasing sheep in Navarre, did not so readily succumb as his friend Favre to the spell of the odd and elderly third party who had fought against the Xaviers at Pamplona and afterwards smirched his honour of a Basque gentleman by vagrancy and brushes with the Inquisition. Besides, he was plainly no athlete and knew nothing but a little dog Latin, while he, Francis, had won distinction in the University sports and would shortly be expounding Aristotle in the University halls. What Ignatius discerned in Francis at that stage to make him worth a siege lasting nearly three years is hidden from us, but certainly it was not the ability to expound Aristotle. Deep calls to deep, and a great heart is quick to recognize, even under veils, its fellow. Francis put up a stout resistance, one measure of which, taken on February 13th, 1531, was to send to Spain for an attestation of his nobility, drawn up in solemn legal form. His brothers put the matter off until too late, for when the document arrived he had capitulated and been some time already in the hands of Ignatius. One breach after another that patient besieger made in his defences, now relieving his chronic poverty, now helping him to find pupils, now doing him other services, always friendly, always smiling, always ready to listen when Francis was in the mood to tell his dreams. They had once been his own dreams, success,

[1] M.H.S.J., *Epistolæ Broëti*, p. 453.

fame, the credit of a great name upon earth, so memory went spying for him behind the lines of Navarre. He bided his time, watched for the sortie of pride, and then flung his question: *What doth it profit a man . . .?* Inexorably, he forced the ambitions of Francis into the infinite, until, on a day when all the bells of Heaven rang, they returned reversed, like the curve of a hyperbola. Even so, his convert did not become a saint overnight, for, though the scales had fallen from his eyes, he still needed, like St. Paul, the novitiate of the desert.

Two friends, two boys, Diego Laynez and Alfonso Salmeron, had been students in Alcalá at the same time as Ignatius. He was the first person they encountered in the streets of Paris when they arrived there together in 1533, still little more than boys,[1] with not enough French to order their dinners. He was to be a godsend to them in more ways than they imagined. The mere fact that they had ventured to Paris at all must have kindled the interest of Ignatius, who soon discovered in them very able minds and that ardour of the sun-baked Spanish uplands so easily turned into heroism. In a brief time, they became his permanent disciples. The next recruit was a certain Nicholas, a wandering scholar, so poor that he owned not even a family name and is called Bobadilla after the little Valencian village where he came, brusque and generous, into the world. In after years, Francis, the hidalgo, used to be quietly amused by Father Nicholas's addiction in apostolic activities to "personas de mucha sustancia."[2] Contrasted with him was his friend, Simon

---

[1] Laynez, of Jewish descent on his father's side, was twenty-one, and Salmeron eighteen.

[2] M.H.S.J., *Monumenta Xaveriana*, vol. I, p. 227.

Rodriguez, a Portuguese of noble blood and head-strong character who joined Ignatius to cause him the gravest anxiety and to keep throughout it all his unwavering affection. One other whom Ignatius would fain have gathered to the little fold at this time was Jerome Nadal. a man of twenty-seven from Palma in Majorca. He visited him in hospital when sick, sent Laynez and Favre to talk with him, won over his confessor, took him for walks and read to him, all to no purpose. Nadal remained suspicious, saying to himself, "I do not want to join these people, for who knows but that one day they will fall into the hands of the Inquisitors?"[1] So they did, and so, ten years later, did Jerome, for all his caution, fall into the hands of Ignatius, to become his second self and the propagator of his spirit throughout the whole Society of Jesus.

That same year, 1534, at Easter, Ignatius outstripped his brilliant young disciples in the academic race and graduated a master of arts of Paris. Never surely there or elsewhere was an M.A. more dearly won or more like a decoration for heroism in face of enemies, such enemies as advancing years, destitution, ill-health, natural repugnance, and even the devil disguised as an angel of light.[2] Stronger than all these things had been his one ally, his passion for the glory of God and the salvation of men.

---

[1] M.H.S.J., *Epistolæ P. Hieronymi Nadal*, vol. I, p. 3.

[2] In Paris, he told his Roman sons, "the same temptation assailed him which troubled him before at Barcelona when he was studying grammar; a multitude of spiritual considerations rose in his mind while the master was lecturing, so that he could not listen attentively." Eventually, he ridded himself of the pleasing distractions much in the same way as he had repulsed the consoling thoughts which invaded his hours for sleep at Manresa.

Now, with the six who had left their nets to follow him, he could plan more effectively for the promotion of those holy aims.[1] Favre, his compass at rest, with Ignatius "unum in desideriis et voluntate," was ordained in July, and the others determined likewise to prepare for the priesthood. Rodriguez gives the fullest account of their deliberations, to which he was a party. No question had as yet arisen about founding a new religious order. Their only ambition was to work for the glory of God as a little band of brothers, that, and "to die gladly at need," adds the witness, "for any cause whatever pertaining to God's greater service and veneration." Like as with their Father, their thoughts became pilgrims and fondly turned towards Jerusalem. It was agreed that when they had finished their studies and become priests they would all go there together, and then on that holy ground decide by vote whether they ought to stay permanently labouring for the conversion of the Turks, or to return, God's greater glory being the only determinant of their election. Further, they agreed that if, after trying their very best to find a passage to Palestine, a year went by without prospect of success, they would then abandon that project and, going to Rome, offer themselves to the Pope to be sent anywhere he liked to choose, "including lands subject to the Turks or other tyrants who hated the Christian religion."[2]

To clinch their resolve, which was "no flare up of

[1] But he did not impose his ideas on the others. He acted towards them, all this time, not as a superior, but as an elder brother, with a vote in their consultations no weightier than theirs.

[2] M.H.S.J., *Epistolæ Broëti*, p. 458. Rodriguez' work, reproduced in this volume of the *Monumenta*, is entitled *De Origine et Progressu Societatis Jesu*. It is, at a very long remove, a kind of *Fioretti* of the early Jesuits.

religious zeal, no spurt of unstable emotion, but the matured purpose of a man who had now spent thirteen years preparing himself to prove his love of God,"[1] the seven brethren decided to bind themselves by vows of poverty and chastity, as well as to go to Jerusalem. On the feast of the Assumption, 1534, they repaired together at dawn to a little unused chapel half-way up the slopes of Montmartre, and there, unobserved except by God, burned their boats behind them during a Mass celebrated by Favre. It was the quietest ceremony, that laying of the foundation stone of the Society of Jesus, so quiet that not even the seven themselves, building better than they knew, had an inkling of its historic significance. Afterwards they kept holiday by the fountain of St. Denis at the foot of the hill, and, having tired the sun with talking, went their several ways in the dusk, "praising and blessing God." It was then, in the vacation, that Francis Xavier made the Spiritual Exercises for the first time, with such penitential fervour as nearly cost him the use of his limbs. Thus would he atone for the vanity of his athleticism.[2] Living apart from one another, the brethren were made a community by the bond of their vow, by mutual visits and invitations to little festive meals, and by a simple rule of life which enjoined a daily meditation or contemplation, an examination of conscience twice a day, and a weekly Confession and Communion.

[1] Sedgwick, *Ignatius Loyola*, London, 1923, p. 144. This book of deep learning worn as lightly as a flower is, like Van Dyke's biography of Ignatius, a triumph of impartiality. The two books are easily the fairest Protestant accounts of Ignatius ever written, and, as history, are far superior to many Catholic accounts. Sedgwick argues strenuously for the year 1495 rather than 1491 as the date of the Saint's birth.

[2] M.H.S.J., *Epistolæ Broëti*, p. 454; *Scripta de S. Ignatio*, vol. I, p. 304.

With the beginning of the new term, they entered on the study of theology, which Ignatius had already been pursuing for some time under the Dominicans in the rue Saint-Jacques. There it must have been that he learned first to revere St. Thomas whom afterwards he was to constitute the chosen doctor of theology in his Society. But he finished only eighteen months of his course. Long years of self-imposed austerity and privation had so gravely injured his stomach that the doctors could do nothing except suggest his "native air" as a possible last hope. He was the more willing to try their prescription because a journey into Spain would give him the chance to atone among his own people for the follies of his youth, as well as enable him to visit the families of his disciples, and, as their attorney, to settle their affairs. So off he went, in the spring of 1535, mounted on a little pony which they had bought for him.[1] It had been agreed among them that from Spain he should proceed to Italy, where, at Venice, the others might join him on the conclusion of their studies.

In his pocket Ignatius carried the first extant letter of St. Francis Xavier, addressed to his brother Juan. Francis had then been three years on his heavenly adventure, which, in view of what follows, is a comforting thing to remember. Apparently he had many times written to Juan for help in his dire poverty, and Juan, a poor man himself, had left the letters unanswered. This fresh appeal is a very human document, flustered and fierce, but showing gleams already of the golden diplomacy which after-

---

[1] This fortunate animal, which Ignatius left as a present to the hospice of the poor at Azpeitia, trots later on into chapter VI, where its dignity and merit are recorded.

wards became its writer's great weapon for winning men. He assumes now that Juan *had* sent him assistance, and for its non-arrival blames that unfailing stand-by of the generous, as well as refuge of the nefarious, the postmaster-general. Then an angry Francis, the old Francis, so punctilious where honour was concerned, makes a last appearance, as he refers to tale-bearers who had traduced him to his brother: "My excess of feeling, Sir, was caused by thought of the great pain which you suffered through the reports of wicked and despicable men. I greatly desire to identify those fellows in order to pay them out as they deserve. . . . God knows the pain I endure at having to put off punishing them according to their deserts. My only comfort is in the maxim: *Quod differtur non aufertur* —postponing is not abandoning."[1] But this treasurable anger of Francis was inspired chiefly by gratitude, for the good name of Ignatius also had become involved, and Ignatius was his angel. "I assure you upon my honour," he tells his brother, "that never in my life will I be able to repay my great debt to him, both for helping me many times with money and with friends, and for having caused me to separate from evil companions whose character in my inexperience I did not recognize. . . ."[2] I beg you

[1] Perhaps the reader will like to have the last sentences in the original: "Dios save la pena que passo en diferirles el pago de la pena que merescen. Mas solo esto me da consuelo, que *quod differtur non aufertur.*" The first copyists of the Saint's letters were shocked by these words and suppressed them.

[2] Long afterwards in India, Francis confessed to another Father that, before meeting Ignatius, he had been kept from debauchery at Paris, not by the fear of God, but by the fear of loathsome disease. He had also incurred the danger of heresy from companionship with men of unsound views. His very amiability had been his snare.

therefore to give him such welcome as you would give to myself. . . . Believe me, if he were the kind of man they represented to you, he would not have gone to your Lordship's house to deliver himself into your hands. . . . I also most earnestly entreat you to deal and converse with Señor Iñigo, and to hearken to what he may tell you. Take my word for it, you will derive great benefit from his counsel and conversation. . . . Now, once again, I beseech you not to fail in this matter, but, as a favour to me, give the same credit to all that he will tell you on my behalf as you would to myself, speaking with you face to face."[1]

Ignatius's rest-cure in his native air would have horrified the good doctors, for, instead of going to the castle of his ancestors where the fatted calf had been killed and all other preparations made to welcome home the prodigal, he sought a lodging in the poor-house of Azpeitia, just outside the Loyola domain. From that headquarters he carried on a three months' breathless, unremitting campaign for God and the Ten Commandments in his native parish, at first to the chagrin of its seignorial lord, his brother Martin. He designed to hold daily classes in Christian doctrine for children. "Nobody will come to your classes," said Martin. "One is enough for me," answered Ignatius. In the event, hundreds came, crowding in from miles around. Being, like Zachæus, a little man, just under five feet two inches in his stockings, he used sometimes to climb into a tree to address them. This was his way of interpreting the doctor's orders to take his native air. Of course, he broke down, but not before he had spiritually transformed that little world of his

[1] M.H.S.J., *Monumenta Xaveriana*, vol. I, pp. 202–6.

childhood, and made its poor people happy by a regular system of contributions for their relief.[1]

Then, in July 1535, began his pilgrimage of friendship, which took him, always on foot, half over Spain, from Pamplona round by Toledo to Valencia. Very likely he met with no good reception from the Xavier family, for it can hardly be a coincidence that they should suddenly just then have remembered the request for a patent of his nobility which Francis had made to them more than four years before. The inquiry which they set on foot so belatedly resulted, after the judicial examination of dozens of witnesses, in the following grand declaration: "We, the Emperor, Queen and King, acting on the advice of the justices of our *Corte Mayor*, do by this our present definitive sentence pronounce and declare the said Don Francisco de Jasso y de Xavier to be a nobleman, hidalgo and gentleman of ancient origin and lineage, . . . and that as such the said Francisco and his sons and lineal descendants may and shall use and enjoy all the prerogatives, exemptions, honours, offices, rights of assembly and challenge, liberties, privileges, lands and rents which all gentlemen, nobles and *hijosdalgo* have used and enjoyed and enjoy . . . in this our Kingdom of Navarre and everywhere else."[2] It was all a waste of parchment, for

[1] In his sober, scholarly but un-indexed book, *Saint Ignace de Loyola* (Paris, 1934), Père Dudon, S.J., devotes a long and instructive chapter, based on official records, to this Azpeitian interlude. Ignatius showed himself strenuously opposed to mendicancy, except when adopted on religious grounds or out of genuine necessity. He even secured the passing of local laws against habitual beggars, for whom he had made other provision.

[2] M.H.S.J., *Monumenta Xaveriana*, vol. II, p. 83. There is much else, especially about "insignas y armas de gentileza y nobleza." The depositions of the witnesses occupy nearly sixty pages in this volume, which shows that kind hearts were decidedly not more than coronets in Navarre.

47

Francis when he received it in 1536, together with a notice of his appointment as a canon of Pamplona, was well on the way to taking out a patent of nobility in the courts of Heaven.

Having visited the families of Laynez and Salmeron—poor Bobadilla does not appear to have had a family—Ignatius felt that he must not leave Spain without seeing "the baccalaureat de Castro" who had been his disciple in the early days in Paris and afterwards joined a Carthusian monastery near Valencia. To walk a hundred miles to see a friend was nothing to Ignatius. At Valencia well-wishers warned him that Turkish pirates were roving the seas, "but they were unable to raise the slightest hesitation in his mind, though they said much to frighten him." He went on board a great ship bound for Genoa, faced imminent death in a tempest, landed, and promptly ran into an even worse adventure in the Apennines. His crawl on hands and knees along a narrow precipice high above a river between Genoa and Bologna, caused him, he says, "the severest bodily suffering he ever endured."[1] And the river claimed him in the end for "lo, he fell from a foot-bridge just as he was entering Bologna, and was so wet and begrimed with mud that the onlookers made of him a spectacle and laughing-stock. He went about the whole town of Bologna, from one gate to another, seeking alms, without being given a farthing." And it was only a fortnight from Christmas Day. He had intended to go on with his theology at this great centre of learning, but, after a week in hospital "with chills and fever and

[1] As Sedgwick points out, this may well have happened on the wild precipitous hill of Bismantova which Dante used to illustrate the difficulty of his climb on hands and knees up the Mount of Purgatory.

pains in the stomach,"[1] thought it better to continue his journey to Venice where he arrived in the last days of 1535, and promptly "devoted himself to giving the Exercises and to other spiritual intercourse." Among those who benefited from such guidance were a cousin of Cardinal Contarini, the Spanish consul to the Venetian Republic, and a refugee Oxford master of arts.[2] He also made one new disciple by the Exercises at this time, an Andalusian priest named Diego Hoces who was the first Jesuit to die and is remembered for the night which he spent in prison and chains at Padua "so joyfully that he did nothing but laugh the whole night long."[3] But to balance these successes, God permitted that he should fall foul, in perfect innocence, of the great Gian Pietro Carafa, who later, as Pope Paul IV, did very much to trouble the peace of the nascent Society of Jesus.

A great man is best represented in his letters, but, alas, those of Ignatius, six thousand strong, must, like himself, go begging in these narrow pages. Still, not to be as mean as the Bolognesi, we may give a few lines of two letters written from Venice to a troubled Benedictine nun in Barcelona: "You ask me to take charge of your soul for the love of God Our Lord. It is true that for many years now His Divine Majesty, without merit of mine, has given me the desire to content as fully as I can all men and women who walk according to His good will and pleasure, and to serve those that labour in His service. . . .

---

[1] M.H.S.J., *Epistolæ et instructiones*, vol. I, p. 93.

[2] This third man, John Helyar, has his modest place in the *Dictionary of National Biography* (vol. XXV, p. 381).

[3] M.H.S.J., *Scripta de Sancto Ignatio*, vol. I, p. 119. The story comes from Laynez.

I am very glad to tell you what I feel in the Lord, and if in anything it appears harsh, that will be against the devil who seeks to disturb you, rather than against yourself. The enemy disturbs you in two ways, not so much by making you fall into sin that would separate you from God, as by keeping you from God's greater service, and troubling your peace. His first way is to put before you and persuade you into a false humility, and his second, to suggest an extreme fear of God by which you become excessively held and occupied. . . . Your own words afford apt testimony to his methods, for after telling me of some weaknesses and apprehensions which bear on the matter, you say 'I am a poor kind of religious and merely *seem* desirous of serving Christ Our Lord.' You do not dare to say 'I desire to serve Christ Our Lord,' or, 'the Lord gives me the desire to serve Him,' but only, 'I seem to have the desire.' Now, if you consider carefully, you will see that those desires to serve Our Lord are not of your creation, but given to you by Him, . . . so you ought to say and to confess fearlessly that you are His servant and that you would die rather than abandon His service. If the enemy puts the thought of justice before me, I immediately retort with the thought of mercy; if he suggests mercy, I allege justice. So we must proceed to avoid being troubled, and to give the mocker a dose of his own medicine. . . . Above all, remember that your Lord loves you, a thing of which I have no doubt, and answer Him with the same love. Disregard altogether bad, impure, or sensual thoughts, weaknesses, or spiritual weariness, when these are against your will, since neither St. Peter nor St. Paul ever procured complete or partial immunity from the intrusion of such thoughts. . . . For just as I shall not be saved by the good works of the good angels, so shall I not be damned on account of the evil thoughts and frailties which the bad angels, the world, and the flesh represent to me. Only my soul does God Our Lord desire to be in conformity with His Divine Majesty, for the soul thus conformed brings it about that the body must, willy-nilly, subject itself to the Divine Will. In this consists our major warfare and such is the pleasure of the supreme Eternal Goodness. May He of His infinite grace and loving kindness keep us always in His hands. Poor in goodness, Inigo."[1]

In his private hours during the year which he spent alone in Venice, Ignatius went on with the study of theology. He had to fend for himself in that *selva oscura*, but was saved by his friends in Spain from the necessity of begging his bread. Once again, he became an object of suspicion to the ecclesiastical authorities, "and many people declared that he had been burnt in effigy in Paris and in Spain." Unluckily for these detractors, the judge who tried the case had recently made the Spiritual Exercises under the guidance of the accused and pronounced a resounding sentence in his favour. As the year drew to a close, the Saint became more and more anxious about his companions, for France and the Empire were again at war. He appealed to his friend, the Domini-

---

[1] M.H.S.J., *Epistolæ et instructiones*, vol. I, pp. 99–109. Only a few of the letters of Ignatius, twenty-four to be precise, have been translated into English, and these not too accurately. A marvellously clever version of them in classical Latin was published at Bologna in 1804, made by A.R.M., "olim Societatis Jesu sacerdos." The initials are those of Father Roch Menchaca, a survivor of the suppressed Society who ate out his heart for love of the dead mother that bore him. But he lived to rejoice in her resurrection.

can confessor of the Queen of France, to "help and favour them by every means in his power, for the service and reverence of God Our Lord," but they had already set out in the teeth of much opposition from those who loved them, and could their Father have seen them on the road he would immediately have recovered his equanimity.

They were expert and wary travellers, nine in number now, as three others, attracted by the spiritual charm of Favre, had joined them, Claude Le Jay, Paschase Broet,[1] and Jean Codure. All had taken the master's degree before leaving. As the war had made the direct route to Italy too dangerous, they went northward by Meaux into neutral Lorraine, and then through part of Germany and Protestant Switzerland to their destination. War or no war, they enjoyed themselves. "So happy were they," says Rodriguez, himself one of the nine, "that their feet seemed not to be touching the ground at all."[2] They wore the dress of university students, except that they had girdles to make walking easier and carried rosaries round their necks. On each man's back was a leather wallet containing a Bible, a breviary and his private papers. This constituted their entire luggage. Not one day of the journey's fifty did the three of them who were priests, Favre, Le Jay, and Broet, fail to say Mass, which in the conditions must have meant very clever manœuvring.[3] Five Spaniards and four Frenchmen, they were nicely fitted to negotiate territories disputed by France

[1] This was his own invariable spelling of his name, not Brouet, as usually found in English books.

[2] *De Origine*, etc. in M.H.S.J., *Epistolæ Broëti*, p. 463. Other quotations about the journey, given without reference, are from this source.

[3] Laynez is the witness here, M.H.S.J., *Scripta de Sancto Ignatio*, vol. I, p. 113.

and Spain. When stopped by French troops, the Spaniards held their tongues and let Favre or Broet do the talking; when Spanish troops appeared, the Frenchmen kept silent and left everything to Francis Xavier or Layncz. They had separate identity cards, so to speak, for each encounter, "Students of Paris on pilgrimage to St. Nicholas-du-Port," or "Spanish gentlemen on pilgrimage to Loreto," both of which designations were perfectly correct. On reaching the French frontier the non-priests all went to Confession and Holy Communion, "quasi ultimum ei vale facientes"—as a last good-bye. They spent three days in Metz whose people declared that they could not have come by land but must "have flown down out of the skies, so great and grave were the perils of the journey." Certainly, such a walk in mid-winter, amidst the turmoils of war, was no mean feat. None of them knew German, so after leaving Lorraine they often got lost through being unable to ask for directions. When at last they reached Basle, they were "tired out with walking, half dead from their great exertions, and almost undone by the rigour of the cold and the snow." But they soon picked up, and accepted with alacrity any challenges to debate which the Protestants offered them. At a town sixteen miles from Constance the local pastor, an ex-priest with a wife and large family, came to their inn accompanied by six or seven of his most eminent parishioners. A terrific debate on religion followed until the pastor, who was a jovial person, felt the need of his supper and employed Virgil to express his sentiments:

Et, jam nox humida cœlo
Præcipitat, suadentque cadentia sidera *cœnam*.

"Let us all sit down together at the same table," said the Protestants. "Certainly not, what do you take us for?" replied the Catholics. The pastor smiled, and in that matter, at any rate, he had the better of the argument. After their separate suppers, the debate was resumed with the greatest vigour, indeed with such fierceness and skill by one of the Jesuits (almost certainly Laynez) that the pastor lost his temper and threatened to have all nine of them clapped into gaol the following morning.[1] However, they got away, and, after some further adventures amid the Alpine snows, reached Venice on January 8th, 1537, where "with great delight of soul they found Ignatius awaiting them."

As ships did not sail to Palestine at that season, the eleven men, as they now were, decided without more ado to divide into two parties and offer their services to two Venetian hospitals, leaving until the spring a contemplated journey to Rome to obtain the Pope's blessing on their pilgrimage. Rodriguez gives the programme of their daily and nightly work at the hospitals: "To tend the patients, make the beds, sweep the floors, scrub the dirt, wash the pots, dig the graves, carry the coffins, read the services and bury the dead." Often, he says, they, the nurses, were ravenously hungry and scarcely able to stand from fatigue. For two and a half months this went on, one story of which time may be given in Rodriguez' own words, as it is usually told in an inaccurate or toned-down version suited to modern squeamishness: "At the

---

[1] "La brutalité de l'animal germanique fait crever le masque de théologien," says André Bellessort (St. François Xavier, p. 55), but that seems more of a political than an ethical judgment of the parson! Laynez could be very provocative.

Hospital of the Incurables, there was a leper, or a man covered from head to foot with loathsome sores that resembled leprosy. Calling one of the Fathers, he said, 'Be good enough to scratch my back.' The Father diligently applied himself to this task, but while engaged on it began to fear, in a paroxysm of horror and nausea, lest he might contract the contagious disease. However, more anxious to break himself and to stifle the rebellion of nature than to take precautions against future contingencies, he scraped together the pus with his fingers, and, putting them in his mouth, licked and sucked them." That Father, so called by anticipation, was Francis Xavier.[1]

By the middle of Lent the roads were deemed sufficiently passable for the long journey to Rome, but that turned out to be an optimistic weather forecast. Ignatius remained behind because he did not think himself a *persona grata* to

[1] M.H.S.J., *Epistolæ Broëti*, p. 475; Polanco, *Chronicon*, vol. I, p. 57. In Paris St. Ignatius had overcome his dread of the plague, which might have hindered his charity, by similarly drastic means. Once, after visiting and consoling a plague-stricken man, he found that his hand, which had touched the man's wounds, was paining him. Thinking that he had contracted the terrible disease, he was overcome with feelings of horror which he could not shake off, until, mastering himself, he thrust his fingers into his mouth, saying: "If you have plague in your hand, then get it in your mouth also." This story is from his confessions or autobiography, and shows again the similarity of his and Xavier's characters. "We must remember," writes the non-Catholic Professor Van Dyke, "that what they did seemed just as dangerous to them as it does to us—and just as disgusting; for they were both Basque nobles, a class of people noted for cleanliness. As patriots in time of war steel themselves to face dirt, hardship and death through months or years for the sake of their country, so these men of delicate conscience and iron will were fixed on dying daily all the years of their life in the great war between God and evil. No discipline seemed too hard if it fitted them for this service. They asked for no relief except from sin and any human shrinking which might weaken them for this duty" (*Ignatius Loyola*, pp. 110–11).

two important personages at the Papal Court, Dr. Ortiz, the counsel for Queen Catherine of Aragon in the divorce case, and Cardinal Carafa, the future Pope Paul IV. His nine brethren travelled three by three, mixing their nationalities, and with a priest to each group. It was Lent, so they fasted all the way, and on some days even starved. It rained incessantly and once, after splashing for miles through mud and water which in places came up to their arm-pits, they were driven by hunger to eating pine-cones—*nuces pineas deturbant, frangunt, edunt.* One Sunday, they walked twenty-eight miles barefooted in the rain, without any food except a crust of bread in the morning. From Ravenna, where they arrived "wet, tired out, and almost dead with hunger," they went in some sort of boat to Ancona, having obtained their fare by pawning a breviary. At Ancona, Rodriguez saw Laynez[1] in the square, barefooted, among the market-women, receiving with the greatest humility from one a radish, from another an apple, from a third a cabbage or similar vegetable. Good Father Simon says that he too secured some fruit on this occasion, namely a conviction of his "utter unworthiness to be in such saintly company." They begged enough not only to provide them with "a merry little meal of the poor together," but to redeem their breviary from the pawnbroker. Then they journeyed on to Loreto where they spent three days in devotions. Near Tolentino, their next stopping place, Rodriguez trudged wearily through the muddiest parts of the road,

---

[1] Biographers of St. Francis Xavier usually claim him as the hero of this scene, but from the description of his talents, "ipsius eximiam erudi-tionem, singularemque doctrinam copulatam cum egregio ingenio," it was more likely Laynez. Rodriguez is provokingly anonymous throughout.

saying to himself "I can't get any wetter or muddier than I am already." But they had luck in the town, for a stranger spontaneously put enough money in their hands to provide them with a supper of bread, wine and figs, *et ad suam etiam pauperibus portionem tribuendam.*

In Rome, the Dr. Ortiz whom Ignatius was afraid of proved the best friend of the wayfarers. Through his influence they were invited by Pope Paul III to talk theology during his dinner and so pleased His Holiness that he not only willingly blessed their proposed pilgrimage, while expressing a doubt as to its being feasible, but also granted them a faculty to receive Holy Orders from any bishop available, "on the sufficient patrimony of their learning." From the Pope and from some Spanish merchants in Rome they received, entirely unsolicited, the sum of 210 ducats, which they transmitted by a bill of exchange to Venice to pay for their passage to Jerusalem. When, a few months later, Jerusalem receded into the unattainable owing to war between Venice and the Turks, every penny of this money was returned to its donors.

One night, on the journey home, Laynez and Francis Xavier were sleeping side by side in some hospice when Francis, waking as from a nightmare, exclaimed: "Jesus, how crushed I feel! Do you know what I dreamt? I was carrying on my back an Indian and he was so heavy I could not lift him."[1] Dear St. Francis, he had no suspicion then that one day, not in a dream, his back would be broken lifting Indians. When he and the rest reached Venice they resumed their old employments in the hospitals and renewed the vows of Montmartre before the

[1] This detail is reported by Ribadeneira who had it from Laynez. *Scripta de Sancto Ignatio,* vol. I, p. 382.

57

Papal Legate, Jerome Verallo. Then, on June 24th, 1537, five of the six who were not priests,[1] including Ignatius and Francis, received Holy Orders from the Bishop of Arbe. They were in no hurry to say their first Mass because they considered it too great a thing to be undertaken until they had prepared their souls by a long period of penance and prayer. Ignatius himself deferred the event for eighteen months, until Christmas Day, 1538, and his Masses afterwards caused him such emotion that his eyesight was gravely affected by the abundance of his tears. He and his disciples therefore determined to leave Venice and seek seclusion for forty days in places where they were not known, Ignatius, Favre and Laynez going to Vicenza, Xavier and Salmeron to Monselice near Padua, Le Jay and Rodriguez to Bassano, Broet and Bobadilla to Verona, and Hoces and Codure to Treviso.

Of the first three's adventures at Vicenza we have the following account from Ignatius: "They lit upon a house without the city which had neither door nor window, and dwelt therein, sleeping on some straw collected by themselves. Two of the three went to beg in the city twice a day, but gained hardly enough to keep life in them. Their usual food, when they had it, was a little bread baked by the one who stayed at home. They spent forty days in this fashion, giving themselves up to prayer and nothing else. Master John Codure arrived after the forty days were over, and they four resolved to begin preaching. They all began to preach the same day and hour in the different squares of the town, first making a great outcry and waving their caps to call the people round them. Their preaching provoked much talk in the city

---

[1] Salmeron was still too young.

and stirred up devotion in many of the citizens; and at this time plenty of food was bestowed on them." Exactly similar were the housekeeping experiences of Xavier and Salmeron at Monselice, as detailed by the delightful first biographer of Francis, Torsellini: "Having found in a private place a desolate and ruinated cottage, he thatched the roof thereof with straw and so made himself a little sorry habitation, wherein he tooke the more delight because it represented to him the manger of Christ his Saviour and His great poverty. . . . He lay upon the bare ground with straw under him in the forsaid hovel, exposed to rayne, wind and weather. . . . This is certain, that the little which he begged would hardly find him bread, to which if perchance he got a little oyle or other meate, he thought he had then made a dainty meale indeed."[1] At Bassano, Le Jay and Rodriguez lived with a certain hermit named Anthony, very much in the style of the original Anthony. When news reached Ignatius that Rodriguez had fallen dangerously ill, he immediately, "though himself in a fever, set forth to visit him, going at such a pace that Favre, his companion, could not keep up with him."

In the course of the autumn, Ignatius re-assembled his companions at Vicenza where they took up again as a community their austerities and apostolic activities. The villagers among whom they went used to laugh at their funny Italian, but they never minded. Francis Xavier and

[1] *The Admirable Life of S. Francis Xavier*, written in Latin by Horatius Tursellinus (1596); translated into English by T.F., Paris 1632, pp. 30–1. "Oeuvre d'humaniste," writes Père Brou, S.J., referring to this book, "un peu trop influencé par ses modèles classiques." Père Brou's own *St. François Xavier*, two vols., Paris, 1912, is the standard modern biography, and one unlikely ever to be superseded.

Rodriguez fell ill and were put in the same hospital bed, "which was narrow enough," says the second patient. They had a little contest of charity, those two, one of them, tormented with fever, thinking only how to keep his shivering bed-fellow warm, and the other scheming to remove the blankets that oppressed his burning companion. As the winter approached and the Turkish war continued, it became evident to all that their chances of reaching Palestine within the year stipulated for in their vow had become remote almost to vanishing point. They therefore took a great decision, crossing, as it were, a spiritual Rubicon. Ignatius, Favre and Laynez were to go to Rome and put themselves at the disposal of the Pope, while the others dispersed in pairs to various Italian university cities, "to see whether Our Lord desired to call any student to our institute."[1] In this *diaspora* Siena fell to Broet and Salmeron, Ferrara to Le Jay and Rodriguez, Padua to Codure and Hoces, and Bologna to Xavier and Bobadilla.

Gradually, almost unrealized by themselves, the lines of those men's lives were assuming a definite pattern. Before separating, they deliberated as to what they should answer if asked the name of their little brotherhood. So far, they had been dubbed popularly *Iniguistas* from the Spanish name of their leader, who, however, was the last man to want to fix his name on anything. "They began to pray and think," writes their intimate, Polanco, "what title would best suit them, and considering that over them they had no head but Jesus Christ, whom alone they desired to serve, it seemed right that they should adopt the name of Him Who was their head and

[1] Laynez in *Scripta de Sancto Ignatio*, vol. I, p. 118

60

that their congregation should be called the Society of Jesus."[1] On his way to Rome, at a little place named Storta about nine miles from the city, Ignatius, praying in a deserted chapel, was visited by Our Lord carrying His cross, who said to him, *con rostro sereno*, "I shall be favourable to you in Rome." The Saint did not know what the words imported, and, thinking perhaps of St. Peter and his similar vision, surmised that maybe they would be crucified, but the incident increased his desire to have his little company called by the name of Jesus.[2] In Bologna, where he laboured even to the point of complete physical exhaustion for the poor, the sick, the imprisoned, the unfortunate of every condition, Francis Xavier also had his longings and premonitions. One who met him often at this time, a man named Jerome Domenech, afterwards himself a Jesuit, related that "almost always he brought their conversation round to the subject of India and the conversion of the gentiles, showing a great fervour of desire to go there."[3] Portuguese expansion in India was the big foreign news of the day, and, as the dream of Palestine faded, Francis sent his heart round the Cape of Good Hope to comfort it. Perhaps he did not then know that Diaz, its discoverer, had originally named the promontory, *Cabo de todos los tormentos*—Cape of all the storms. In due course he would find a grim appropriateness in that title as applied to his own apostolic activities.

In Ferrara, his brethren, Le Jay and Rodriguez, were

---

[1] *Chronicon*, vol. I, p. 72.

[2] Laynez, who was with Ignatius at the time, in *Scripta de Sancto Ignatio*, vol. I, p. 378.

[3] *Scripta de Sancto Ignatio*, vol. I, p. 382.

experiencing already storms a-plenty. They worked in the midst of fog, bitter cold, and drenching rains, returning at night to the poorest hospice in the city, a big gloomy institution built of clay bricks, "damp as could be and open to all the winds of heaven." Worse than its inhuman discomfort was its matron, "a shrewish old dame," who spied on her poor charges all the time and compelled the men among them, including the two Paris M.A.'s, to submit to her inspection, stark naked, before they got into their miserable beds. From this indignity, as well as from semi-starvation, the Jesuit pair were rescued by no less a lady than Vittoria Colonna, Michael Angelo's poet friend, who had become interested in them from seeing them at their devotions.[1]

Ignatius and his reconnoitring party succeeded better than they had anticipated in Rome. Many persons volunteered to make the Spiritual Exercises, including the Sienese ambassador, Tolomei, also of Vittoria Colonna's circle, Cardinal Gaspar Contarini, and portly Dr. Ortiz whom the Saint took to Monte Cassino for greater seclusion.[2] From this expedition he brought back a notable recruit in the person of Francis Strada, a young Spaniard recently cashiered by Gian Pietro Carafa, that good hater of all things Spanish. Better still, the Pope proved his

---

[1] Rodriguez, in M.H.S.J., *Epistolæ Broëti*, pp. 495-6.

[2] During the forty days which he spent at the mother house of all Benedictines, Ignatius "one day saw in vision the baccalaureat Hoces entering into Heaven, whereat he wept abundantly and was refreshed with great consolation." Hoces died worn out prematurely in the hospital of the poor at Padua. In life he had been no beauty to look at, a poorly-built man of swarthy countenance, but after death, his companion, Codure, avowed that he could not take his eyes from his face, "for it seemed as beautiful as the face of an angel." (*Scripta de Sancto Ignatio*, I, p. 126.)

friendship by appointing Favre and Laynez professors at the Sapienza, and inviting them to fortnightly theological tourneys in his presence. Meantime, the year of waiting for the ship of dreams to Palestine had passed, and the scattered brethren, released from the main provision of their vow, though still cherishing a half-hope of one day seeing Zion, converged on Rome in the spring of 1538 to fulfil their alternative obligation by offering themselves to the Pope. Together again, they all lived in contented penury at a little cottage among vines near the Trinità dei Monti which had been lent to Ignatius, but moved shortly afterwards to a less cramped, though not less humble, abode in the centre of the City. From that house they issued early in May, with due authorization, to preach in various churches or piazzas, to administer the sacraments, and to instruct children in Christian doctrine. Not one of them was an Italian or knew much Italian, so their sermons, except for those of Ignatius who preached in his native tongue at a Spanish church, were more calculated to provoke smiles than good resolutions. But again they did not mind, for, as Laynez put it, "that preaching was at any rate a fine mortification." It also astonished the Romans and did them good to see, against all custom, other priests besides monks or friars occupying the pulpit.[1]

From their experiences and observations at Paris and on the journey to Venice, the Pilgrim Priests, as they called themselves, had become peculiarly alive to the menace of Protestantism. In Italy that menace was no less serious for being underground or taking the insidious

[1] *Scripta de Sancto Ignatio*, vol. I, p. 120; Rodriguez, in *Epistolæ Broëti*, p. 499.

form of veiled propaganda from the pulpit.[1] Of this
they had prompt and disquieting evidence almost as soon
as they arrived in Rome. The chief preacher of that
Lent of 1538 was an eminent member of the Order
from which Luther sprang, by name Fra Agostino. The
Fathers went to hear him and quickly detected that his
theology of grace and free-will was tainted with Lutheran-
ism. St. Ignatius appealed to two of the friar's admirers,
themselves persons of importance in Rome, to reason
with him and advise caution, but the only result of his
charitable endeavour was to draw on himself their implacable hostility. Others of the Fathers expostulated
with the friar in private, and, when that had no effect,
took to refuting his errors in their own sermons. Now,
the man had many friends in high places, and even
enjoyed the favour and protection of Pope Paul III,
always gentle towards heretics. These friends rallied to
him with such effect that for eight months the Pilgrim
Priests, unknown foreigners, stammering bad Italian,
became the butt of every sort of calumny. It was said
that Ignatius himself had been condemned by the Inquisition in Spain, in France, in Venice; that he and his companions were fugitives from justice; that they were a
secret Lutheran sect; that they ought to be burnt at the
stake, or condemned to the galleys. Throughout the
storm, they went on with their work quietly, but it
suffered sad reverses. This was now the eighth time that

---

[1] In the richly documented and splendidly learned introductory volume
of his *Storia della Compagnia di Gesù in Italia,* Father Tacchi Venturi has
shown, texts in hand, the extent, the methods and the considerable success
of the heretical campaign in Italy (*Storia,* vol. I, part I: *La Vita religiosa in
Italia,* Rome, 1910, pp. 307–50).

Ignatius had been accused of heresy, and he told his devoted Barcelona friend, Isabel Roser, that never in all their lives had he and his companions suffered "more violent contradiction or persecution" than during those eight months. Denunciation of them was made to Benedetto Conversini, the Governor of Rome, but at that point Ignatius, not a soldier for nothing, counter-attacked so vigorously that his accuser was banished from the City. The more highly placed detractors, of whom this man was only the tool, then tried to smooth matters over. But Ignatius would not have it, knowing too well how mud adheres unless one has the shield of some easily produced and irrefutable evidence. Once, when similarly charged in Paris and put off with verbal assurances by the judge just before his journey to Spain, "he himself," he tells us, "fetched a notary and witnesses into the house and secured written testimony" to his innocence. He did the same in Rome, well aware that otherwise his case would go by default, and then good-bye to all his long-cherished plans for helping souls. As the Governor hesitated out of regard for the other party to pronounce sentence in full juridical form, Ignatius went personally to the Pope and secured an order for the continuance of the investigation. He was able to put in evidence telling testimonies from the ecclesiastical authorities of Bologna, Siena and Ferrara, where his sons had laboured, but the great moment of the trial came when all three other judges before whom he had been previously arraigned, Dr. Figueroa of Alcalá, Dr. Ori of Paris and Dr. de' Dotti of Venice, filed into court to testify for the accused. They had just arrived in Rome, each on his own business, and without a thought in the world of helping Ignatius

Loyola. Then, at last, sentence was solemnly given that not only had he and his companions incurred no stain on their reputations, but rather were the excellency of their lives and doctrine made the more resplendent by the proceedings.[1] Some years later, as though to endorse the sentence, Fra Agostino fled to Switzerland where he publicly embraced Protestantism and died a Lutheran minister, full of years and heresy. The persecution and its sequel are the last matters referred to by Ignatius in his autobiography, which closes with a snap of relief— "And now Master Nadal can tell you the rest."

---

[1] M.H.S.J., *Scripta de Sancto Ignatio*, vol. I, p. 628; *Epistolæ Broëti*, pp. 502–7; Tacchi Venturi, *Storia della Compagnia di Gesù in Italia*, vol. II, pp. 153–76. This last is a most erudite and detailed account.

CHAPTER III

THE FELLOWSHIP OF HIS SON

A MONTH after the official rehabilitation of Ignatius,[1] he and his companions were appointed by Papal bull instructors in Christian doctrine to all the boys' schools of Rome. But hunger and cold did even more than Governor or Pope to win them what they wanted, a hearing for their message. That winter of 1538 broke all records in Italy. From Christmas Eve until May 25th following, the country remained continuously in the grip of the fiercest frost ever known, diversified by incessant storms of snow and thunder. Soon famine stalked the land, and in Rome itself, through the negligence of the authorities, people perished by the hundred of cold and starvation. "Everywhere in the streets and piazzas the poor lay huddled, frozen to the bone and dying abandoned in the night from hunger. There was no one

---

[1] He wrote a propos of it to Pietro Contarini: "We know indeed that it will not bring us entire immunity from abuse in the future, nor have we ever looked for such immunity. . . . Never shall we be troubled, God helping us, at hearing ourselves described as ignorant, uncultured men, unable to speak the language, nor even if we are called bad men, deceivers and waverers. What grieved us was that the doctrine itself which we preached should have been declared unsound and our way of life evil, neither of which is ours but Christ's and the Church's. But of this enough. . . ." (M.H.S.J., *Epistolæ et instructiones*, vol. I, p. 136).

to care for them, no one to shelter them, no one to have pity on their misery."[1] Even the Lady Charity had fallen a victim to the weather.

The Pilgrim Priests were living then in their third Roman home, a large ramshackle building, reputedly haunted, near the Torre del Melangolo, where now stands the Palazzo Mario Delfini. Into this house they gathered the stricken people, "going out at night to seek them in the piazzas, and bring them home and wash their feet." The sick they put in their own beds, and for the others begged bundles of hay from their friends, as well as the necessary food and fuel, carrying these things on their backs through the streets. At times they had as many as three or four hundred guests crowded somehow under their roof, whom they fed and comforted, and lovingly initiated into their own secret of consolation. Besides these casuals, the Fathers also came to the rescue of about two thousand starving people, marooned in their miserable tenements, helping them with moneys given to Ignatius for the support of his brethren, "until not a single farthing was left in the house."[2]

The ten men had offered their services to the Pope and the Pope had graciously accepted them, but, at least until the first months of 1539, they appear still to have retained a last lingering hope of being able to make the pilgrimage to Jerusalem. Once, on their fortnightly visits to His Holiness to regale him during dinner-time with his beloved disquisitions on theology, he suddenly said to

---

[1] Rodriguez, an eye-witness, in *Epistolæ Broëti*, p. 500.

[2] M.H.S.J., *Epistolæ Broëti*, p. 500; Polanco, *Chronicon*, vol. I, p. 66. The population of Rome in those days was about 40,000.

the four of them then present: "Why is it that you so greatly desire to go to Jerusalem? If you wish to have fruit in the Church of God, then Italy is a good and true Jerusalem."[1] According to Bobadilla who reports it, that little incident was the immediate cause of the Fathers' resolution to devote time to the question of their present status and future plans. But there were other causes also impelling them in the same direction. Ignatius himself had told Isabel Roser that they were being "greatly importuned (*mucho infestados*, were the words he used) by this and that prelate to work for God our Lord in their territories." On March 19th, 1539, Father Paschase Broet received from Cardinal Carafa, acting for the Pope, an order *in virtute sanctæ obedientiæ* to proceed to Siena with a companion chosen by himself, and set about the reformation of a Benedictine abbey in the city. It was to be expected that other such mandates would soon arrive, which in fact they did, so the question became urgent whether the companions were to remain united as heretofore, or to go their ways on the Pope's business independently. They began their deliberations in the early spring of that year, 1539, meeting for the purpose at night when their daily Lenten labours in pulpit and confessional were over. A memorandum of the meetings is still extant in the handwriting of Codure or Favre.[2] "On the first night we met," say they, "the question was proposed whether or not it would be more expedient for us to remain so bound together in one body that no

[1] M.H.S.J., *Bobadillæ Monumenta*, p. 616.

[2] This and the other documents relative to their discussions are published with every refinement of scholarship in the M.H.S.J., *Sancti Ignatii de Loyola Constitutiones Societatis Jesu*, vol. I, Rome, 1934.

partings from one another, however great, could sever
our union. . . . In the end, we came to the conclusion that,
as the most merciful and loving Lord had deigned to
bring us together and bind us to one another, feeble men
of such diverse nationality and character, we ought not
to destroy this union of God but rather daily to strengthen
and confirm it, making ourselves one body in which
each took thought and care for the others, for the greater
fruit of souls. . . ." That point settled, subject always,
they carefully state, to the confirmation and approval of
the Apostolic See, there arose immediately the capital
question of authority in their brotherhood. Should they
remain as they were, a purely voluntary association,
headless and unorganized, or should they add to the vows
of poverty and chastity already taken a third vow of
obedience to one of their own number? It was an extremely difficult question, as may be judged by the
fact that it took them nearly a month of prayer and
constant argument to decide. For one thing, they saw
clearly that such a vow would constitute them religious
in the canonical sense of the word. Now, religious were
not in favour in the Church at that time, and, besides,
did they make the vow, they might be compelled by
the Pope to join one of the established orders, founded
for purposes other than those special ones to which they
had dedicated their young enthusiasm. Not until they
had thoroughly explored these and other objections did
they go on to consider the many advantages of the
proposed vow, especially its "unequalled power to bring
down all pride and arrogance." At length, the pro-
tracted debate, nourished on prayer and conducted with
scrupulous regard for free speech, was ended by a unani-

mous vote in favour of the vow of obedience.[1] The name of Ignatius is not mentioned in the Memorandum, and, so far as this or any other available evidence goes, his influence counted for exactly ten per cent, and no more, of the forces that brought about the great decision.

Having resolved, then, if the Pope approved, to transform their little voluntary association into a new religious order, for that was what their acceptance of the vow of obedience amounted to, the Fathers set about defining the aims, the conditions of membership and the form of government which would characterize this order, already named by them the Company or Society of Jesus. The aims, as debated and agreed to unanimously, were extremely simple and extremely practical. From their experiences in three countries, these good, earnest realists had become convinced that nothing was more necessary to the Church than the instruction of her children in the elements of faith and duty. The ignorance then prevalent was appalling, and the clergy, both regular and secular, had, on the whole, become so slack or faint-hearted that little or nothing was being done to dissipate it. Consequently, the Fathers voted the first "Constitution" of their new Society in the following words: "That children or any others whomsoever are to be taught the Commandments of God." Out of nine resolutions taken between April 15th and May 23rd, 1539, five deal with this one point, laying it down, among other things, that

---

[1] M.H.S.J., *Constitutiones*, vol. I, pp. 1–7. To ensure individual freedom the Fathers gave an undertaking to refrain from asking one another's views or even mentioning the matter at all outside the time devoted to their common discussions: "ut nulla alterius persuasione alius traheretur et flecteretur magis ad obediendum quam ad non obediendum, vel contra."

the instructions are to last for an hour at a time and to be given on at least forty separate days in the course of the year. It was decided too, Bobadilla alone dissenting, that these stipulations should come under the vow of obedience and bind under mortal sin.

With regard to the training of new members, a vital matter to every religious order, the Fathers made an innovation by requiring such men to engage for three months before their formal noviceship in spiritual exercises, in undertaking pilgrimages, and in the service of the poor in hospitals. This lengthening of the traditional time of probation, afterwards extended to two years in all, was meant, as Ignatius explained, to compensate for various protective features of the older orders, "clausura, quietud, reposo," which the new order, with its active aims, felt obliged to forgo. Other matters relative to the admittance or dismissal of novices were determined at a meeting on June 11th, as also that there should be "one superior in the whole Society, elected for life," and that the brethren might accept houses or churches for their use, "on condition that they assumed no right of property over them."

By June 24th, the Fathers, reduced to six in number through the absence on Papal business of Broet and Rodriguez in Siena and Favre and Laynez in Parma, considered that the time had come to present a summary of their resolutions for the judgment of the Holy See. This venerable document which contains in germ the later Jesuit Constitutions begins as follows: "Let him who would fight for God under the banner of the Cross and serve the Lord alone and His Vicar on earth in our Society, which we desire to be distinguished by the name of Jesus, bear in mind that, after a solemn vow of perpetual chastity, he is part of a community founded primarily for the task of advancing souls in Christian life and doctrine, and of propagating the faith by the ministry of the word, by spiritual exercises, by works of charity, and, expressly, by the instruction of children and unlettered persons in Christian principles. First and foremost, he is to have God always before his eyes, and then the constitutions of this his order which are, as it were, a way to God, striving with all his might towards the attainment of this end which God has proposed to him, according to the measure of each one's grace and the grade of his vocation. The determination of each one's grade, as well as the selection and assignment of employments is to rest entirely in the hands of the superior to be chosen by us . . ., who shall have power, in council with the brethren, to make constitutions conducive to the end proposed to us, a majority of the votes being always juridically decisive. For matters of more serious and enduring importance, the council will consist of the greater part of the whole Society which the superior can conveniently summon, but for lesser and temporary affairs it will be made up of all those who happen to be present in the place where our superior resides. With him will rest all right to command and all executive authority."

The second article of the charter deals with the special vow of obedience to the Pope, "by which," write the Fathers, "the companions are to be so bound that they must immediately, without any shuffling or excuse, undertake whatsoever His Holiness commands appertaining to the progress of souls and the propagation of the faith, whether he sends us to the Turks, or to the New World, or to the Lutherans, or to others whomsoever, infidels or Catholics. . . . And lest perchance there might grow up amongst us any ambition for or repugnance to particular missions or countries of this kind, each must promise that he will never, either directly or indirectly, treat with the Pope about them, but leave all care of the matter to God, to His Vicar, and to the superior of the Society, which superior shall, like the rest, promise in his turn not to try to influence the Pope one way or the other, without the advice of the Society, concerning any mission that may be laid upon himself."

The third article is an assertion of the reciprocal duties of superior and subjects, theirs, to give prompt and constant obedience, "acknowledging and *quantum decet*, venerating in him Christ, as it were, present," and he, "to be ever mindful in his government of the kindness, meekness and charity of Christ." Here again, the scheme so dear to the Fathers' hearts of instructing children and others who needed it in the rudiments of the faith comes to the fore. "It is necessary in the highest degree," they lay down, "that the superior and council should be diligently vigilant in this matter, since in our neighbours' souls the edifice of faith cannot arise without a foundation, and, on the other hand, there may be a danger among ourselves lest someone, on account of his greater learning, should seek to avoid this office, as one at first sight less attractive, when in reality there is none more fruitful, either for the edification of our neighbour or for the exercise of our own charity and humility."

The fourth article deals with the poverty to be practised in the new order. "As we have learned by experiience," say the Fathers, "that a way of living utterly removed from all contagion of avarice and as like as possible to evangelical poverty is sweeter, purer, and better calculated to edify our neighbour, and as we also know that Our Lord Jesus Christ will provide the necessaries of life for His servants who seek only the Kingdom of God, each and all are to make a vow of perpetual poverty, declaring that they cannot, either individually or as a community, acquire a legal right to any income or real property for the Society's upkeep or use, but are content to enjoy the use alone of things necessary to life, by the consent of the owners." Only one exception, prompted by the far-sighted Laynez, was admitted, in favour of endowments for houses of study wherein future members of the order might receive their preliminary education.

The fifth and last article introduced a notable innovation, destined for a great deal of criticism. So traditional had the singing of the Divine Office in choir become in the older orders that it seemed to be almost of the essence of the religious life. Now, the Pilgrim Priests proposed to found a new order without this distinctive and beautiful feature which wedded music to the service of God. It was a bold change to make, but even the most devoted lover of the liturgy will admit that their reason for it was not unworthy of true Christians: "All priests of our Society are bound to recite the Office according to the Church's rites, but not in choir lest they be withdrawn from those works of charity to which we have wholly dedicated ourselves." They even went the length of giving up music in their services altogether, "having found that it hindered them not a little in the pursuit of their vocation, which required that they should spend a great part of the day, and often of the night, in helping the sick, physically and spiritually." But that particular item of renunciation was not accepted by the Pope, so Jesuits still have organs in their churches, and yield to none in the solemnity of their Eucharistic liturgy. Besides choir and its consoling offices, the Fathers also relinquished, or, to use a better verb, speaking of men led by one who had been a soldier, sacrificed any claim to a distinctive uniform. Finally, if they made no ruling with regard to the fasts and other austere practices traditional in the religious life, that, they declared, and their personal histories declared too, was not from any dis-esteem of them, but only because they had already imposed so many fresh burdens, from which they would not have members of their order to escape by alleging penance as an excuse.[1]

When ready, the document embodying their hopes was entrusted by Ignatius to his good friend and devoted client, Cardinal Contarini, for presentation to the Pope, who ordered it to be submitted to the Master of the Sacred Palace, the Dominican, Father Thomas Badia. This saintly and learned religious, described by another famous cardinal as having "buono il giudizio, migliore la volontà, bonissima la conscienza,"[2] reported after the most careful scrutiny that the entire project of the new order seemed to him devout and holy, whereupon the Pope gave it his preliminary verbal approbation. That was the first milestone passed, but the Pilgrim Priests, who, innocent of the law's delays, thought it their destina-

---

[1] M.H.S.J., *Constitutiones Societatis Jesu*, vol. I, pp. 16–20.

[2] Aleandro, cited by Tacchi Venturi, *Storia*, II, 296. Badia was confessor to both Contarini and Aleandro, and became a cardinal himself in 1542.

tion,[1] had still a long way to go before they could call themselves members of the Society of Jesus. In the Sacred College at this time was a very eminent cardinal named Girolamo Ghinucci, to whom fell the duty of drafting Papal bulls and briefs. While approving in general of the five articles submitted, this expert of the Curia expressed himself as being very dubious about the wisdom of excluding choir duties and penances according to rule or of admitting the special vow of obedience to the Pope. The first, he thought, might give a handle to the Lutherans and confirm them in their errors, while the second seemed superfluous as being already a general Christian obligation. An *impasse* was thus created, Contarini holding out for the five articles in their integrity, and Ghinucci with equal resolution maintaining his objections. As judge between them, the Pope turned to another distinguished canonist, Bartolomeo Guidiccioni,[2] who declared at one and the same time his theoretical approval of the five articles as they stood and his determined practical opposition to the whole idea of a new religious order. Indeed, it was known that he favoured the suppression of all existing orders of men except four, the Benedictines, the Cistercians, the Franciscans and the Dominicans.[3] As the Pope had a great and well-founded

[1] Writing on September 24th, 1539, Ignatius himself told his brother Beltran joyfully that their whole way of life had been approved and confirmed by the Holy Father, who had given them "a complete faculty to draw up constitutions" (*Epistolæ et instructiones*, I, p. 149).

[2] To the merits of this austere and outspoken septuagenarian Tacchi Venturi pays four pages of warm tribute (*Storia*, II, 309–12).

[3] Guidiccioni was a very hammer of monks. From a manuscript of his advocating a general council to reform ecclesiastical abuses, it would appear that he desired to have, not four orders of regulars, but only one, corresponding to the general class of secular priests. His objection to the diversity

esteem for this arbiter of his own choosing,[1] he could not reasonably ignore his judgment, and it therefore seemed to many that the last had been heard of the projected Society of Jesus.

But it did not seem so to Ignatius. From Montserrat in 1521 to Rome in 1538 he never once, so far as is known, entertained the idea of founding a new religious order. What he did was to wait patiently on the will of God, content to be led by paths which he knew not to a goal unrevealed. In that summer of 1539 he reached the long journey's end. Whether or not the Pope exclaimed on reading the first charter of the Pilgrim Priests, *Digitus Dei est hic*, Ignatius saw the finger of God in it with absolute certitude. He therefore resorted to his usual tactics in difficulties, praying as though everything depended on God, and working as though everything depended on human effort. With only ten priests to say them, he vowed three thousand Masses for a change in the heart of Cardinal Guidiccioni. By March 18th, 1541, when the issue had been six months decided, Francis Xavier, on his way to India, announces that to date he has said 250 of the Masses, and with such consolation that he intends to offer others all his life "por Monsenor reverendissimo."[2] But Ignatius brought more than prayers to bear on the unyielding Monsenor. The Duke of Ferrara

---

of orders arose from what he calls "their abominable dissensions, quarrels and contentions, both among themselves and with the secular clergy." (Document in Tacchi Venturi, *Storia*, vol. I, part II, pp. 208–14).

[1] Guidiccioni was created cardinal and appointed Vicar of Rome in December of that same year, 1539.

[2] M.H.S.J., Laynez in *Epistolæ et instructiones*, vol. I, p. 122; and Rodriguez in *Epistolæ Broëti*, p. 515; *Monumenta Xaveriana*, vol. I, p. 245.

who had already, in his profound regard for Le Jay, used his influence to protect the good name of the Companions, now on the appeal of the same Father, prompted by Ignatius, enlisted in their interests the powerful help of his brother, Cardinal Ippolito d'Este. At Bologna, Francis Xavier, similarly inspired, won the enthusiastic co-operation of Cardinal Ferreri, while from the Archbishop of Siena came a letter praising to the skies the character and work of Father Paschase Broet.[1] The most strenuous moves of all, though, were made by the Anziani or senators of the Republic of Parma where Guidiccioni had been vicar-general a few years earlier, and where Favre and Laynez were at the moment doing wonders for the faith. In a warmly worded letter to their ambassador in Rome, Federico del Prato, the good senators exhorted him to be urgent with the Cardinal, beseeching him in their name to give way on the subject of the five articles. Not content with that, they wrote also to Costanza Farnese, who had much influence with Pope Paul, telling her that by the shining example and indefatigable labours of Favre and Laynez "si vede la città tutta convertita," and begging her humbly to favour with His Holiness the "honestissima petitione" of the two men and their brethren.[2]

---

[1] M.H.S.J., *Epistolæ Broëti*, p. 385; *Monumenta Xaveriana*, vol. I, pp. 208–9. The testimonial to Broet is worth quoting: "Ea est Paschasii vestri, at potius nostri, vitæ integritas, morum suavitas, ut omnibus gratus jucundusque sit, mihi vero gratissimus, et in eo munere, quo hic fungitur, est adeo vehemens, ut summa ejus cum laude oculos omnium in se converterit, nam verbis hortatur, exemplis juvat, humilitate allicit, charitate ad bene beateque vivendum inflammat" (*Epistolæ Broëti*, pp. 203–4).

[2] Texts from the municipal archives of Parma in Tacchi Venturi, *Storia*, vol. I, part II, pp. 194–200.

As a result of these *démarches* in Heaven and on earth Cardinal Guidiccioni came to terms, though not until a year of crushing anxiety had passed over the head of Ignatius. The verbal approbation of the Pope was given on September 3rd, 1539, but the bull establishing the Society of Jesus bore the date, September 27th, 1540. In the meantime, however dark the omens, the Saint never lost his confidence, as may be seen by the fact that he obtained from Francis Xavier and Simon Rodriguez, before they left Rome in March 1540, their votes, secret and carefully sealed, for the election of the first Jesuit General. Guidiccioni's terms were that the numbers of the new order should be limited provisionally to sixty, and on this condition, readily accepted by Ignatius, Pope Paul III signed at his palace of San Marco the Bull, *Regimini militantis Ecclesiæ*, establishing the Society of Jesus. This famous document, which, after a stylized curial opening, mentions the names and nationalities of all ten companions, is in substance a recapitulation of the five articles, with the reference to sung Masses and penances of rule omitted. These articles, says the Pope, "We, of our Apostolic authority, approve, confirm, and bless, . . . taking under our protection and that of the Apostolic See the companions themselves, and granting to them licence and power to draw up among themselves such particular constitutions as they shall judge to be conformed to the purpose of this Society, to the glory of Jesus Christ Our Lord, and to the good of the neighbour, *non obstantibus . . . quibusvis aliis constitutionibus et ordinationibus apostolicis cæterisque contrariis quibuscumque.*"[1]

Meanwhile, between its oral and its written confirma-

[1] M.H.S.J., *Constitutiones*, vol. I, pp. 24–31.

tion, things had not stood still with the infant Society. Indeed, Ignatius found it difficult to keep a single one of his men in Rome, so great was the demand for them elsewhere, and informed the Archbishop of Siena in August 1540 that it had become almost a whole-time occupation to be their adviser by correspondence at their various posts "in Portugal or in the Indies, in Spain, in Paris, in Ireland, in Naples, in Parma, in Placenza, in Brescia and in the March of Ancona."[1] At first, the most perambulatory of the brethren was the Frenchman Favre who evangelized in the course of two years, 1539–41, places as far apart as Parma, Brescia, Worms, Speyer, Ratisbon, Saragossa, Alcalá and Madrid. At the abortive Conference of Worms between the Catholics and Protestants, he was theologian to the Papal Legate and told Ignatius that he felt "great shoots of love and charity" penetrate his soul for the German people. Referring to the prohibition laid on the Catholics from dealings with the Lutherans, he exclaimed: "God knows how much it would delight me to have leave to converse with them, and especially with their chief man, Philip Melanchthon."[2]

But Favre's big initial field of apostolic activities was tame and almost parochial compared with some others that soon beckoned to the sons of Ignatius. First and greatest of these, not mentioned in the five articles but appearing in the bull, *Regimini*, was the famed and fabled El Dorado "quas Indias vocant." As early as November 1538, their former academic superior, the Portuguese Diego de Gouvea, Principal of the Collège de Sainte-Barbe, Paris, had approached the brethren with

---

[1] *Epistolæ et instructiones*, vol. I, p. 159.
[2] M.H.S.J., *Fabri Monumenta*, pp. 50, 58.

a suggestion that some of them might sail as missionaries to Portugal's new empire in India. In reply, Broet, who spoke for all ten, told him that they had already been invited to sail to Spain's new empire in America, but that they were the Pope's men and His Holiness had wished them to find their America in Rome. "The distance of the places has no terror for us," he continued, "no more than has the labour of learning a new tongue, might only that which is most pleasing to Christ be done." Now if the Pope were to order us to India, why then—*ibimus gaudentes.*[1] His reply was transmitted by Gouvea to John III, King of Portugal, who, in the August following, instructed his ambassador at Rome, Dom Pedro Mazcarenhas, to make investigations about the virtues and abilities of the priests in question. If these proved satisfactory, and no other way presented itself of obtaining the men for the Indian mission, he was to secure an order from the Pope to that effect and then arrange for their journey to Portugal at the earliest opportunity. One result of the ambassador's inquiry was that he took St. Ignatius for his own confessor. But the Pope, while praising the good intentions of the King and warmly commending the Fathers, declined to put them under a formal command, because "a voyage so long and perilous ought to be undertaken voluntarily." Senhor Mazcarenhas must therefore treat with them himself and report to His Holiness the results of his negotiations. "In this matter," he informed the King, "I had little trouble, for, with great content, they agreed to make the journey, . . . though they could offer me only two men for it, as they

---

[1] M.H.S.J., *Epistolæ et instructiones,* vol. I, pp. 132–3.

number a bare six in Rome now and two others are to be sent by the Pope to Ireland and Scotland."[1]

At that time, March 1540, Ignatius had recruited personally or through those good sergeants, Favre and Laynez, a few more companions, the able and devoted administrator from Lombardy, Pietro Codacio, the saintly ex-publishers, Diego and Stefano de Eguia, the first man on the long list of Jesuit martyrs, Antonio Criminali, the young and ardent Valencian priest, Jerome Domenech, the gentle and lovable Paolo d'Achille, and, to mention no others, the delightful, high-spirited Spanish lad, Pedro Ribadeneira. They were grand material but far too few to meet half the demands on their Father. Of his first disciples only Francis Xavier and Salmeron remained in Rome at the time of the Portuguese King's application. Salmeron had already been set apart for the Pope's newly planned mission to Ireland, and as for Francis, we are given this picture of him by Rodriguez: "When I saw him in Rome looking so frail, thin, and practically worn out, I judged that he could never recover his previous health and strength; indeed, I nearly persuaded myself that he would be of no further use for any work whatever."[2] But Ignatius found something for this dearest of his sons to do; he made him the first secretary of the adumbrated Society of Jesus. To judge by some remarks of the genial young Strada, himself, though not yet a priest, rapidly obtaining fame as an orator, Francis was an incompetent secretary. "I marvel that I have received

[1] Correspondence in appendix to *Epistolæ et instructiones*, vol. I, pp. 737–41. When told of their readiness to go, the Pope issued a formal order on the matter.

[2] *Epistolæ Broëti*, p. 491.

no reply to my other letters," writes he from Montepulciano in November 1539. "If I liked I could throw all the blame on Señor Maestro Francisco who has undertaken the task of writing for all. But, to be kind to the man, I excuse him this time, only entreating him to remember that, if the winter cold has rendered his hands too numb to write, the heat of fire, which has the quality of making cold things warm, will remedy the situation and give him fingers apt and able to wield a pen without shivering. This I write, entertaining myself with Señor Maestro Francisco as though I was in his company and talking to him face to face. Please do not misinterpret my manner of speaking, because, as a matter of fact, owing to the intense cold here, I have been obliged to light a little fire myself in order to thaw out my hands for this letter."[1]

In consequence of his ill-health, and perhaps, also, because Ignatius could not bear to part with him, Francis was not among the first two chosen for the Indian adventure. That honour fell to the obvious Simon Rodriguez, a Portuguese all on fire for the foreign missions, and to Nicholas Bobadilla, who, tough and enterprising, seemed born to affront hardships and dangers. But he had fallen grievously ill in Naples while engaged at the Pope's behest on the delicate task of reconciling Joanna of Aragon with her husband Ascanio Colonna. In the hospital he heard a doctor say of him to a nurse: "That man is going to his tomb." Recalled to Rome by Ignatius, the fever again prostrated him and destroyed all hope of his being fit for the voyage to India. It was a providential fever. Ignatius himself lay in bed ill at the time. Summoning Francis,

[1] M.H.S.J., *Epistolæ mixtæ*, vol. I, pp. 40–1.

he said to him: "Master Francis, you know that by order of the Pope two of us are to go to India, and also that Master Bobadilla, who was chosen, cannot go on account of his illness, nor can the Ambassador wait any longer. This is your enterprise." We have the very words which Francis used in his instant reply: "Pues, sus! Hemé aqui!" They are untranslatable literally, but mean, "Splendid, I'm your man!"[1]

That little dialogue between the two saints was spoken on March 14th and the Ambassador left for Lisbon on the 16th, so Francis had two days in which to settle his affairs and say good-bye to his friends until eternity. On the 15th, he drew up three short documents, one affirming in advance his approval of all that should be decided with regard to rules and constitutions, a second containing the formula of his vows, and the third registering his vote for the first superior-general of the Society to be. That same day a young, unknown priest offered himself to Ignatius as a humble coadjutor of the men going to India. So obscure were his origins that only his baptismal name has survived, but later we find this gentle, quietly heroic Micer Paul of Camerino acting the part of a Timothy to the Apostle of the Indies. For his wardrobe, the Apostle took "ciertos calcones viejos," some ancient breeches, which, with a threadbare cassock, an indescribable cassock in Ribadeneira's opinion, made up his entire baggage.[2] By March 31st he was in Bologna, from which place he wrote in the following terms to Ignatius and Codacio: "On Easter Day I received your letter . . . and with it so much joy and consolation as is known unto Our Lord. Since, I think, in this life only by correspon-

---

[1] *Scripta de Sancto Ignatio*, vol. I, p. 381.   [2] *Loc. cit.*

dence shall we meet again (in the next, *facie ad faciem*
with many an embrace!), it remains for us during the
little time left to take frequent looks at one another
through the medium of letters. . . . The Lord Ambassador heaps on me so many favours that I should never
finish writing of them, and I know not how I would be
able to allow it, were it not for the thought, nay, the
practical certainty, that in the Indies I shall pay off the
debt at the price of no less than my life. . . . Would you
give my greetings to Madonna Faustina de' Jancolini and
tell her that I have said Mass for her Vincenzo and
mine,[1] and that tomorrow I shall say another for herself.
She may rest assured that I shall never forget her, even
when I am in the Indies. Remind her from me, Micer
Pedro, my dearest brother,[2] to keep the promise she made
me to go to Confession and Communion, and to let me
know if she has done so and how often. If she wishes to
give pleasure to Vincenzo, hers and mine, tell her from
me to forgive those who killed her son, as Vincenzo
is interceding much for them in Heaven."[3]

From Bologna via Modena and Reggio the cavalcade
wended its way to Parma, where Francis hoped to be
able to say good-bye to his oldest friend, Favre. Finding
that Favre had left for Brescia the very day of his arrival,
he meditated going on there to see him but was dissuaded

---

[1] This young friend of Francis, the only son of Faustina, had been
murdered in Rome. His mother was the earliest benefactress of the Society
there, having bequeathed to the "poveri preti di Jesu Christo" her house
in the Piazza Colonna, "on condition that no woman, young or old, poor
or rich or religious, ever set foot in it." The "poveri preti" declined the
gift.

[2] Father Pietro Codacio.

[3] M.H.S.J., *Monumenta Xaveriana*, vol. I, pp. 208–9.

by the Ambassador. "God grant," wrote Favre referring
to their disappointed tryst, "that if we are never to see
one another again in this world we may rejoice together
in the next, remembering these partings endured only for
Christ."[1] Francis, by all that we hear of him, was a man
deeply affectionate, who treasured old ties and friendships.
It was noticed that his ecstasies while saying Mass came
over him at the Memento for the Living. Near his
ancestral home there is an eminence still called *Las Penas
del A Dios*, the Sorrows of Good-bye, because he is sup-
posed to have climbed to it to look his last on Castle
Xavier. However that may have been, it is not wholly
fanciful to think that, as he traversed the Basque lands,
"God saw this long road all scattered with *Penas del A
Dios*."[2] Lisbon was reached in mid-June after a three
months' journey, memorable to Francis, not for any
spring-time glories of Alps or Pyrenees, but for the mile-
stones of his absolutions and the sweet landmarks of his
communings with God. Rodriguez had gone ahead and
was already hard at work in the hot city, where, despite
King John's attempts to make him comfortable, he insisted
on begging his bread and living with the poor in hospices.
"Immediately on arriving in Lisbon," wrote Francis, "I
went to Master Simon who that very day was expecting
the access of a quartan ague. My coming was such a joy
to him and seeing him such a joy to me that the two joys
combined cast out the fever, which now for a month has

[1] *Fabri Monumenta*, p. 31.
[2] Cros, *Saint François de Xavier, sa vie et ses lettres*, vol. I, p. 162. The
story that, in a spirit of renunciation, he declined to turn aside to visit his
mother at the Castle (Coleridge, *The Life and Letters of St. Francis Xavier*,
vol. I, p. 65) is nonsense, as his mother had been dead then for eleven
years.

not returned. He is very well and having much fruit of his labours."[1] Both men had much fruit of their labours, so much, that the King, whose court they soon transformed, held them back from India for eight long months and in the end allowed only Francis to make the journey. For the present we may leave them to their endless confessions, their sermons, their retreats, their work for the poor and the hapless prisoners of the Inquisition, and return to Ignatius in his house near the Torre del Melangolo.[2]

Five months went by after the issue of the bull, *Regimini*, before Ignatius was able by Papal consent to detach sufficient of his men from various tenacious bishops to make possible the election of his Order's first superior and the discussion of its constitutions. On March 4th, 1541, six of them, Ignatius, Salmeron, Broet, Le Jay, Laynez and Codure, fell to work, it being impossible to retrieve Bobadilla from Calabria, Favre from Germany, or Rodriguez and Xavier from Portugal. Moreover, Lent had begun and those six eager men felt the call of it like a clarion, so at the very first meeting it was decided that Ignatius and Codure should draw up a scheme for combined discussion later, while the rest gave themselves heartily to the labour for souls which they loved.

[1] *Monumenta Xaveriana*, vol. I, p. 213.

[2] Among the letters of Francis at this time the most revealing are those to his uncle, known as the Doctor of Navarre, who was then a professor at the University of Coimbra. Their spirit is in the following lines: "My soul received so much joy and consolation from your letter of October 25th that nothing but the sight of you, longed for by me these many days, could have given me more rest. . . . I say nothing of the love that binds me to you. The Lord, who alone searches the secrets of both our hearts, knows how very dear you are to me" (*Monumenta Xaveriana*, vol. I, pp. 324–6).

Ignatius and Codure produced a schedule of forty-nine points dealing in greater detail with the matters presented more largely in the five chapters. As an instance of the detail, among the ten ordinances with regard to dress is one forbidding the general superior or any professed father "to go shod outside the house in *pantuflos*," or to have a mule for his private transport. The capital distinction of grades in the Society of Jesus, professed and non-professed or spiritual coadjutors, is more marked here than in the articles, and received its final juridical form later in the Constitutions.[1] All forty-nine points met with approval from the Fathers in council and became an interim code for the Society until the Constitutions were written and promulgated.[2]

The last important business requiring attention was the election of the Society's superior. So far, in the words of Polanco, "Ignatius had held the rudder of this little ship, but in the guise of a father who had begotten all according to the spirit and won their completest confidence by his prudence and charity, not as though he possessed any legitimate power to command."[3] He ruled not by law but by love, and, away from him on their missions, the brethren had managed very well by taking it in turn for a week or a month to be superior. But such idyllic arrangements were not suited to a rapidly expand-

---

[1] Besides an extra fourth vow of obedience to the Pope professed Fathers take a series of simple vows to safeguard the poverty prescribed in the Constitutions, to refrain from the least attempt to secure office inside or outside the Society, and to refuse ecclesiastical dignities, such as bishoprics or the purple of cardinals, unless solemnly ordered to accept them by the Pope.

[2] M.H.S.J., *Constitutiones*, vol. I, pp. lxxii–lxxviii, 33–48.

[3] *Chronicon*, vol. I, p. 90.

ing organization bound by the terms of its existence to advance its flag into any part of the earth that the Pope might indicate. It is this intimate dependence on the Holy See which explains the novel features of the Society of Jesus, its abandonment of choir and other monastic features, its two grades of membership, and, above all, its centralization of power in the hands of a general, as contrasted with the more federal constitutions of the older orders. The little election was very solemnly conducted. During three days the six Fathers gave themselves up to prayer for guidance in their choice. Then their sealed votes, together with those of the absentees previously obtained, except Bobadilla's,[1] were placed in a box and left to be, as it were, consecrated by a further three days of prayer. At length the time arrived to scrutinize them, which is a thing, perhaps, that the readers of this book also may like to do, so here they are in substance: *Ignatius*—"Jesus. Excluding myself, I give my vote in Our Lord to him who receives a majority of votes to be the superior. I have given it indeterminately for good reasons, but if the Society thinks otherwise, or that it is better and more to the glory of God for me to particularize, I am ready to do so." *Xavier*—"I, Francisco, say and affirm, *nullo modo suasus ab homine*, . . . that the one to be elected general in our Society is, in my judgment, our old leader and true father, Don Ignatio, who brought us together with no little labour, . . . and that, after his death, his successor is to be Father Peter Favre. . . ." *Favre* —"Concerning the first superior-general to whom we are to vow obedience, I give my vote to Ignatius, and in his

[1] He was ill at the time and did not send in a vote. Also he was a peculiar, if zealous, man, with notions of his own about most things.

absence by death, which God forbid, to Master Francis Xavier. . . ." *Laynez*—"Jesus, Maria. I, Diego Laynez, induced only by zeal for the glory of the Lord and the salvation of my soul, elect Father Ignatius Loyola as my superior and the superior of the Society of Jesus." *Salmeron*—"In the name of Jesus Christ, Amen. I, Alfonso Salmeron, most unworthy of this Society, after prayer to God and mature consideration, elect for superior of the whole congregation Ignatius of Loyola, who, as he begot us all in Christ and fed us with milk when little ones, will, now that we are grown up, bring us the solid food of obedience and guide us to the rich and abundant pastures of Paradise . . . , so that we may truly say, *et nos populus pascuæ ejus et oves manus ejus*, and he, joyfully for his part, *Domine, ex his quos dedisti mihi, non perdidi ex eis quemquam.* Which may Jesus, the Good Shepherd, deign to grant unto us. Amen." *Rodriguez*— "To the praise of God and His Virgin Mother. It seems to me, according to such light as, all unworthy, I possess, that Ignatius is the one whom we ought to choose from among us as president and ruler, and that if by some mischance or death he is not available, then Peter Favre should succeed in his place, . . . asserting, most dear Brethren, that I have not been persuaded to this by anybody, whether directly or indirectly, but act of my own free will and choice, as I am confident you also will do. . . . And when, dearest Brethren, the Lord will have happily fulfilled your desires, remember your brothers, and lift up your hearts for them also." *Le Jay*—"I judge and desire that Ignatius, whom now these many years God has given us all for a father, should be elected superior of our Society . . . , and to his rule, after God and the saints,

I now submit myself body and soul most willingly."
Broet—"In the name of Our Lord Jesus Christ. Amen.
I, Paschase Broet, elect as superior-general Father Ignatius
of Loyola." *Codure*—"Jesus, Maria. . . . Considering
only the greater glory of God and good of the whole
Society, I judge that he whom I have always known as a
most ardent promoter of God's honour and the salvation
of souls ought to be placed over others because he has
always made himself the least of all and ministered to all.
I mean reverend Father Ignatius of Loyola."[1]

From his vote, it is quite plain that Ignatius, who knew
his men through and through, expected to be elected.
In explanation of his antecedent refusal to accept the
honour he has left the only writing which he ever penned
concerning himself, except such incidental references as
are to be found in his letters. He "made a speech," he
says, "according to the feelings of his soul, affirming
that he had a greater desire and will to be governed
than to govern; that he could not discover in his soul
sufficient strength to rule himself, much less to rule
others. Considering this, and his many evil habits past
and present, as well as his many sins, faults and miseries,
he declared and declares that he does not accept such an
office, nor would he ever be able to accept it until he
had more light on the subject than he then possessed.
He begged and entreated them much in the Lord to consider the matter with greater diligence for three or four
days more, commending themselves more earnestly to
God Our Lord in order to find someone better suited

[1] M.H.S.J., *Monumenta Ignatiana*, vol. II, p. 5; *Xaveriana*, vol. I, p. 812;
Fabri, p. 51; *Lainii*, vol. VIII, p. 638; *Epistolæ Salmeronis*, vol. I, p. 1;
Epistolæ Broëti, pp. 519, 886, 1, 418.

and more useful to all for the task." After four days the Fathers accordingly voted again, with exactly the same result. Ignatius then, "having examined both sides of the question in the light of God our Lord's greater service, replied that, to avoid extremes and for the greater peace of his conscience, he would put the matter in the hands of his confessor, Father Theodore, friar of San Pietro de Montorio, making to him a general confession of all his sins . . . and giving him a description of all his infirmities and bodily miseries. That done, it would be for the confessor to order him in the name of Christ Our Lord, taking into account his entire life past and present, either to accept or to refuse this burden." The Saint then spent three days at San Pietro alone with his confessor who at the end gave judgment for acceptance. Not even that satisfied him, however, so he begged Father Theodore to commend the question to God for a little while longer, and thereupon with a quiet soul to put his opinion in writing and send it to the brethren. Afterwards he returned home. The confessor's sealed decision arrived three days later and was to the effect that Ignatius ought to undertake the business and government of the Society. Then at last he gave in, and issued instructions that on the first Friday after Easter, April 22nd, 1541, all would make the stations of the Seven Churches of Rome, pronouncing their vows in St. Paul's according to the bull granted by the Pope.[1]

[1] M.H.S.J., *Scripta de Sancto Ignatio*, vol. II, pp. 4–8. Both Sedgwick and Van Dyke are at pains to safeguard Ignatius from the imputation of insincerity, but the Saint, whom even the outlandish bigot, George Borrow, recognized for "a great, portentous man, honest withal," hardly requires defending, at least to anybody with the slightest real knowledge of his character.

The vows taken on that occasion during a Mass celebrated by Ignatius are, except for a few inessential changes of phrasing, identical with those still made by all professed Fathers of the Society of Jesus: "I, Ignatius Loyola, promise to Almighty God and to the Pope, His Vicar upon earth, before His Virgin Mother and the whole court of Heaven, and in the presence of the Society, perpetual poverty, chastity and obedience, according to the manner of life set forth in the Bull of the Society of Our Lord Jesus, and in the Constitutions declared or to be promulgated, of the same Society. Moreover, I promise special obedience to the Supreme Pontiff with regard to the missions mentioned in the Bull, and likewise to be diligent to see that children are taught the rudiments of the faith, according to the same Bull and Constitutions." Having read the formula, Ignatius consumed the Sacred Host and then turned towards his companions who each individually pronounced the vows, substituting for the words "et Summo Pontifici, ejus in terris Vicario," these others, "et tibi, Reverende Pater, locum Dei tenenti." Finally, they all received Holy Communion, and, after their thanksgiving, went in turn to embrace Ignatius and give him the kiss of peace, "not without great devotion, feeling, and tears."[1]

A few months later, in June, the new Society received from the Pope through the good offices of Father Codacio its first church and parish, Santa Maria della Strada—Our Lady of the Road. It was a very appropriate title for the mother-church of an essentially missionary order, which put the emphasis in its constitutions, not on peace nor even

[1] The description is entirely from the pen of Ignatius, as in the last reference.

on the sanctification of its own members, but on work of every kind for the salvation of souls. "I remember often hearing our Father say," wrote Gonzales, "that he wanted none in the Society just to save their own souls, if, beyond this, they did not all make ready to save the souls of other people."[1] The work that went on at Santa Maria della Strada was the kind that does not come under the caption of news, though it made news then to hear priests preaching so simply and earnestly the great neglected truths, or to watch them, masters of Paris, so eagerly teaching the small ragamuffins of Rome the Ten Commandments. Later, in the Constitutions of his Order, St. Ignatius laid it down that each of his sons ought to be, as it were, a sort of heavenly Autolycus, with a keen, speculative eye for the unconsidered trifles of humanity, for orphans and outcasts and the disinherited poor. In Rome, even when burdened with the ever-increasing cares of his office as superior, he reserved half of his heart for such people and was instrumental in revivifying or newly establishing confraternities to care for neglected children, the sick poor, and those saddest prodigals of the human family, women of the streets. That last must have been a work dear to Our Lady of the Road. It was sponsored by a confraternity composed of cardinals, bishops and other eminent persons who displayed a perhaps natural timidity in coming to grips with the problem of founding a house of refuge for the Magdalens. In the little piazza in front of the Jesuit church Father Codacio had been conducting excavations, and prided himself on the fine heap of old marble blocks, the remains

[1] M.H.S.J., *Memoriale P. Consalvi* in *Scripta de Sancto Ignatio*, vol. II, p. 232.

of some buried temple, which he had unearthed. "Sell the stones, Peter," said Ignatius to him one day, "and give me a hundred gold crowns out of what you get for them." He then presented himself with the money at a meeting of the illustrious *Compagnia della Grazia* and said: "Here are a hundred crowns. If nobody wishes to be ahead of me in starting this work, let them at least follow me." They did, and that was how the famous Casa de Santa Marta for repentant prostitutes came into existence, Ignatius himself being given the entire spiritual charge of the institution.[1] Many there were to tell him that he merely wasted his time seeking those lost sheep and trying to reform them. "There's where you're wrong," he answered the doubters, "for were I able by the utmost exertion and diligence to persuade one human being to refrain from sin for a single night *propter Dominum meum Jesum Christum*, I would omit absolutely nothing to ensure that God should not be offended during that time, even if I knew that the sinner would immediately afterwards return to his sin."[2]

[1] Ribadeneira, in *Scripta de Sancto Ignatio*, vol. I, p. 357; Tacchi Venturi, *Storia*, vol. I, part II, p. 292. St. Martha's brought on the devoted head of its chaplain a whole flood of abominable calumny.

[2] Ribadeneira, *l.c.*, p. 356. The vocation of Pedro Ribadeneira and his training by Ignatius, whose first biographer he became, are episodes of Jesuit history too well known to be repeated in any detail. Pedro, a fourteen-year-old and very hot-headed page in the train of Cardinal Alessandro Farnese, had been advised by Dr. Ortiz to seek out Ignatius if ever he got into trouble, which did not take long to happen. Having played truant one day from his duties, he was afraid to return to the Cardinal and, with his heart in his mouth, knocked at the door pointed out to him by Ortiz as the home of Ignatius. He was received with so much kindness and understanding by the Saint that he offered himself altogether to the Society and became the joy and the torment of the Fathers, progressing through many escapades to great eminence in the service of God. One of his recollections

In his government of the Society of Jesus the same invincible spirit manifested itself. Sixty years ago when much less than half his extant letters had been printed, a writer in the secular *Revue Historique* ventured the opinion that "perhaps no other founder of a religious order did so much *épistolairement* to extend and consolidate his work as Ignatius Loyola." With more than nine thousand printed pages of the Saint's letters and instructions now available to us in the Jesuit *Monumenta Historica*, we can safely eliminate the cautious "perhaps" from that judgment. And it was not only letters that demanded his energy, but the far heavier and more responsible task of drafting his young Order's constitutions on which all its future depended.[1] His first appointed helper, Codure, "il buen Magistro Juan," escaped a dreaded journey to Ireland by going to Heaven instead in 1541, and then he had to wait six years before finding his other Juan, the ideal secretary, Polanco.[2] It is certain,

---

from those early days was of seeing Ignatius teaching catechism in Santa Maria della Strada. "I, a boy, admonished him, a holy man of fifty," he says, "that there were many mistakes in his speech, and many things to be rectified, because he spoke a Spanish sort of Italian. 'Good,' he replied, 'note down, if you please, anything you think wrong, so as to be able to warn me.' I therefore took to observing him carefully and made notes of the foreign words he used, of his mispronunciations, and of other such faults . . ., but there were so many that I got tired of the task and told him so. Then said he: 'Pues, Pedro, que haremos á Dios?'—Well Pedro, what *are* we to do for God?" (*Scripta*, vol. I, p. 358).

[1] That Ignatius and Ignatius alone, though helped very largely in the drafting and even inspired occasionally by Polanco, was the author of the Constitutions, has been proved beyond a shadow of doubt by the editors of the *Monumenta* (*Constitutiones Societatis Jesu*, vol. II, Rome, 1936, pp. cxlvi–cxc).

[2] The assiduity of this remarkable man may be judged from the fact that his extremely prosy but invaluable *Chronicon* of early Jesuit activities runs to six volumes, containing 4,515 pages, in the *Monumenta*.

however, that he began the long labour alone as early as
1544, not with his pen, indeed, but in the travail of his
soul. By some heavenly chance, a kind of spiritual diary
which he kept for twelve months at this time escaped the
general destruction to which he condemned his private
papers. It is entirely a record of the graces accorded to
him, such an entry as this for February 2nd, 1544, being
typical: "Abundance of devotion at Mass, with tears,
and an increase of confidence in Our Lady." This and
the following four entries all contain the cryptic phrase,
"y mas a no nada," which is explained on February 8th
by the words "no tener renta alguna," not to have an
income of any kind, allowing us to discern his main preoccupation in these intimate and profoundly mystical
colloquies with God. For forty days he continued to
seek earnestly the guidance of Heaven on that one point
of the poverty suitable to his Order. As the phrase "mas
a no nada" indicates by its peculiar reinforcement of nega-
tives, the whole bent of his soul was for the dependent,
hand-to-mouth poverty which has no assured dividends,
however small, to rely on, and that, in fact, became the
law for the professed members of his Society. Sometimes,
as he confides to the paper, he was unable to begin the
Judica of his Mass through excess of emotion; at other
times, he would lose power to pronounce the words as he
went on. *Con muchas logrimas* is the burden of the whole
story. "We see in these notes the movements of a soul
constantly preoccupied to bring the arguments and con-
clusions of the most concentrated human reflection into
accord with the inspirations of grace, a soul by turns
exalted and illuminated, or anxious, perplexed, undecided,
in which case it returns with unwearying insistence to the

Master of souls; we see one filled and saturated with sweet devotion, or stumbling gropingly through the dark night of the mystics, bewildered, hesitant, convinced, broken-hearted, and then, once again, serene. No sooner does he think that he has grasped the solution than it escapes him, but he finds it again with tears in the heart of the Blessed Trinity and in the intercession of the Saints."[1]

Ignatius told Gonzales, the confidant of his autobiography, that "visions fell to his lot with exceeding frequency when he was fashioning the Constitutions . . . , sometimes of God the Father, sometimes of the Trinity of Persons, sometimes of the Most Blessed Virgin, now interceding, now approving."[2] But human industry was not neglected for all that, and Ignatius made a deep study, not only of the ecclesiastical legislation bearing on his problems, but of the venerable rules of St. Augustine, St. Benedict, St. Francis, St. Dominic, and other great monastic patriarchs. Though no part of those rules is embodied *verbatim* in the Jesuit Constitutions, yet there are many similarities due to the fact that all stem from the same parent trunk of the New Testament. In particular, the Ignatian doctrine of obedience, so often harshly criticized and condemned, is substantially the same as that

[1] Bernoville. *Les Jésuites*, Paris, 1934, pp. 104–5. This book by a French *littérateur* of Basque extraction is one of the most sympathetic and understanding ever written about the Society of Jesus. It is not, however, a history of the Society.

[2] *Scripta de Sancto Ignatio*, vol. I, pp. 97–8. While speaking to Gonzales, the Saint had with him the leaves of his so-called diary. "I besought him," writes the Father, "to let me have a short loan of the papers, but he would not." We are more privileged than the good man, for we may study the papers at our leisure in the Madrid edition of the Jesuit Constitutions edited by Father de la Torre in 1892, or in the second of the two volumes devoted to them in the *Monumenta*, pp. 86–158.

contained in the fifth chapter of the Rule of St. Benedict, nor does anything that Ignatius says on the subject go beyond the following declaration of the Father of Western monasticism: "If perchance any heavy or impossible commands are laid on a brother, let him receive the order of the Superior with all meekness and obedience. But should the weight of the burden seem altogether to exceed the measure of his strength, let him patiently and opportunely put before the Superior the reasons why it is impossible for him to bear it, in no spirit of pride or resistance or contradiction. Supposing, then, that after this representation the order of the Prior remains what it was, the subject is to know that it is expedient for him, and to obey, relying out of charity on the help of God."[1]

Were it not known by external criteria that the same man, and he Ignatius, composed both the *Spiritual Exercises* and the Jesuit Constitutions, we might be convinced of the fact by their internal resemblances. Those well-known Ignatian clichés, his obsessions as we might almost call them, *majus Dei obsequium, majus Dei servitium, major Dei gloria*, pervade both works. It has been estimated that the phrase "the greater glory of God" recurs 259 times in the Constitutions, or about once to each manuscript page. The reason for this frequency is because the entire legislation of the work tends in every detail to the fulfilment of the one supreme law and end, God's greater

[1] *Regula Sancti Benedicti*, cap. LXVIII. As for the famous "perinde ac cadaver," or as Ignatius wrote it, "como si fuisse un cuerpo muerto," St. Bonaventure affirms that St. Francis of Assisi "put down the similitude of a dead body as an example of obedience" (*Legenda de Vita S. Francisci* cap. 6), and many centuries earlier,the author of the *Constitutiones monasticæ*, long believed to be St. Basil, used the example of a workman's tool which permits itself to be employed however the user wishes.

service, and, this whether the question be about admitting candidates for the Order (part I), or dismissing them (part II), or forming them to virtue (part III), or training them for the work of helping souls (part IV), or binding them more closely to their Order when trained (part V), or securing their subsequent progress in the way of God (part VI), or disposing of them as labourers in God's vine-yard (part VII), or maintaining their union with one another and with their superior-general (part VIII), or governing them as an Order (part IX), or the increasing and conservng of that Order in its good estate (part X). "Ignatius does not over-emphasize machinery but some-times seems almost to overlook it. . . . His view of the Order is personal and not at all mechanical. Men must make it and not formulas. He saw its unity not simply as a similarity of regulations but chiefly as a unity of spirit. He evidently did not look on the rules as iron-clad. He provides especially for exceptions, and the exceptions he names are manifestly to keep the spirit at the expense of the letter. All through these laboriously wrought-out rules for the guidance of an intricate enterprise for doing good to his fellows, there shines a simple sincerity, at times very touching, and an unshakable trust in God. This man wishes his followers to be pure in heart, poor in spirit, merciful, to hunger and thirst after righteousness to strive always to make peace."[1]

[1] Van Dyke, *Ignatius Loyola*, pp. 156–7. And compare Sedgwick, p. 223: "Protestants have declaimed against him what they call the iron constraint put upon the human soul. But if one stops to think, how does the Jesuit training differ, unless perhaps in conscientious intensity, from that at West Point or Saint-Cyr? In a military academy the whole weight of authority comes down on the individual soul. Substitute the flag for the cross, country for church, famous generals and marshals for saints and martyrs,

The writing of the Constitutions cost Ignatius three years of intense application, after which he submitted them in 1551 to the judgment of such Fathers as he could summon to Rome, revised them in accordance with their suggestions, and then sent them to be tested experimentally for a long period in Spain, Portugal, and other countries. He was so far from being an autocrat that he went to his grave two years before they became the law of the Society of Jesus.

---

honour for grace, and you will find that the constraint in either case is very much the same. Obedience is of equal obligation, the word of the superior as indisputable, the period of preparation about as long. As for liberty of thought, there is no more room for patriotic agnosticism in West Point than for religious agnosticism in a Jesuit College. . . . The difference is that we have lost our belief in supernatural religion, but not as yet our faith in nationality. But whatever the plausibility of this comparison, there is, in truth, something humanly sacrilegious in coldly criticizing a document every clause of which was prayed over with tears, and offered to the Lord."

CHAPTER IV

ALL THINGS TO ALL MEN

"IT is to be observed," writes Ignatius in the Constitutions, "that the intention of the vow wherewith the Society has bound itself unreservedly to obedience to the Supreme Vicar of Christ, is that we repair to whatever part of the world he shall determine to send us for the greater glory of God and the succour of souls, whether among the faithful or infidels; nor did the Society mean any particular region, but that it might be dispersed in divers regions and places throughout the world."[1] God took the Saint at his word, for, before he died in 1556, his men had crossed all the seas of the world and landed in Britain, Ireland, India, Japan, Brazil, Abyssinia and China.

The mission to Britain and Ireland was a lost cause from the very start, and had no results except to reveal the inexhaustible patience of St. Ignatius. In 1536 the Irish Catholics revolted when Henry VIII endeavoured to impose his schism upon their country. But, divided among themselves, they were easily beaten in detail by the more cohesive English. By 1539 when their last champion, Con O'Neill, succumbed, all seemed over. O'Neill in desperation appealed to the Pope for assistance, and then it was that Paul III, urged by Robert

[1] Part VII, c.i., n.1.

Wauchope, archbishop-elect of Armagh, determined to send two nuncios invested with full apostolic authority to the stricken island. There followed a busy drafting of bulls and faculties, and then long delays and revisions of the bulls, due to various causes of which the chief was the scarcity of news from Ireland. To Rome that country was indeed a misty island, a *terra incognita* blacked-out by the great bulk of schismatic England. A message from its people, faithful but beleaguered, might take as long as six months to cross a Europe in turmoil with the wars of France and the Empire. And France was the ally of Ireland's enemy. Still, the Pope persisted in his design to send nuncios, though nobody had very clear ideas as to what they might be expected to achieve. At all events, their going would be a gesture of sympathy, and sympathy counts for something in stiffening a people's resolution. The two men eventually chosen for the mission were Broet and Salmeron. Ignatius, as much in the dark as everybody else but bent on being helpful, drew up in September 1541 three sets of instructions for the guidance of that valiant pair who, as like as not, had never before given a thought to Ireland. One of these, headed "Del modo de negociar y conversar in Domino," is worth quoting for the light which it sheds, if not on Ireland, on the diplomatic methods of Ignatius.

"In dealing with all persons," writes the Saint "and especially with equals or inferiors, according to their dignity or authority, speak little and reluctantly, listen long and willingly. Let farewells be brisk and courteous. In conversing with persons of rank or power consider first, in order to win their affection for the greater service of God Our Lord, of what temperament they are and adapt yourselves thereto. If a man is passionate, with a quick, vivacious manner of speech, do you also speak of good and holy things in a similar style, eschewing grave, solemn or melancholy airs. With those, on the other hand, who by nature are circumspect, reticent, and slow in conversation, you will be just the same, for that is what pleases them. *Omnia omnibus factus sum.* Note that when two hasty-tempered people converse, there is the greatest danger, if they be not completely like-minded, of disagreement and heat in their discourses, so one who is conscious of a quick temper ought to go well armed by self-examination and resolutions to endure and keep calm, especially if he knows the other to be weak in self-control. . . . In all speech with others by which we desire to win them and put them in the net for the greater service of God Our Lord, let us follow the method adopted by our enemy, the devil, in his dealings with a good man, he all for evil purposes, we all for good. For he goes in by the other's door to come out by his own, not contradicting but approving his habits, taking stock of his soul and drawing it to good and holy thoughts that please its devotion, until, little by little, he works round to come out his own way, luring the soul, *sub specie boni*, into some obstacle of error or illusion. . . . In like manner, we, for our good purpose, may applaud or agree with another in regard to some matter in itself innocent, passing over other things of a bad complexion, so as to win his sympathy and further our good purpose. . . . With such as we find tempted or sad we should conduct ourselves affably, speaking more at length and showing greater contentment and joy interiorly and exteriorly, in order to go counter to their depression.

In all dealings with others, especially when acting as peace-makers or giving spiritual advice, it is necessary to be guarded, remembering that everything one says may or will become public. In the dispatch of business be liberal with time, that is to say, if you promise something for to-morrow, do it, if possible, to-day."[1]

The other two much longer instructions deal with the journey and its contingencies. "Do not have a mule or a horse," says Ignatius. "In board and lodging always aim at a becoming simplicity, . . . making shift with a half or a third, as you can best manage, of the ordinary expenses. Have no money whatever in your hands or keeping, but entrust anything which you receive for the journey to some honest, good people of the same place, that they may distribute it freely among the poor and apply it to other pious purposes, as will seem to them most for the service of God Our Lord." As far as possible, they must beg their way to Ireland, where it would be their duty "to assist that country in spiritual matters and to relieve, as well as they could, the conscience of the Supreme Pontiff" who felt sorely concerned for the fate of his children in the farthest West. On arrival, they are to visit the Catholic lay leaders, "praising in the name of His Holiness their constancy and zeal" and also the bishops whom, if remiss in duty, they will "admonish and exhort to better conduct." Priests are to be watched to see whether they administer the sacraments regularly and fittingly, in particular Confession and Communion. "Observe also," continues Ignatius, "whether the word of God is preached in a Catholic spirit, and give to its ministers all the instruction and help in your power.

[1] M.H.S.J., *Epistolæ et instructiones*, vol. I, pp. 179–80.

Moreover, do you teach the people yourselves. . . . If you hear of any heretical preacher or parish priest, consider how he can be deprived of the opportunity to harm others and, for your part, endeavour to reclaim him by showing him the truth in a spirit of gentleness. . . . Try to strengthen in the faith those who are sick . . . and exhort them to Confession without giving occasion either for servile fear or for presumption. . . . If you could introduce grammar schools in some places and find efficient Catholic masters for them, it would be a great remedy for the great ignorance of the country. . . . And it would be a good thing, too, to provide *Monti della pietà* for the assistance of the poor, and hospitals and other pious institutions. . . . In all the aforesaid works of charity . . . proceed, according to our Institute, without accepting remuneration of any kind or even any alms for the work you do. . . . In so far as it is necessary for the glory of God and the common good to risk your lives, you must not refuse to do so, but without rashness or tempting of God. Generally speaking, you will use all possible dexterity and prudence not to be captured by the King's ministers."[1]

So, in the zeal of his heart, Ignatius wrote and counselled, thinking Ireland another Guipuzcoa which needed only exhorting to be well. But the wounds of the country, half inflicted from without and half received in the house of her friends, went far too deep for mere spiritual G.P.'s such as Broet and Salmeron to heal. Fine men both, tall and distinguished-looking in their beards red and black,[2] they were, for all their devotion, on a hopeless quest, as Cardinal Beaton warned them when they

[1] *Epistolæ et instructiones*, vol. I, pp. 727–30.   [2] *Epistolæ Broëti*, p. 197.

107

encountered him at Lyons. "He advised us," wrote Broet, "on no account to proceed with our journey and business, firstly, because, said he, all the cities, towns, forts and castles were in the English King's hands; secondly, because almost all the harbours were held by his soldiers; and thirdly, because the Irish were of all mankind the wildest people, barbarians incapable of any discipline whatsoever." That judgment of a Scot who was himself no great credit to the Catholic religion[1] undoubtedly warped the minds of the two Jesuits, who, however, decided to go on and see what they should see. They sailed from a port in Flanders, were thrown twice on the English coast where they had to remain in hiding for ten or twelve days, and, at last, on December 31st, 1541, reached Edinburgh.

From Edinburgh on February 2nd, 1542, Salmeron addressed a long letter to St. Ignatius, explaining the situation: "After two days of rest Master Paschase and I went to the King [James V] to deliver to him the Brief of His Holiness. He replied in very gracious and friendly terms, saying that he would provide us with letters of introduction to the Irish chieftains and also with a guide to conduct us safely to our destination. . . .[2] We have had the greatest difficulty in obtaining information about Irish affairs here, greater even, I think, than in Rome. It is doubtful information too, one saying one thing, and another a different, for not a man have we found able

[1] Beaton, Primate of Scotland, had six illegitimate children, and was most savagely done to death only four years later by his own countrymen.

[2] The French Ambassador to the Scottish Court, Jean de Mervillier, and some Scots who had known the Jesuits in Rome gave the King and Mary of Guise a very favourable account of them, which explains the royal benevolence.

to enlighten us from his personal experience. Almost everybody advises us not to go, including the Archbishop of Glasgow, and the French Ambassador has been urging the King and Queen to prevent us, on the ground that we would be risking our lives uselessly. . . . On top of this, three Irish priests *en route* for Rome have told us that the two principal chieftains of their country, O'Donnell and O'Neill, recently submitted to the King, and that O'Neill delivered his son up to him as a hostage. . . . Another thing we learned from them was that the few remaining Catholics still faithful to the Pope have fled to the mountains where they engage in daily warfare among themselves. . . . Before deciding, we wanted to have some news from people who knew more, and from other Irishmen, so we made up our minds that Master Paschase should go to Glasgow, . . . where, they told us, Irishmen came very frequently to study or to trade. But he was just as badly off there as here, for never a merchant or student turned up. He therefore went on fifteen miles to another port called Irvine, where ships from Ireland arrive, to obtain better information about our affair. Before leaving Glasgow, he wrote saying that if he could find a ship sailing soon from Irvine to Ireland he would take it, having put off his gown and dressed himself in an Irish kilt. Otherwise he would return here. . . . He is back now, after waiting twelve days in vain for a ship, but he learned what he wanted to know from various merchants and some Irishmen. According to their report, the affairs of Ireland are not as painted here, . . . so we are going together to do what Master Paschase wanted to do, namely *explorare Hyberniam.* . . ."[1]

[1] M.H.S.J., *Epistolæ Salmeronis*, vol. I, pp. 2–9.

Perhaps it will be agreed now that those two innocents abroad entertained no private prejudices and were purely concerned to carry out the Pope's commission to the best of their ability. They landed somewhere in Ireland on February 23rd and quickly found that the hypothesis on which their mission had been planned, the survival of some measure of Irish independence, was purely imaginary. Only a month before, Henry had assumed the title of King of Ireland. The O'Neills and O'Donnells, who, two years earlier, had risen in arms rather than submit to his violence, now owned him for "Supreme Head, under Christ, of the Church of England and Ireland." But there was much worse than that, for of the thirty dioceses in Ireland at the time no less than twenty-two rested in the hands of bishops who had disavowed the Pope's authority and sworn allegiance to the Tudor tyrant.[1] In those circumstances, a man would need to have been a major prophet to foretell the future of the faith in Ireland. Broet and Salmeron were not prophets but bewildered foreigners who saw and noted the blatant evil while missing the hidden, intensely active leaven of good. They remained in Ireland only thirty-four days, and it takes a good while longer than a month to make out Irishmen. In their dispirited report to Cardinal Cervini, afterwards Pope Marcellus II, they attribute all the troubles of the country and the failure of their mission to the inter-tribal shindies which the warriors of Ireland in their famous generations have certainly always loved far more than was good for themselves or for their people. These feuds, says Salmeron, were "de tal digestion" that only God could

[1] Ronan, *The Reformation in Dublin*, London, 1926, pp. 303-7.

heal them. Both he and Broet picture the moral state of the country in the blackest colours, but they can only have learned these things from hearsay, and Ireland is well known to be a place where tall stories have ever abounded for the quizzing of earnest-minded foreigners. Back in Scotland again, they were greeted with amazement by those who had tried to dissuade them from going and expected to see them no more "usque in diem resurrectionis."

On the return journey to Rome they looked so woebegone in their tattered and grimy gowns that they were arrested as spies and thrown into prison at Lyons, much to the delight of the English Ambassador, Lord Paget, who happened to be in the town. It was their last of many adventures and risks run to carry out, in the spirit of their vow, an impossible undertaking. "God be praised for everything," concluded Salmeron, "the time of our stay in Ireland was not without its share of the cross of Christ Our Lord, for we went hungry and thirsty, and had no place to lay our heads nor even in which to say a Pater Noster in peace. However, it was all little enough compared with what we deserve for our sins, and we would go through it again gladly, and more than it, if so we might continue to render Christ Our Lord some service. Besides, it was Lent and the right time for penance."[1]

In Paris on his way back Broet fell in with a colony of sixteen Jesuit scholastics, sent there by Ignatius to study at the University. They were the seed of the future French province which Father Paschase himself was destined to govern for ten years (1552–62) of great labour

[1] M.H.S.J., *Epistolæ Salmeronis*, vol. I, p. 13; *Epistolæ Broëti*, pp. 23–31.

and abundant adversity. But Italy had ten years of him first during which he sweated without a pause to bring men and women nearer to the Lord whom he loved. Typical of his activities is this little note to Francis Xavier from Faenza in 1545: "When I came here first I found many poor and sick folk to visit. Seeing that nothing was being done for them, I approached a number of estimable gentlemen and now between us we have founded a society called the *Compagnia della charità*, whose members will visit the sick poor throughout the city and provide for them, first, spiritually, by exhorting them to go to Confession and Communion, then, corporally, by finding them all necessaries of life during their illness, including a doctor and medicines."[1]

That letter takes us back to St. Francis who had been sailing the Atlantic and Indian Oceans at the same time that Broet and Salmeron were on the North and Irish Seas. He had gone like them as Legate of the Pope, but to islands and countries even less known in Rome than Ireland. And he had gone with as little show, accepting only of all King John's rich offerings to him "a few books necessary in the Indies and a cloak or two of rough material against the cold of the Cabo de Buena Esperança." When the King's gentleman, the Conde de Castañeda, begged him at least to take a personal servant to do his washing and cooking, as such employments would diminish his ambassadorial dignity, he replied: "Señor Conde, it is this dignity and authority of yours which has reduced the Church of God to her present plight . . . , and the best means to acquire true dignity is

[1] *Epistolæ Broëti*, pp. 33–5. Broet was the first of Jesuit regional superiors called provincials, being appointed to that office for Italy by Ignatius in 1551.

to wash one's own clout and boil one's own pot, without being beholden to anybody."¹ He embarked on his thirty-fifth birthday, April 7th, 1541, from the quay of the Tagus known as the Place of Tears. His ship, a great lumbering galleon called the *Santiago*, carried several hundred souls, including three Jesuit companions, and the new Governor of India, Martin da Sousa—"a very good man and much esteemed in the Indies," according to Francis who thought no evil of anybody, but, in fact, one of the murkiest ruffians in the whole grim history of Portuguese colonization. That halo for a buccaneer was sent in a letter to Ignatius and the Roman Fathers which contained also a most touching petition for guidance and a cry of the heart for news: "When you write to us in the Indies, write of each and all by name, as it will be only once a year. And write at great length, *muy à largo*, so that we may have enough to read for eight days."²

¹ *Monumenta Xaveriana*, vol. II, pp. 836–7.

² *Monumenta Xaveriana*, vol. I, p. 247. Vessels sailed from Lisbon to India only each spring. The Jesuit companions of Francis were Micer Paul of Camerino, priest, Francisco Mansilhas, scholastic, and Diego Rodriguez, lay-brother. Of Mansilhas, a sort of Jesuit Brother Giles, he wrote: "It is a fact that he has a larger store of zeal, goodness, and simplicity than of exceptional learning. Unless Micer Paul can communicate to him some of his own abundant knowledge, I am afraid we won't know what to do about getting him ordained in the Indies. To forestall trouble, he desires very much that you would obtain him a dispensation . . . to be ordained on the title of voluntary poverty and very ample simplicity. His goodness and his *santa simplicidad* do really make up for his ignorance. If only he had talked as much with Bobadilla as he did with Caceres, we might not be in our present predicament but see him moving in full sail over the Scriptures and uttering oracles with every breath. Micer Paul desires very much to obtain from His Holiness the favour that each time he says Mass he may be able to release one soul from Purgatory" (*l.c.*, pp. 244–5).

If we expect Francis to provide us with a diary of his voyaging, we do not know him at all. He had his own interests, but they were centred so exclusively on men's souls that in his 127 extant letters, written close by jungles or on perilous seas, not a single elephant trumpets, not a tiger roars, not a shark shows a fin. In this again he is the image of him whom from Cochin he lovingly addressed as "Padre mio *in Christi visceribus* unico," Ignatius. The most that he will say of himself is a generality, such as these lines from Mozambique to the Roman Fathers: "I was sea-sick for two months, and suffered sorely during forty days off the coast of Guinea owing to our being heavily becalmed. But God Our Lord deigned to show us great mercy by bringing us to an island where we are to this day. I am sure that it will make you rejoice *in Domino* to know that God Our Lord has been pleased to find use for us as servants of His servants. Immediately on arriving here, we took charge of the poor sick folk who came in the squadron.[1] My time has been spent hearing their Confessions, giving them Communion, and helping them to die happily. . . . Micer Paul and Micer Mansilhas busied themselves with their bodily needs and all of us did what we could for the poor people, according to our meagre and feeble capacity. As for the fruit, God knows that, since it is He who produces all of it. It is no small comfort to us that at last the Governor and all the nobles of the armada understand our desires to be very different from any craving for human favour, and purely *propter Deum*. The trials and troubles were, in fact, of such a kind that, left to myself, I would

[1] Ships to the East sailed in armadas, and there were four other vessels with the *Santiago*.

not have dared them a single day for all the world. . . .
We ask you all for the love of Our Lord to remember
us particularly in your prayers and Holy Sacrifices, since
you know what poor metal we are. . . . I would love to
go on writing, but at present I am prevented by illness.
To-day they bled me for the seventh time, and I am mid-
dling well, praise be to God."[1]

To judge by the accounts of other travellers who made
the voyage to India at that period, conditions on board
the *Santiago* must have closely resembled those of slave
and convict ships at a later time. Indeed, many of the
Santiago's passengers *were* slaves and convicts. It was
usual for them to die like flies on the journey, and a
doctor on the vessel regarded it as a plain miracle, "due
to the virtue and care of the said Father Francis," that
only forty-one of his shipmates succumbed. "I used
often to watch him," says this man, "at his work of
charity and zeal. He begged alms aboard for the sick
and poor, and himself looked after those who were prostrated. Never, even for a moment, did he leave off hearing confessions, teaching Christian doctrine, and tending
the sick, and all this *magna vultus hilaritate*." Another
witness, a certain "Magister Joannes uxoratus," blessings
on his connubial memory, gives the following picture of
Francis at Mozambique: "Owing to his incessant labours
for the sick at the hospital where he lived, and also for
people of the ship outside, the Father fell into a fever which
tormented him sorely. I paid him a visit and urged him
to stop work for a while, as he was a sick man himself.
Otherwise it might be the death of him, and, in any case,
he would have his chance again when he got well. He

---

[1] *Monumenta Xaveriana*, vol. I, pp. 247–9.

answered me that he must watch that night with a certain brother who lay in great danger of both body and soul, but that afterwards he would call a halt. Now this brother was a seaman who had been delirious for some days. The following morning while visiting the sick at the hospital, I also looked in on the Father in his tiny berth and found the seaman laid on the Father's own bed, which if I remember rightly, was a sort of rope hammock, with a ragged coverlet, a pillow of kinds, and nothing else. The Father was sitting beside the bed on a coil of rope, . . . talking with the seaman, who had come out of his delirium and made his confession. . . . He died that evening after receiving Holy Communion, whereat the said Father was full of happiness. Indeed, he always seemed happy, even when overwhelmed with work."[1]

On the voyage beyond Mozambique, off the Kenya coast at Malindi, Francis received the one big thrill of his seafaring. It was the sight of a stone cross set up there forty years before by Vasco da Gama on his way to win Portugal an empire. This other man, adventuring to win Christ an empire, wrote of the *padrao*: "Only God Our Lord knows the consolation I received . . . at beholding the cross standing there alone, victorious, in the midst of Islam." In Socotra, a further stage on, he gave himself, puzzled and pitiful, to the service of the derelict and persecuted Nestorian Christians, who had forgotten how to baptize and knew no intelligible prayers except the one word, *Alleluia*. He besought da Sousa to let him stay and work for these poor people, but the Governor, who valued him as a protection against shipwreck, would not

[1] *Monumenta Xaveriana*, vol. II, p. 235 (the doctor), pp. 254–5 (Magister Joannes).

hear of it. At last, on May 6th, 1542, more than a year
after leaving Lisbon, he was in his land of heart's desire,
at Goa, the capital of Portuguese India. As usual, his
first impressions were enthusiastic. Goa, he wrote home,
was a "cosa para ver," a sight worth seeing, with its
multitude of churches and its plenty of priests, especially
Franciscans, who had settled there after the conquest of
the town by the great Albuquerque in 1510. One had
reason to thank God heartily that the name of Christ
should thus be honoured in such distant lands and among
so many heathen.

When Francis wrote in that strain he had not seen one
of the principal sights of the city, the slave-market, close
by the cathedral, where Kaffirs raided from Mozambique
and luckless native Hindus were paraded, pummelled,
and sold at a maximum price of exactly thirty pieces of
silver. It was the most appropriate price imaginable.
And Francis had not witnessed how these slaves were
treated by their so-called Christian masters, had not
noted, as did a later French traveller, that, when bastina-
doing them, the masters "counted the blows on their
rosary-beads." Nor did Francis know yet that Goa
was a very Babylon of iniquity. Just ten years later,
Camoëns, the Homer of Portugal's heroic age, came to
Goa, and crystallized the horror of his noble soul in a
sonnet entitled *Babylon and Sion*, meaning Goa and Lisbon.
It is worth a dozen descriptions:

> Here where fecundity of Babel frames
> Stuff for all ills wherewith the world doth teem;
> Where loyal love is slurred with disesteem;
> Where Venus all controls and all defames;
> Where vice's vaunts are counted virtue's shames;

Where Tyranny o'er Honour lords supreme;
Where blind and erring sovereignty doth deem
That God for deeds will be content with names;

Here in this world where whatso is, is wrong,
Where Birth and Worth and Wisdom begging go
To doors of Avarice and Villainy—
Trammelled in the foul chaos, I prolong
My days, because I must. Woe to me! Woe!
Sion, had I not memory of thee![1]

It is the deep tragedy of Francis Xavier's life that so much of his matchless heroism had to go begging because the men of his own race and faith in the Indies were such unmitigated scoundrels. The motto of Sion for her empire in the East was "the service of God Our Lord and our own advantage",[2] but Goanese Babylon kept only its second half in honour and remembrance.

Like Camoëns Francis had his Sion far away, that poor house near the Torre del Melangolo where dwelt Ignatius and the brethren. He must often have felt lonely in Babylon. Four months after arrival he sent home his heart in this fashion: "For the love and service of God Our Lord, dear Brothers, I beseech you to write to me in detail about every single member of our Society, for as I have no hope now of ever seeing you again *facie ad faciem*, let me do so at least through a glass darkly, that is, by means of your letters. Do not deny me this favour, unworthy as I am. Remember that God Our Lord made

[1] Translated by Richard Garnett.
[2] So King Manuel who despatched Vasco da Gama on his famous expedition (*A Journal of the First Voyage of Vasco da Gama*, Hakluyt Society, 1898, p. 113).

you worthy, so that I, through you, might hope for
and obtain much merit and refreshment."[1] Like St. Paul,
Francis was meant by God to be a pathfinder rather than
a stationary Apostle. He has been described as a man
consumed with a divine impatience, a saint in a hurry.
Sometimes he has been accused of restlessness, but God
knows, as he would say himself, that his vagabondage was
not due to an itch for change or a desire for more interesting labours. He must go to open doors, he said, and God
knows too what each door cost him in privation and
suffering. If he spent only five months in Goa, they were,
at any rate, months never to be forgotten by the sick, the
poor, the slaves, the outcasts, the half-baked converts
from heathenism who had become Christians "for the
sake of a new hat, or a shirt, or to escape the gallows."[2]
He set up his tent among the sick at Albuquerque's hospital,
and there his practice was to sleep on the floor by the bed
of any man dangerously ill, "so as to be able to help him
at night."[3] His other great interest was in prisoners.
Goa had three gaols, "the nastiest and foulest places in
the world," full of slaves, escaped galley-birds, and other
riff-raff. Of these the Saint constituted himself chaplain
and almoner, begging for them at rich houses and ex-
pending on their poor starved souls all his own private
treasure of devotion. Just like a saint, he quickly ferreted
out yet another class of unfortunates, the most pitiable
of any, the lepers. "On Sundays," he told his Roman
brethren, "I have been going outside the city to say Mass

[1] *Monumenta Xaveriana*, vol. I, p. 259.

[2] Father Lancilotti to St. Ignatius, October 1547, in *Selectæ Indiarum
Epistolæ*, Florence, 1887, p. 25.

[3] This story comes from the governor of the hospital at the time (*Monumenta Xaveriana*, vol. II, p. 842).

for people afflicted with leprosy. Every one in the lazar-house has now made his confession to me and received Holy Communion. . . . They have become my friends, my very good friends."[1] But his chief and best-loved avocation here and everywhere was the humble indispensable schoolmaster's task of teaching children, and near children such as slaves, their catechism. To gather his young audience, he went through the streets, vigorously ringing a little bell like a muffin-man. The children, brown and black, followed him excitedly in swarms. He addressed them in a kind of Portuguese patois which he had learned, and sang or chanted the Creed, the Pater Noster, the Commandments, and other fundamentals of Christian doctrine "so that the little ones might the better retain them." One who knew him recorded that this method brought the Commandments an unwonted popularity, as the fisherman took to singing them at his nets and the peasant, while tilling his little farm, "for his entertainment and recreation."[2]

At the end of September, 1542, Francis set out for Cape Comorin and the coast of the pearl-fishers, drawn there by pity for a people who had been hastily baptized eight years before and then left shepherdless. It was a long voyage by sea to this torrid and sterile country[3] but all that he took with him was a piece of leather with which to mend his shoes and an umbrella.[4] The umbrella was

[1] *Monumenta Xaveriana*, vol. I, p. 258.

[2] Father Emmanuel Texeira, in *Monumenta Xaveriana*, vol. I, pp. 843–4.

[3] A voyage of at least six hundred miles, which, to and fro, Francis repeated thirteen times in the following ten years.

[4] Even these things he was persuaded to take, says Texeira, only "por mucha importunacion" on the part of his friends (*l.c.*, p. 850).

very necessary against the implacable sun of Malabar.
Francis, who disliked heat and found the relatively reasonable sun of Lisbon appalling, must have been glad that
he brought it. His two years on the Fishery Coast were a
continual broiling, yet he moved about so much that it is
difficult to keep track of him. He slept and ate anywhere
and anyhow, on the burning sand or in miserable native
huts that stank of rats and bats and snakes. His food was
the native food, rice seasoned with pepper, or, when times
were good, a little fish. He cooked it himself. After a
long day's work in the sun, he contented himself with
two or three hours' sleep. Indeed, the mosquitoes, more
redoubtable than rats or snakes, saw to it anyhow that he
spent most of the night awake. But his worst trouble was
the language. Old writers, and more modern ones too,
often tell us that he had the gift of tongues and did not
need to waste his precious time learning languages. Well,
hear Francis himself, speaking of his first approaches to
the poor, benighted Paravas, who knew nothing whatever of the religion which they had adopted except that it
guaranteed them Portuguese protection against Arab
raiders. "They did not understand me nor I them," he
reported sadly, "because their native tongue is Malabar
and mine is Basque.'[1] A few years later he is writing in a

[1] "Y la mia bizcaina" (*Monumenta Xaveriana*, vol. I, p. 279). On this
André Bellessort writes: "On s'est demandé pourquoi il n'avait pas
mis le castillan ou le portugais. Mais il sourit en écrivant ces mots, et d'un
sourire mélancolique. Il ne serait pas plus dénué devant les Hindous, s'il
n'avait jamais parlé d'autre langue que celle de son village natal. Son
ignorance le replace dans la condition d'un petit enfant. Il faut qu'il refasse
son éducation, qu'il réapprenne à assembler des syllabes; et, tout naturelle-
ment, le souvenir de sa langue basque lui revient à la mémoire" (*Saint
François Xavier*, pp. 113–14).

similar vein: "I go among this people without an inter-preter, . . . so you can imagine the exhortations I shall be able to make, they not understanding me and I under-standing them even less. . . . I baptize the new-born babies and others who come my way. For this there is no need of an interpreter. Also, the poor make me under-stand their distress without an interpreter, as I can see it for myself."[1]

In a letter seventeen pages long to his Roman brethren, Francis gives some idea of how he wrestled with the language problem. He picked out a few more intelligent natives who had a smattering of Portuguese. To these he repeated in that tongue the words accompanying the Sign of the Cross, the Creed, the Commandments, the Our Father, the Hail Mary, the Salve Regina, and the Con-fiteor. The natives slowly and painfully put the formu-laries and prayers into some sort of Tamil, and then Francis, still more slowly and painfully, learned the Tamil by heart.[2] So, he says, "after many meetings and great travail we produced our prayers, . . . and when I had fixed them in memory, I went through the whole place with a bell in my hand, gathering all the boys and men that I could, and teaching them twice a day for a month." Was not that month's toil a lovelier miracle than any gift of tongues? The children were his great stand-by. "They would not let me say my Office," he told St. Ignatius, "nor eat nor sleep unless I taught them some prayers, and then I began to understand *quoniam talium est regnum*

[1] *Monumenta Xaveriana*, vol. I, p. 337.

[2] Tamil is a language of infinite phonetic nuances. To vary the nuance of pronunciation is to change the meaning of a word or to render it entirely unintelligible. St. Francis had therefore to learn, not only the words, but the exact stress or lilt to be given to each when spoken.

cælorum." He trained them to be little apostles themselves and to teach their fathers and mothers and all the
family and neighbours what they had learned in the
school.[1] His lessons were conducted in the following
way: "To begin with, I say the First Commandment
and all repeat it after me. That done, we all say together,
'Jesus Christ, Son of God, give us the grace to love Thee
above all things.' When we have asked that grace, we
all in unison say a *Pater Noster*, and then, 'Holy Mary,
Mother of Jesus Christ, obtain for us grace from thy
Son to be able to observe the First Commandment,'
which petition to Our Lady we follow up with an *Ave
Maria.* This same order we keep for the nine other Commandments, and, just as we say twelve *Pater Nosters* and
twelve *Ave Marias* in honour of the twelve articles of the
Creed, asking of God Our Lord grace to believe them
firmly and undoubtingly, so we say ten *Pater Nosters*
and ten *Ave Marias* in honour of the Ten Commandments, begging God Our Lord to give us grace to
keep them." It is in this great letter, so confused
and repetitive, yet so charged with emotion,[2] that
Francis, seeing the vast fields around him white
for the harvest, uttered his piercing appeal: "Many a
time it has come into my mind to go to the study-halls

[1] *Monumenta Xaveriana*, vol. I, pp. 280, 274.

[2] Of the letters in general Père Brou well says: "Les amateurs de beau
langage et de composition savante ne trouveraient là que phrases souvent
embrouillées, à peine correctes, écrites au courant de la plume par un
homme dont tous les moments sont dûs au prochain. . . . On s'imagine le
voir, dictant ou écrivant sa lettre, à chaque instant interrompu, et reprenant,
comme il le peut, le fil de ses idées. Il ne cherche qu'une chose, soulager
son cœur, dire à ses frères combien il les aime, les appeler au secours, leur
communiquer un peu du feu divin qui le dévore. . . ." (*St. François Xavier*,
vol. I, p. 184).

of your parts, particularly to the University of Paris, and shout aloud like a man beside himself to those of the Sorbonne who have more learning than desire to employ their learning fruitfully how many souls are missing Heaven and going to Hell through their negligence. . . . So great is the multitude which turns to the faith in this land where I wander that often my arms are wearied with baptizing, and I have no voice left through so frequently repeating the Creed and the Commandments. . . ."[1] A short while later his arms must have been almost paralysed, for up and down the dreary, inhospitable land of Travancore he baptized in the course of a single month more than ten thousand persons. Taking a twelve-hour day, that would have worked out at about one baptism every two minutes for thirty days consecutively.[2]

The letter announcing that portentous event was written at Cochin on January 27th, 1545, and began with the following greeting to the Roman Jesuits: "God Our Lord knows how much more my soul would be comforted by a sight of you than by writing these letters, that are so uncertain owing to the great distance from here to Rome. But since it is God Our Lord who has separated us in such far-apart places and we are so united in one love and spirit, the bodily severance cannot, I am sure, cause any lessening of love or care in those who love one another in the Lord. For, as I fancy, we see one

---

[1] *Monumenta Xaveriana*, vol. I, pp. 282, 285–6.

[2] The figure is his own—"En un mes baptizé mas de diez mil personas" (*Monumenta Xaveriana*, vol. I, p. 367). This was his only mass conversion, and he took infinite pains to see that the new Christians had priests and catechists to instruct them. It was a Pentecostal event which we have no right to criticize in view of St. Peter's example on the first Pentecost Sunday (*Acts*, ii, 41).

another almost always, even if we do not have our old familiar intercourse. The memory of the past when established in Christ supplies, as it were, an intuitive knowledge. That so constant thought of you all which is in my soul, is more your creation than mine, since it is your continual devoted prayers and acceptable sacrifices for me, *triste peccador*, which imprints on my soul, *charissimos en Xº hermanos mios y únicos*, your undying memory."[1] From Cochin, too, Francis wrote to the Queen of Portugal, begging that the "Slipper Money" of four hundred crowns a year which she derived from the Pearl Fisheries might be diverted to the support of his catechists, since "she could have no fitter shoes or pantofles to climbe to Heaven than the Christian children of the Piscarian Coast."[2] Finally, during this period of incessant movement, when he went about "barefooted, in a much tattered gown, . . . very humble and simple, . . . cracking a joke with people he met,"[3] he wrote twenty-six letters to Mansilhas, the untheological, whom he had brought from Goa to be his deputy and catechist. They are the most intimate of his letters, and reveal a Francis playful, tender, sad, desperately concerned for the welfare, physical as well as spiritual, of his Paravas, angry with the Portuguese for their depredations, human enough to be discouraged, half-minded to seek peace in the land of Prester John, "where one can serve God Our Lord without anybody persecuting him." Fearing that his honest but rather stolid henchman might be too severe with the pearl-fishers, he said:

[1] *Monumenta Xaveriana*, vol. I, p. 366.

[2] Torsellini, *The Admirable Life of St. Francis Xavier*, p. 140.

[3] M.H.S.J., *Epistolæ Mixtæ*, vol. I, p. 231; *Monumenta Xaveriana*, vol. II, p. 372.

"Learn to bear with and to succour their frailties very patiently, holding to the hope that if they are not good now, they will be some day. And if you don't succeed with them as you would wish, be content with what you can, like myself."[1]

The year 1545 was one of crisis for Francis. Wild tribes from the hills had carried slaughter among his peaceable Paravas, and a local rajah had massacred six hundred new Christians on the island of Manar. Their Apostle ran every sort of risk, shouldered every sort of burden, to help them or to avenge them. In search of Portuguese assistance he walked or voyaged to Cochin, to Goa, to Bassein north of Bombay, to Negapatam. From Cochin he addressed a long letter of burning protest to the King of Portugal against the wickedness of his officials,[2] but nothing came of it. Perplexed and disheartened, he felt, after four months of prayers and tears at the reputed shrine of St. Thomas the Apostle, that God wanted him to move on, especially as three of his brethren were coming from Europe to take up the burden of India. His commission was to all Portugal's eastern conquests, so beyond India Malacca beckoned, and be-

---

[1] *Monumenta Xaveriana*, vol. I, p. 314. Speaking of the Portuguese officials, he wrote to Father Simon Rodriguez: "I am astounded at the way they discover so many new moods, tenses and participles for that piratical verb, *rapio*" (*l.c.*, p. 375). Rapine was indeed the main attraction of India for many of these gentry. It is horrible to read in Barros, the official historian of Portuguese colonization and himself Treasurer of the Indies in 1532, such sentiments as these: "The Portuguese as lords of the sea by the power of their fleets may justly compel all Moors and Gentiles to take out safe-conducts under penalty of confiscation and death. The Moors and Gentiles are outside the law of Jesus Christ. . . . We Christians have no duties towards them" (*Asia Portugueza*, decade I, book I, chapter i).

[2] *Monumenta Xaveriana*, vol. I, pp. 356–61.

yond Malacca, the Moluccas, the Spice Islands, *fons et origo* of all the famous explorations.[1] So strong was the urge in him eastwards that he said: "If Portuguese ships do not sail this year to Malacca, I shall go on a Moorish or heathen ship, or in a native *catamaran*." By the last days of September 1545, he had crossed two thousand miles of perilous seas to his goal, where a letter from St. Ignatius reached him, two years and five months old. For three months he laboured in his usual style at Malacca, chiefly among the Portuguese colonists who needed converting no less than did the native Malays. Often, there were so many confessions to be heard that for two or three days on end he had no time to swallow even a mouthful of food and went completely fasting. His nights in a little cell at the hospital he spent almost entirely in prayer, only towards dawn snatching some sleep on the floor with his head resting on a cobble-stone.[2] "He made himself everybody's intimate friend by the great pleasantness of his conversation. Very often he used to join men at their games and diversions, showing a keen interest in the play. If, out of respect for him, they desisted, he would very agreeably invite them to continue, saying that they were soldiers and had no need to live like monks . . . He made a habit of inviting himself to dinner, now with

---

[1] "In the Name of God. Amen! In the year 1497 King Dom Manuel, the first of that name in Portugal, dispatched four ships to make discoveries and go in search of spices" (*A Journal of the First Voyages of Vasco da Gama*, p. 1). The spice trade, the richest of all trades, had been till then in the hands of the Arabs and Venetians. Vasco da Gama's voyage changed all that and, indeed, revolutionized European commerce.

[2] *Monumenta Xaveriana*, vol. II, p. 334. The witnesses to his nightly devotions had watched him through a rent in the palm-leaf curtain of his cell.

this person, now with that, going to their houses with the greatest friendliness. He used to compliment them on their dishes and service and would ask to have the cook brought in, when he would courteously offer her his congratulations. . . . So easy was his manner in every company that with soldiers he seemed to be a soldier and with merchants a merchant. All of them, not only the Portuguese, but their slaves and servants, loved the Father greatly."[1]

Then he was off again on New Year's Day, 1546, over another two thousand miles of stormy, pirate-ridden seas to the lands of pepper and cloves. Until June he laboured in Amboina, tramping the island jungles with a hymn in Malay on his lips to attract the shy natives from their huts. Afterwards he had himself paddled from one island to another of that beautiful but terrifying archipelago where life teems in its most flamboyant and most sinister forms. He told those who tried to deter him that if they would not give him a boat he would swim. One set of islands, the Moro group, was reputed to have Christians, but the Portuguese warned him not to venture there, as the natives were head-hunters and poisoners, who, at need, would serve up their own fathers for dinner. He spent three months all alone among those poor savages, and at the end declared that their islands ought not to be called *islas de Moro* but *islas de esperar en Dios* —islands of hope in God.[2] Twenty years later, his brethren,

---

[1] *Monumenta Xaveriana* vol. I, p. 68. This testimony was taken from men who had worked with St. Francis.

[2] *Monumenta Xaveriana*, vol. I, pp. 426–7. Letter to the Roman Jesuits. While he was saying Mass on one of the islands, an earthquake nearly overturned his altar.

going in by the door which he had opened, turned all the reputed head-hunters into fervent Christians.

In mid-April, 1547, Francis decided that the time had come, not to go on, but to go back. There were no more outposts of Portuguese empire for him to visit, and he must organize the mission of Malacca where three of his brethren were expected; must see how his beloved converts of Comorin and Travancore progressed; must lend a helping hand to the sorely pressed Fathers of Goa; must, if God willed, take up again his project, before frustrated, of evangelizing Ceylon. At Malacca, where monsoons detained him for five months, he met destiny in the shape of a Japanese murderer named Yajiro, who, tormented by remorse, had sought him out on the advice of some Portuguese mariners. Zipangu, the Land of the Rising Sun, had been discovered only six years then and no European had as yet penetrated it. Francis was thrilled to the core by what he heard from the Portuguese merchants of the mysterious islands, and by what he saw of Yajiro. "If all Japanese are like him, so desirous to learn," he wrote, "I think they are the most inquiring people of all countries known. . . . I asked him whether the Japanese would become Christians if I went with him to his country, and he replied that they would not do so immediately, but would first ask me many questions and see what answers I gave and how much I knew. Above all, they would want to see whether my life corresponded with my teaching. If I did these two things, spoke well, satisfying their questions, and lived without their finding anything to blame in my conduct, then, half a year after first meeting me, the king, the nobility and all other people of good judgment would become Christians. . . . All the Portuguese merchants who have come from Japan assure me that by going there I could render God Our Lord much service, and more than among the peoples of India, because the Japanese are a race greatly given to the exercise of reason. From what I am feeling in my soul, I think that I myself or some other member of the Society will go to Japan within two years, although it is a voyage of the greatest peril owing to the sea being very tempestuous and overrun with Chinese pirates. Consequently many ships are lost, so pray to God Our Lord, dear Fathers and Brothers, for those who may go thither. . . ."[1]

His return to India gave Francis small comfort, as the evils incidental to empire-building seemed to have increased in his absence. A mood of great despondency came over him, revealed in three letters which he sent to Europe from Cochin. "God is aware, *Pater charissime*," he wrote to St. Ignatius, "how I long to set eyes on you again in this life that I might tell you of many things which require your help and attention. I see out here very many of the Society and I know that we sorely

---

[1] *Monumenta Xaveriana*, vol. I, pp. 434–5. Letter to the Roman Jesuits, which is full of the Saint's attachment to and profound love for the Society of Jesus. He puts his whole hope of salvation in the prayers of his brethren and attributes to them his protection in all the dangers and difficulties he had faced. "When I begin to speak of the *Sancta Compañía de Jesús*," he says, "I do not know how to extricate myself from such a delightful occupation nor how to stop writing. But I see that I must stop, . . as the ships are about to sail. I know of no better way to conclude than by confessing to all of you *quod si oblitus unquam fuero Societatis nominis Jesu oblivioni detur dextera mea*. . . . May God show me so much mercy through your merits as to give me, according to my poor capacity, an understanding of the debt which I owe to the Society, not a full understanding because I am not equal to it, but some realization, even if only a little." (pp. 436–7.)

need a physician for our souls. I do earnestly implore you by Jesus Our Lord, *Pater optime*, to be mindful also of these your sons in India, and to send out some man pre-eminent in virtue and sanctity whose vigour and briskness may stir me from my lethargy." In a plain-spoken but intensely respectful letter to King John of Portugal, he advocated the use of strong measures against the Portuguese officials who hindered the spread of the faith in India, even suggesting that their ill-gotten fortunes should be confiscated. As things were, he had little hope of receiving encouragement from the officials to make new converts or to keep steadfast those already won, and so he was thinking of going to Japan. His letter to Simon Rodriguez, then Provincial of the Portuguese Jesuits, was mainly a cry for more workers, men of such a stamp that they could safely be sent alone or in company wherever a chance offered for the greater service of God Our Lord, whether to Malacca, China, Japan or Pegu. "As for the King," he continues, "it seems to me, and God grant me to be mistaken, that at the hour of his death the good man will find himself to have fallen very short with regard to India. . . . If I thought that he thoroughly realized the sincerity of my love for him, I would beg him as a favour . . . to spend daily a quarter of an hour asking God Our Lord to give him a better understanding and interior realization of Christ's words: What doth it profit a man if he gain the whole world and suffer the loss of his soul? . . . It is time, dear Brother Simon, to undeceive the King. . . ."[1] But however sad at heart Francis may have been at that time, it did not appear in

---

[1] *Monumenta Xaveriana*, vol. I, pp. 448, 452-3, 457-8. Pegu was a kingdom in Lower Burma.

his conversation. "He sempre com ha boqua chea de riso," testified one who knew him—he was always as though he had his mouth full of laughter.[1]

From Cochin the Saint hurried to visit and encourage his six brethren working among the pearl-fishers under the leadership of the young Italian Jesuit, Antonio Criminali, whose character was almost as sweet and lovable as his own. "Believe me, he is indeed a holy soul, and born for the missions here," wrote Francis to Ignatius. Five months after that tribute was paid to him, Padre Antonio, aged twenty-nine, fell mortally wounded by the lances of Madura tribesmen. He died because he would not desert his flock, the first of nearly a thousand Jesuit martyrs. The letter of Francis mentioning him went off with another to Ignatius which concluded as follows: "So I come to an end, begging you, kneeling on the ground while I write as though you were present before me, *Padre mio di mi anima observantissimo*, of your charity to commend me much to God in your holy Sacrifices and prayers. . . . Your least and most useless son, Francisco."[2] This period of the Saint's life is one jumble of journeyings—Kandy (Ceylon), Goa, Bassein, Goa, the Fishery Coast, Cochin, Goa, Cochin, Bassein, Goa— nearly five thousand miles in the aggregate. His experiences of native customs and characters were very similar

[1] *Monumenta Xaveriana*, vol. II, p. 270.

[2] *Monumenta Xaveriana*, vol. I, p. 482. Details about the holy life and heroic death of Antonio Criminali are given by his contemporaries in *Selectae Indiarum Epistolae*, pp. 91, 98–9. He was a man of great family affection, devoted throughout life to this little list of people drawn up by himself—"patre, tutti fratelli, sorella, cugnati, cusini, cusine, parenti et amici." To 1914, the number of Jesuits who died by violence for the faith was computed officially at 907.

to those recorded in *Mother India*, and they made him
yearn all the more for Japan. Every detail he was able to
learn about that country fascinated him, for instance the
writing. One day, watching his young convert, Yajiro,
at work, and seeing how his brush went from the top
of the page downwards instead of from left to right, he
said: "Why don't you write in our fashion?" The
convert put down his brush: "The question should be,
Father, why do not you of Europe write as we of Japan?
For, as the head of a man is above and his feet below,
so it is but natural that he should write from above
downwards." Francis passed on this piece of Oriental
logic to Ignatius.[1]

But even more than Indian obscenity did Portuguese
rapacity drive his thoughts to Japan. From Cochin in
January, 1549, he wrote an astonishing letter to King
John III, a letter that gives the measure of his indignation,
because he was naturally so courteous and deferential:
"Senhor, . . . it is a sort of martyrdom to have patience
and watch being destroyed what one has built up with so
much labour. . . . Experience has taught me that Your
Highness has no power in India to spread the faith of
Christ, while you have power to take away and enjoy
all the country's temporal riches. You must pardon me
for speaking so plainly, as the disinterested affection I bear
you compels me to it. . . . Knowing what happens here,
Senhor, I have no hope of their carrying out the commands and provisions which are needed in favour of
Christianity, and therefore I am, as it were, fleeing to
Japan, so as not to lose more time. . . . May Our Lord

[1] *Monumenta Xaveriana*, vol. I, p. 484. All the Saint's dealings with
Yajiro are charming.

give you to know His holy will and grace to accomplish it perfectly, as would be your desire at the hour of death. . . . This hour is nearer than Your Highness imagines, so be prepared, for kingdoms and seignories finish and have an end. It will be a novel thing, unknown in Your Highness's existence, to see yourself at the hour of death dispossessed of your kingdoms and seignories, and entering into others where you may have the new experience, which God avert, of being ordered out of Paradise." Francis must have been perplexed in the extreme to write such a letter, but there is this to be said for him, that the main purpose of it was to secure the King's favour for two good servants of God and Portugal, a Franciscan Father and an Armenian Bishop. Two other letters to the same monarch, now the property of the well-known booksellers, Maggs, of Berkeley Square, London, show the Saint pleading for no less than thirty-four Portuguese officials, each of whom is mentioned by name and his record extolled. Francis entreats the King to pardon him "for being so importunate in recommending so many persons."[1]

---

[1] The letter textually cited is in *Monumenta Xaveriana*, vol. I, pp. 509–12. The other two, not in that collection, have been edited by Georg Schurhammer, S.J., in the *Archivum Historicum Societatis Jesu*, 1933, fasc. I. There is a translation of the *Monumenta* letter in Pieris and Fitzler's interesting volume, *Ceylon and Portugal*, part I, Leipzig 1927. The documents there gathered together cast a lurid light on the tortuous intrigues of the Portuguese in Ceylon. The local "Captain," André de Sousa, himself decidedly no angel, complains bitterly to the Governor of the Indies at Goa about the conduct of his underlings. They are "utterly reckless and out of hand," he says, and for his part he desires no greater favour than permission to leave "a land so evil as Ceylon" (p. 152).

CHAPTER V

AFAR UNTO THE GENTILES

IT was a busy time for St. Francis and full of stress, that eve of his plunge into the unknown. Thwartings had become his portion, as they must ever be of men so single-minded in their aims. One cherished aim of his was to come to the rescue of the poor, abandoned Nestorian Christians in Socotra whom he had never forgotten. Two zealous men were ready to sail there at his orders in January 1549, but Governor da Sa vetoed the project as likely to irritate the Moslems and so disturb the peaceful traffic of the Portuguese. Thus it happened that for a matter of pepper and cloves Christianity died out to its last *Alleluia* on the forsaken island. There were many Socotras in the hard experience of Francis, and they explain his eagerness for Japan where were no Christian-hating Arabs nor suave, persistent Jews, nor predatory Portuguese to barter the souls of men for merchandize. A year and more he had been planning and preparing his expedition with as much forethought as any of the great sea-captains. There was nothing in the least reckless or haphazard about it. From Bishop Albuquerque of Goa, ordinary of the most scattered and extensive diocese on earth, and from Governor da Sa, he had procured magniloquent letters of credence, written on parchment, for presentation to the sovereign of Japan. They constituted him ambassador of

Portugal, and at Malacca he was to receive from Portugal's representative all the material assistance that he needed. At last, in April 1549, he entered at Goa upon the first stage of his six-thousand-mile voyage,[1] accompanied by Father Cosmo de Torres, Brother Juan Fernandez, and three Japanese converts, including Yajiro, recently baptized with great éclat and rejoicing in the name of Paul of Holy Faith. On the last day of May they docked at Malacca, where for a year Father Perez had been toiling single-handed, in continual pain and absolute contentment. "It fills me with confusion," wrote Francis, "to see all the good done by one man so frail and full of suffering." The last letter which he wrote on earth was addressed to this heroic invalid.[2] He heard, too, inspiring news of Father Beira's fine work among the head-hunting savages of Moro, and himself began hunting for Portuguese adjectives to express his delight and admiration.

But not all the Jesuits who had been sent out to him from Europe brought with them ready-to-wear haloes, and it required the uttermost *finesse* of his charity to manage some of his polyglot subjects. The strange, exciting

[1] Before going he bequeathed to his brethren as a last legacy an instruction for their guidance, filling ten printed pages. There is little order in his counsels and the style of them is often as repetitive as a small schoolboy's essay. The wonder, however, is, not that he, an M.A. of Paris, wrote so confusedly, but that he found time to write at all. Besides, through the faulty form, the spirit triumphantly shines out, a spirit at once so masculine and so tender that it gave wings to the burdens it imposed. "In conversation," he advises, "be pleasant and merry, so that people may not be deterred by timidity from profiting of your ministry. Let your words be affable and kind, and even when you have to reprove . . . do it with love and graciously. . . ." (*Monumenta Xaveriana*, vol. I, pp. 870–80). It was his own way.

[2] *Monumenta Xaveriana*, vol. I, pp. 559, 807–10.

College of St. Paul at Goa which they ruled contained close on a hundred varieties of Oriental humanity, Hindus, Malays, Kaffirs, Ethiopians, Sinhalese, Japanese and China-men, some the sons of princes and others boys purchased for a few silver crowns in the slave-market of Bassein. These, in the large hopes of Francis, were to be the future apostles of their countrymen. They needed to be guided with both firmness and affection, but unfortunately the College Rector, Father Antonio Gomes, could not supply the second requirement. He was a brusque imperious person, much esteemed in the social circles of Goa for his elegant sermons. One of his bright ideas was to send back to Portugal in chains any young Jesuits who grew restive under his autocratic rule. Also, he showed a disposition to cavil with the religious of other Orders who had been in India long before the Jesuits. Poor Francis hardly knew what to do, for when he tried to remove Gomes from his post, there arose such a clamour of influential voices that he was obliged to desist. "Antonio," he wrote from Malacca, "I strongly commend to you charity, friendship and love with all the holy friars of the Orders of St. Francis and St. Dominic. You must be very devoted to them all, and beware of letting any cause of disedification arise between you and them. . . . From time to time, you will pay them visits, so that they may see how you love them."[1] He showed the greatest forbearance towards this highly gifted, cross-grained man and wasted enough charity on him to make a saint out of a head-hunter. But he did not cure him.

Another letter of those Malaccan days reveals the Apostolic Nuncio to the East in the role of matchmaker, full of eagerness for a wedding between his "grande

[1] *Monumenta Xaveriana*, vol. I, pp. 522–3.

amigo," Christopher Carvalho, a wealthy, unattached
colonist, and the penniless daughter of a widowed lady
in Goa whom he calls "Nossa Mãy"—Our Mother—
because in better times she had been generous to his
brethren. The good Christopher was willing, so it only
remained for Micer Paul of Camerino and Antonio Gomes
to win the consent of the young lady. "I beg of you," he
writes to the two Fathers, "to work for it in such a way
that this marriage may be brought about. It would give
me much joy and contentment to see the orphan girl,
who is such a good daughter, protected, and Nossa Mãy's
poverty relieved. . . . Do please give great attention to
the affair. . . . May Our Lord unite us in His glory, for
here below I do not know when we shall see one another
again."[1]

Altogether there are extant a dozen letters written by
Francis from Malacca on this occasion, which we owe to
the fact that no ships were then sailing direct to Japan.
The merchants would have been delighted to take a saint
on board with them, but, if he came, he must be content
to winter somewhere on the Chinese coast, since trade,
they said, required that order in their navigation. The
good Captain of Malacca, Pedro da Gama, son of the great
Vasco and truly a Portuguese without guile, endeavoured
to persuade him to accept the offer, but Francis had his
own trade, his heavenly trade, to consider, and could not
bear the thought of lying idle many months at some
secret rendezvous of mammon. Pedro did his best in the
circumstances, providing him with thirty bushels of the
finest Malaccan pepper for sale in Japan to obtain funds to

---

[1] *Monumenta Xaveriana*, vol. I, pp. 566–8. He wrote to Nossa Mãy also,
but that letter has not been preserved.

build a chapel, and also with "many beautiful and costly presents for the King of Japan, that, softened thereby, he may show himself more disposed to admit us and let us stay in his Kingdom."[1] Assisted by the excellent Pedro, Francis eventually lighted on a Chinese junk about to put to sea, whose captain, nicknamed with some reason *Ladrão*, the Pirate, agreed to take him and his party direct to Japan for a good consideration. It happened that this picturesque Celestial had a wife and some property in Malacca both whom and which he would never see again, da Gama warned him, if he broke the contract.

Francis tells the story of the voyage in the longest letter which he ever wrote: ".... We embarked on the afternoon of St. John's Day [June 24th] in the ship of a heathen Chinese merchant, . . . with wind and weather in our favour, by the goodness of God. But the heathen are very inconstant, so the Captain began to change his mind about going to Japan and to stop without need at the islands which he came upon. The two things that annoyed us most on our voyage were first, to see that we failed to take advantage of the good weather and wind which God Our Lord gave us, . . . and second, the great and constant idolatrous worship and sacrifices offered, without our being able to prevent them, by the Captain and his heathen crew to the idol which they carried on the ship. . . . On the route to China, a hundred leagues from Malacca, we touched at

---

[1] *Monumenta Xaveriana*, vol. I, p. 529. Letter from Francis to the King of Portugal in which, with typical gratitude, he dilates on the great merits of Captain da Gama, who, he says, "could not have treated us better had we been his own blood brothers." He begs His Majesty to requite Pedro's services, since he would always be too poor himself to repay the great debt which he owed him. The value of the presents was 200 *cruzados* (*ib.* p. 520). What they were we shall see later on.

an island and took on rudders and other timber necessary for the great tempests of the Chinese seas. Then they cast lots, after first making many sacrifices and feasts to the idol with a multitude of prostrations, and asked whether the wind would be favourable or no. The lot fell out that we were to have good weather and should not wait longer. So we weighed anchor and set sail, all of us rejoicing greatly. The heathen put their trust in the idol, which they devoutly venerated on the poop of the ship in the midst of lighted tapers and incense fumes of eagle-wood, but we trusted in God, the Creator of heaven and earth, and in Jesus Christ His Son, for whose love and service we were come to this part of the world. . . . As we pursued our way, the heathen began casting lots again and inquiring of the idol whether the ship would return from Japan to Malacca. The answer was that we would go to Japan but not return to Malacca. As a consequence, they became diffident about going to Japan and were in a mind to winter in China and wait for another year.

"As we slowly sailed along, while close to Cochin-China . . . we met with two disasters on one day, the Eve of St. Mary Magdalen [July 21st]. Heavy seas were running and there was a high wind, so we anchored. The well of the ship happened to be open through carelessness and Manuel, our Chinese companion . . . fell down it. . . . With great difficulty we drew him out, but he was unconscious for a good while. . . . The storm raged unabated, tossing the ship so violently that a daughter of the Captain fell into the sea . . . and was drowned under her father's eyes. . . . All that day and night, the heathen, crying and lamenting, made, without pause, great sacrifices and feasts to the idol, killing many birds and giving it food and

140

drink. In the lots which they cast, they asked the idol why the captain's daughter had died, and the answer came that she would not have done so, nor have fallen into the sea, if our Manuel had died. . . . You see the peril in which our lives were placed by these lots of the devil. . . . When the seas abated we weighed anchor and set off again, all of us in great sadness. . . . In a few days we arrived at the port of Canton in China, where both Captain and crew deemed it well to spend the winter. We alone resisted, . . . saying that we would write to the Captain of Malacca and inform the Portuguese how they had cheated us and broken their promise. It pleased God Our Lord to give them the will to go, . . . so in a few days we reached another port of China, Chiian-chow. There they had determined to winter, . . . but as they stood ready to enter the port a sail hove in sight with information that it was full of pirates and a death-trap for ships.[1] . . . The Captain therefore decided to keep away. Now it was a head wind back to Canton but a stern wind to go on to Japan, so, against their wills, Captain and sailors were forced to come to Japan. Neither the devil nor his ministers had power to prevent our coming, and God it was who brought us to this longed-for land. On the feast of the Assumption, 1549, . . . we came to the port of Kagoshima, the native place of Paul of Holy Faith, whose relatives, as well as all others there, received us with much love."[2]

Francis was delighted by his first contacts with the Japanese. The hidalgo in him had not completely died,

[1] Dog does not eat dog, so more likely the ships in the harbour were police junks which *Ladrão* had reason to avoid.

[2] *Monumenta Xaveriana*, vol. I, pp. 572–601.

and he speaks with a kind of suppressed enthusiasm about the sense of honour which gave dignity even to the poorest in that land of the very poor: "They are a people of great honour, of honour to be marvelled at. They esteem honour more than anything else. . . . In general they are poor, but neither the nobles nor the common people consider poverty a reproach. One thing about them, not, I think, to be found among Christians, is that nobles however poor and commoners however rich honour a very poor noble just as much as if he were very wealthy. Not for anything would a very poor nobleman marry into a plebeian caste, not even for a fortune. It would seem to them a loss of honour to marry into a lower caste, and they esteem honour more than riches. They are very courteous among themselves. . . . They are a people who brook no insults nor slighting words. . . . I would have you know one thing that you may give great thanks to God Our Lord, this island of Japan is very well disposed for a large development of our holy faith in it." So Francis, the incurable optimist, relying chiefly on the report of that convert murderer, Yajiro, who was about as safe a guide to his country's social customs and religious aspirations as would be some Cornish peasant to the spirit and genius of England. It was a weakness of Francis that he trusted too much and indeed loved too well an illiterate vagabond of unstable character who could hardly write his own name correctly.[1]   But he had nobody else except this broken reed to rely on. With him he went to school again, trying desperately hard to learn the language. "May it please God Our Lord," he wrote, "to give us language, so that we may be able to speak of His busi-

[1] *Monumenta Xaveriana*, vol. I, p. 119.

ness. . . . Now, we are among the people like statues,
silent, while they talk and discourse at large around us.
We must become as little children to learn the language,
and God grant that we may imitate the little ones, too,
in simplicity and purity of soul. . . . I think that this winter
we shall employ our time in drawing up an exposition of
the articles of faith in Japanese for printing. As all the
chief people here can read and write, this will be a means
of extending our holy faith widely, since we cannot come
to everybody's rescue." That is just what Francis would
love to have been able to do, come to everybody's rescue.
Already, in this his first letter from Japan, he is talking
eloquently to his brethren in Goa of the fine opportunities
that lay open to them in China. "You could go there,"
he says, "in all security, under the safe-conduct of the
King of Japan, who, we trust in God, will be our friend,
for I would have you know that the King of Japan is a
friend of the King of China. . . . We live in good hopes
that if God Our Lord gives us another ten years, we shall
see great things done in these parts by men coming from
your parts. . . ." Dear sanguine Saint, it would take more
than ten years, but the great things would indeed be done
and all under the impetus of his own infectious heroism.

Francis might talk easily of the King of Japan, meaning
its effective ruler, but in practice the difficulty was to dis-
tinguish that elusive personage among the host of Daimyô
or tribal chieftains who all gave themselves regal airs.
Japan at the time was in a state of completest anarchy.
Whirl, as in the Olympus of Aristophanes, was the real
King, having shorn the lawful Divine Emperor or *Dairi*
of all his authority and relegated him, like an unvalued
family heirloom, to a tawdry shrine in Kyoto, with none,

except a few faithful women and half-starved retainers to do him reverence. These were things that Francis did not hear from his mentor, Yajiro, but rather purely imaginary tales of Japan's wonderful universities. He kept an open mind about those institutions which, in fact, turned out to be merely huge Buddhist monasteries with schools attached. All that pleasant Japanese autumn and biting winter, when he confessed that he was "dying of the cold," he worked very hard trying to master Japanese. As at Cape Comorin he had enlisted the pearl-fishers to make for him an exposition of Christian doctrine in Tamil which he then learned by heart, so in Kagoshima he and Brother Fernandez elaborated with Yajiro's assistance a Japanese one, full of pathetic solecisms. This he went about the streets reciting to anyone who would listen. He was a man in whom love had completely cast out fear, so he did not hesitate to venture uninvited into the Buddhist monasteries and give the astonished monks his lesson. One of them, a gentle old abbot named Ninjit, became his friend, but, though they had many amicable conversations interpreted by Yajiro, Francis did not succeed in making him a Christian. He says wistfully that the abbot's name meant "Heart of Truth." Buddhism takes the heart out of truth and, as Ninjit himself afterwards acknowledged with regret, he understood very little of his charming visitor's arguments.[1] The results of the campaign in Kagoshima were sadly different from those which he had obtained among the Paravas of Cape Comorin. There, as an old Jesuit chronicler named Sousa expressed it, he had fished with a net, but in Japan he was obliged to fish

[1] Documents in Cros, *Saint François de Xavier, sa vie et ses lettres*, vol. II, pp. 77–9.

with a line. It was very slow work that fishing, a bite
here and a bite there, until after a year at it the three men
had made a catch of only about a hundred souls.[1] As for
the whole populations which Yajiro had assured Francis
would become Christians in six months, there was not a
sign of them. Still, in the midst of that Laodicean environ-
ment, his patience never gave out, nor his cheerfulness,
though he was in fact a virtual prisoner in Kagoshima.
Yajiro, when questioned by the local Daimyô, Shimazu,
had not minimized the standing of his beloved Master
with the *Nambanjin* or Barbarians of the South, as the
Portuguese were contemptuously named in Japan. Shimazu accordingly deferred on one pretext or another the
permission asked by Francis to repair to the court of the
Emperor, and put his holy eagerness in a cage to act as a
bait for merchantmen.

His letters from the odd, austere, timber town of Kagoshima, where people rejoiced in black and mourned in
white, disclose the extraordinary range of his charity.
His heart is everywhere at once, in the dread islands of
the Celebes and Banda Seas, at Malacca, on the Fishery
Coast, in Goa, in Ormuz, in Coimbra, in Rome. He
shows himself as avid for details of the lives and work of
his brethren in those places as though around him there
did not swarm the strangest world ever seen by a European,
and he needed not to spend a large part of his time squat-
ting cross-legged on a mat in his little house, trying to
satisfy its insatiable curiosity. In the midst of that preoccupation he found time to be concerned for the welfare
of the slaves and the sick in Goa, and to wonder if Antonio

[1] The figure given in *Monumenta Xaveriana* is 600, but that is a copyist's
error. Francis wrote 100 (vol. I, p. 659).

Gomes was keeping his temper. "For the love of Our Lord," he writes to this man, "I beg you to make yourself very much loved by all the brethren of the Society, as well those in the College as, through your letters, those in other places. . . . I most earnestly beseech you to write to me about your spiritual life. You know how much joy that would give me, how it would console me in the midst of my heavy care and trouble here. What would make me happiest of all would be to know that all the brethren of the Society, both inside and outside the house, love you greatly. It is not enough for me to know that you love them unless I know also that they love you."[1] The huge letter describing his voyage with the Pirate concludes on the same sweet note: "So I end, without ever being able to end writing of the great love which I bear you each and all. If the hearts of those who love one another in Christ could be seen in this present life, believe me, my dearest brothers, you would be seen clearly in mine. . . . I beg you earnestly to have true love in your midst, not allowing any bitterness to grow. Convert part of your zeal into love for one another, and part of your longing to suffer for Christ into forbearance with one another for His love and conquest of all aversions which do not permit this love to grow." But having written his beautiful letters how did Francis dispatch them to India and Europe? By a method typical of him: he walked that winter of 1549 nearly three hundred miles to the coastal town of Hirado where he had learned that a Portuguese ship was at anchor, and delivered them with his own hands to the captain.[2]

[1] *Monumenta Xaveriana*, vol. I, p. 651.
[2] Cros, *S.F.X., sa vie et ses lettres*, vol. II, pp. 55–6. Among the letters

Now the Daimyô of Kagoshima was at mortal enmity with the Daimyô of Hirado and therefore did not appreciate as well as ourselves that winter expedition of Francis. Moreover, Hirado had its ship, but never a Portuguese sail came to gladden his harbour. He began to think that Francis was not the potent siren he had been represented, and the Buddhist priests or bonzes, a proud, depraved, semi-military caste somewhat like the Teutonic knights, fostered his new attitude of suspicion. In the summer of 1550, he issued an edict forbidding under pain of death the further propagation of Christianity in his dominions. It was the signal for the Jesuits to move on in search of the Emperor. Paul of Holy Faith remained in charge at Kagoshima, where, after a few months, he tired of poverty and persecution, and went off to take up the more congenial profession of a river-pirate in China.[1] Francis mercifully never learned that sad news. Before leaving Shimazu's dominions he visited the enormous moated fortress of Ichicu, whose chatelaine with her eldest son and several retainers had become his converts. They made splendid Christians and kept the faith nobly in face of much persecution, without help of priest or sacrament. Twelve years later when, on his endless missionary jour-

was one for Pedro da Gama, which, says Father Perez, his friend, nearly rendered him "distracted with joy." The vicar-general of Malacca sang a Mass in thanksgiving for the arrival of the letters, at which the entire Portuguese colony attended. (Cros, *l.c.*, 70-1).

[1] The evidence is that of Father Froes who became a Jesuit before Francis went to Japan and himself spent more than twenty-four years in that country (Cros, II, 96-7). For the rest, in those Far Eastern waters piracy was regarded very much as Thucydides says the early Greeks regarded it —"an employment that involved no disgrace, but rather brought with it something of honour."

neys, the great Jesuit lay-brother and best physician in Japan, Luis de Almeida, came to the fortress, he found the little community there as fervent as if only that morning St. Francis had left them. They showed him with emotion the gifts of their Apostle, long prayers written in his own hand and enclosed in little sachets, a picture of the Annunciation, an altar-frontal, and a discipline. "Once a week," said the steward, Michael, to Brother Luiz, "I gather the Christians of the fortress together and hand them the discipline so that each may give himself three strokes, not more. Should anyone wish to exceed that number, I do not permit it for fear the discipline might get broken."[1]

In Hirado, which they reached by sea, the Daimyô desired to retain the missionaries for the same reasons that had at first inspired his enemy of Kagoshima. Profiting by the friendliness of this tough robber-baron, they made more converts in a few days than they had done in a year at the other place. But Francis must find the Emperor, so, leaving Father Torres to organize the neophytes, he took, accompanied by Fernandez and a Japanese convert christened Bernard, the long road to Yamaguchi, second largest city of the Kingdom and residence of a powerful and opulent Daimyô named Ouchi Yoshitaka. It was a journey of five hundred miles which they made partly by land, partly by sea, in the early winter. One who knew Japan better than any other European of that age attested that "to pass thus into the heart of the country, in a dress so new and strange, through the midst of Japanese heathenism, without guide or hope save God, was a deed of great

[1] From a letter of Almeida cited in Cros, II, 82–6.

heroism."[1] They had left the presents for the Emperor in the keeping of Father Torres, and took with them as their only baggage two wallets containing a surplice, three or four shirts and an old blanket, this last, says Fernandez, "to cover both of us during the night, as Japanese inns have no beds." They were lucky when they succeeded in obtaining admission to an inn. More usually the keepers of those places drove them away with scorn. In anticipation of such barbarous treatment, their companion Bernard carried a little sack of cooked rice at his girdle, so that anyhow they need not starve. Sometimes in the villages they were pelted with stones.[2] Francis and Fernandez, if not the first, were certainly among the earliest white men to set foot in Yamaguchi and caused a corresponding sensation. Indeed, the populace looked on them with the same gaping wonder that men gaze at some new animal, an okapi or giant panda, but there was no friendliness in their slanting eyes, no real interest even, only a cold, scornful curiosity. When Francis attempted to read to them the carefully conned Japanese lessons on the faith in his note-book, the press of people around him used for the most part to guffaw and mimic his accent, though a few were impressed. He was a great lover of children, but the children of Japan, "probably the most malevolent in the whole world against strangers,"[3] made his stay at Yamaguchi a misery. "Los niños nos perseguian haciendo burla de nosotros"—the children ran after us with shouts of

---

[1] Father Alessandro Valignani in *Monumenta Xaveriana*, vol. I, p. 123. Valignani was the great organizer of early Japanese Christianity.

[2] The evidence is that of Fernandez, in Cros, II, 99–100.

[3] Steicher, *Les Daimyô Chrétiens*, Hong Kong, 1904, p. 6. A fascinating book by a profound student of Japanese history.

derision. It is, perhaps, the saddest sentence he ever wrote.[1] They were invited to the luxurious houses of the *samurai* and *kugi*, the military caste and nobles, but purely as human freaks who might afford those haughty snobs an hour's amusement. Sometimes the insults became so insufferable that Francis, for all his forbearance, turned scarlet and whispered to Fernandez, "Give them as good as you get." That glorious Brother, himself formerly a rich silk-merchant in Spain, did as he was told, but said afterwards: "Each time I answered those Japanese lords in the fashion indicated by the Father, I trembled, expecting to receive for my pains the stroke of a sabre which would sweep my head from my shoulders. . . . Father Francis said to me again and again, 'You ought to mortify in yourself more than anything this fear of death, because by despising death we shall show ourselves superior to this proud people.' " Juan was given plenty of opportunities to put the counsel in practice. The lordly Daimyô desired to see them at his palace where he lived surrounded by all that was fairest, noblest, and vilest in Japan. After the usual ceremonial reverences, Yoshitaka asked a few polite questions about the two men's countries and travels. Then he said: "What is this law you bring to the Japanese?" At a sign from Francis, Brother Juan began to read out of his notebook the story of the creation and fall of man, the Ten Commandments and the judgment of God reserved for sinners. At this point Fernandez paused, because there followed a vigorous and pointed denunciation of the unnatural vices to which the Japanese nobility, including very much the Daimyô himself, were notoriously addicted. Men given to these vices were described by

[1] *Monumenta Xaveriana*, vol. I, p. 660.

Francis in the text as "filthier than pigs, and much lower than dogs and other brute beasts." Inexorably Francis signed to the Brother to continue. Yoshitaka grew red in the face and poor Juan believed that he was about to order off the heads of the pair of them, but he let them go without saying a single word. The behaviour of Francis may not have been tactful, but it was surely magnificent. For two months the indomitable men continued to preach and teach twice daily until every street and square in that city of 50,000 souls had heard them. They hardly made a convert.[1]

Finding their efforts useless, the three men left inhospitable Yamaguchi for Miyako, the present Kyoto, then capital of Japan, on December 17th, 1550. That meant another three hundred miles by land and sea in the dead of winter. The little history of the journey given by Fernandez to Father Luis Froes is very touching: "Often we had the snow up to our knees and further. A man we met on the road said to us, 'If you people are from the land of the gods [India] why don't you tell those above to stop throwing so much snow on the earth?' At night the cold was so sharp and penetrating that Father Francis spread over the two of us the matting that did duty for a bed, but even so we failed to become warm. We had to cross icy rivers whose waters sometimes came up to our girdles. Still, Father Francis on all this journeying went without shoes, and that lasted until we came to a port where we embarked for Sakai. Day and night we remained seated on the deck of the ship in the midst of young merchants who treated us very badly with their tongues. One

[1] Details from the documents in Cros, *St. François de Xavier, sa vie et ses lettres*, vol. II, pp. 103–8.

of them who by chance found the Father sitting in his place became violently angry and poured on him all sorts of abuse. The Father said nothing, but merely looked at the man sadly. Another of these young merchants made a pastime of outraging the Father, addressing him sometimes as though he were a fool and sometimes as though he were a brute beast. On one occasion, Master Francis, with that expression of gentle sadness on his face, said to the man, 'Why do you speak to me thus? Know that I love you very much and would be very happy to teach you the way of salvation.' But the young man made nought of these words."[1] Another writer who also had the story from Brother Fernandez tells what happened to them when they landed at Sakai: "The three travellers were very badly received. Nobody would give them a shelter, and along the streets the people never stopped mocking and insulting them. So bad was it that, being neither able to preach nor to find a place to lay their heads, they took refuge in a pine-wood outside the city and there, at the foot of a tree, built themselves a sort of cabin from dead branches which they found lying about. But not so soon were they to have peace, for bands of children came running to stare at the strangers and flung at them, with plenty of insults, a hail of stones." But they did eventually obtain a little hospitality in the place, and through the kindness of one courteous Japanese obtained places as lackeys in the train of a nobleman going to Miyako. "This nobleman," says Fernandez, "travelled in a palanquin with his pages, while his grooms followed behind on foot. With these latter ran Father Francis turbanned like a Siamese. Never at any time did I see him

[1] Cros, II, 116–17.

looking so gay as on this occasion. Thus, then, at a gallop did he cover the ten leagues which separate Sakai from Miyako."[1]

Francis had arrived at his city of dreams where he hoped to obtain an imperial writ for the naturalization of his Divine Master in Japan. Alas, in eleven days the dreams so long cherished were dead. "He did not find the country disposed as he had desired," says Fernandez, with sad finality. There was no Emperor, only a poor phantom called by that name, and even to him admission was barred when it became known that the strangers had no presents to offer. In a vain effort to obtain an intercessor, they went on yet another journey, braving again the stones and insults of those terrible Japanese children. It was quite fruitless, and Francis thereupon resolved to return to Yamaguchi, whose Daimyô, as far as he could see, was the most powerful ruler in Japan. He would do for an emperor. Again, they went partly by land, partly by sea, making for Hirado as their first objective. "If we had had much to suffer at the beginning of the expedition, going from Hirado to Yamaguchi and thence to Miyako, on account of the bad roads and privations of every description, the sufferings were far greater on the way back, for it was February, the season of severest cold and of most snow and wind. From the inns the Father used to take some dried fruits that they gave him for his money. These he kept in his bosom or in the sleeves of his gown, and when, on our way through the streets, we met little boys, he would give them the fruit with his blessing. . . . Father Francis was more than four months on this double journey, always going on foot and sometimes without

[1] Cros, II, 112–13, 117.

shoes." That again is the account of Fernandez who never says anything about his own sufferings.[1]

In Hirado the Saint took a fresh decision. As, despite what he had been told, the Japanese obviously judged a man by his clothes and despised him for his poor coat, he would remove that source of misunderstanding. He therefore procured for Fernandez and himself from Portuguese friends robes of good, sound stuff, at which not even the most sartorial snob in Japan would turn up his nose. Then, taking his presents for the Daimyô and the two lordly letters of credence, he returned to Yamaguchi, reaching that city in March, 1551. The presents were of thirteen different kinds, including a clock that sounded the hours day and night, an arquebus that could be fired three times without reloading, three beautiful decanters of cut glass, a sort of musical box called a *manicordio*, a piece of brocade, mirrors, and spectacles. One other item not mentioned by any of the printed sources but explicitly set down in the manuscript *History of the Church in Japan* written by the Portuguese Jesuit missionary, Father João Rodrigues, who died at Macao in 1634, was a quantity of European wine. It is pleasant to think of St. Francis introducing port into Japan. Objects such as his presents had never before been seen in Yamaguchi, so they became the talk of the town and even found mention in old national chronicles. The Daimyô was so delighted with them that he offered Francis a handsome sum of money,

[1] Cros, II, 121–2. Less than thirty years later, the Jesuit successor of St. Francis, going in by the door he had opened, made 7,000 converts in Miyako in a few months. Not only that but he built a fine church in honour of the Assumption of Our Lady, "remembering that that was the day when Father Francis Xavier entered Japan" (Father Organtini, in Cros, *l.c.*, 123).

and that being declined to the good gentleman's passing wonder, gave him complete freedom to preach and for residence a pagoda with much land attached, on which Father Torres later built a church.[1] The deed of gift constituting the Jesuits owners of this property stated that the pagoda was made over "to the Bonzes of the West who had come to teach the doctrine of the Holy One, leading to deliverance."[2] In other words, the Daimyô undoubtedly regarded the two Jesuits as being members of some unfamiliar Buddhist sect from India. Francis, on his side, "saw no one but only Jesus" in the documents, so both parties were contented.

What the Saint's life was like at the Buddhist house where he first lodged and then at his pagoda may be gathered from a few lines of his long letter to St. Ignatius dated January 29th, 1552: "Our Fathers going to Japan . . . will be more harassed than many people imagine. At all hours of the day and part of the night they will be importuned with visits and questions; they will be summoned to the house of notables and be unable to decline such invitations. They will have no time to pray or to make a meditation or contemplation; no time for any spiritual recollection; no time to say Mass, at least in the beginning. They will have to occupy themselves so uninterruptedly in answering questions that time will fail them to say their Office, to eat and to sleep."[3] Twice a day, morning and evening, Francis and Fernandez issued to preach in the streets. He used to sit on the high kerb of a well in a cul de sac called *Tonono cogi* and read to the

[1] Cros, II, 138–9, 144.

[2] Charles, *Yamaguchi au temps de François Xavier*, 1937, p. 15.

[3] *Monumenta Xaveriana*, vol. I, p. 669.

people grouped around him from his note book.[1] Then an interminable discussion began, as their auditors used to follow the two men home to continue it to all hours. In spite of the interest which they aroused and the relative respect accorded to them on account of the chiming clock and other presents given to the Daimyô, they made no conversions until one day when Brother Fernandez was preaching and a boorish fellow spat full in his face. "Without showing the least trace of emotion the Brother wiped his face and went on with his lesson. Now in the crowd there was a man of note, a great adversary of Father Francis who never came to listen to him except to contradict. The act of Brother Fernandez brought him such light that, after the instruction, he followed the Brother home and begged Francis to prepare him for baptism. He was the first Christian of Yamaguchi."[2] And so, as Francis said himself with a sigh of gratitude, "after many days and many questions there began to be Christians." In two months he baptized more than five hundred persons, not a few of whom were noblemen.[3]

But his most remarkable convert at this time was not a nobleman. Far from it, he was a poor buffoon and street musician with only one eye and that half-blind, who earned his bowl of rice by playing on his *shamesen*, the Japanese guitar, at fairs, or by making the *samurai* and *kugi* laugh with his good clowning and witty repartees. He was completely illiterate and never to his dying day learned

[1] During his stay in Japan, M. Bellessort, who knows the country so well and has written one of the best modern books about it, discovered the ruins of this "puits de Jacob."

[2] Evidence of an anonymous Jesuit who knew Fernandez, in Cros, II, 140–1.

[3] *Monumenta Xaveriana*, vol. I, p. 664.

so much as the alphabet. Though young, only twenty-five, he had an appearance so grotesque that children used to fly in terror at his approach. Father Froes who knew and loved him well in later years says candidly that he was *de muy ridiculosa fisionomia.*[1] Beneath the rags, however, beat a very upright heart, and behind the ridiculous face was a brain of extraordinary alertness. Of all Francis's listeners he was the most assiduous and intelligent and never did the Saint in his entire career baptize a greater convert than this deformed vagabond who in later years, as Brother Laurence of the Society of Jesus, became one of Japan's outstanding apostles.[2]

"Le Japonais chrétien . . . est certainement un des êtres les plus exquis que la nature et la grâce aient jamais façonnés." So speaks a modern authority on Japan[3] and so of old spoke St. Francis. "The people with whom we have so far had dealings are the best yet discovered," he wrote from Kagoshima, "and in my opinion no people superior to the Japanese will be found among unbelievers." Despite the harsh treatment which they subsequently meted out to him, he never went back on that judgment. Even among the bonzes, whose vices and chicanery he denounced at the risk of his life, with the freedom of a St. John the Baptist, he found virtues to admire and men

[1] In Cros, II, 147.

[2] A charming sketch of this practically unknown Christian hero was given by Pierre Charles, S.J., in a conference delivered at the Gregorian University in presence of the Japanese Ambassador to Italy. It has been published in the inspiring Belgian mission series *Xaveriana,* under the title *Le premier Jésuite Japonais* (12e série, no. 138, Juin, 1935).

[3] Bellessort, *Saint François Xavier,* p. 296. Bellessort has also written *La Société Japonaise* and *Les Journées et les Nuits Japonaises,* fine books based on living experience, which contributed to their author's election to the French Academy.

to make his friends. As for his converts of Yamaguchi, he hardly knows how to praise them sufficiently: "It is wonderful how truly friendly the Christians are. They are always coming to our house to visit us and see whether there is anything we would like them to do for us. The whole nation in general is given to compliments and courtesies, and the Christians seem to excel greatly in this respect, especially with ourselves, because of the profound love which they bear us."[1] If, then, after six months Francis said good-bye to those charming new friends who so much resembled St. Paul's best converts, it was certainly not, as has been sometimes suggested, through any sense of discouragement or frustration. Rather was it for their own sake, for the sake of their people, that he deemed it expedient to go, in order to send them many apostles and to win for God, if he might, the other great empire towards which Japanese eyes were so constantly turned. The Japanese owed everything to China, their script, their arts, their philosophy, their temples, their religion, and at that period of their history they delighted to acknowledge the debt. "The Japanese," said Francis, "hold the Chinese for men of great wisdom as well with regard to rules of conduct and the other world, as concerning the good government of this. So one of the questions they put to us on the subject of the Law of God and the creation of the world was, how, if these things were so, did the Chinese not know of them?" He had nothing to say in reply at the time, but already a tremendous answer was stirring in his heart—he would go and convert China as a short cut to the conversion of Japan. A few months later we find him writing to St.

[1] *Monumenta Xaveriana*, vol. I, pp. 579, 664.

Ignatius: "If no impediments arise in India to hinder my departure, I hope this year, 1552, to go to China, for it is possible that great service to our God may result, not only in China, but in Japan. Once the Japanese knew that the Chinese had received the Law of God they would more rapidly lose faith in their sects. I have the highest hopes that, by means of the Society of Jesus, both the Chinese and the Japanese will abandon their idolatry and adore God and Jesus Christ, Saviour of all nations." He goes on to explain to Ignatius some differences between Japanese and Chinese writing, and to say that he intends putting his little exposition of doctrine into Chinese characters. "I shall use it to make myself understood in China until I know the language of the country." The letter is signed, *Menor hijo y en destierro major, Francisco—* your least and most exiled son, Francis. By this time his dark hair had turned completely white, but his heart remained unageing.[1]

His leave-taking of the beloved disciples in Yamaguchi was similar to that of St. Paul at Miletus, a little sermon, many tears, a loving embrace, and he was gone.[2] But he took them with him in his heart, and his days and nights thereafter were full of schemes and dreams to procure help for Torres and Fernandez, to whom in fullest trust, he had committed the infant church of Japan.

The immediate occasion of his departure was news of the arrival of a Portuguese ship at Funai, the present Oita, capital of Bungo, a province of the great island of Kyushu. The enigmatic Daimyô of that place counted among the

[1] *Monumenta Xaveriana*, vol. I, pp. 672–4, 695.
[2] Rodrigues, *Historia*, from an original Japanese account, cited in Charles, *Yamaguchi*, p. 26.

most powerful in the country. By all the stories he appears to have been a sort of Japanese King David, addicted to fearful sins, including murder, and as quick to repent of them. He certainly had strong religious leanings, whatever his frailties, and he took an immense liking to St. Francis, whose name he adopted, when, after twenty-seven years' hesitation, he finally became a Christian. Francis worked in his town for two months, which, if we are to believe the merry old traveller, Mendez Pinto, were occupied almost entirely in exciting skirmishes with the bonzes. Pinto certainly was in Funai just then, but, incorrigible romancer, he so dramatized the simplest facts that his *Peregrinacioes* have hardly more value for the life of St. Francis than have the Clementine *Recognitions* for the life of St. Peter. One historic fact emerges. A revolution broke out in Yamaguchi at the time, the Daimyô committed *hara-kiri*, and the rebels chose the brother of Bungo's lord for their new ruler. He, too, was an admirer of Francis, so the Saint sailed from Japan in mid-November, 1551, after a sojourn there of two years and three months, with a heart made happy by the knowledge that at least two strong infidels had guaranteed to protect his Christians.[1] There were only a

[1] Father Torres wrote an account of the revolution at Yamaguchi to Francis while it was still in progress: "Everybody is hunting for us to kill us," he said. . . . "The situation is indeed critical. Daily there are pillagings and murders. If things quieten down, we shall ask these *Fidalgos* to confirm the permission which the dead king gave us to exercise our ministry. . . . Should we be prohibited from preaching in public, we shall do so secretly and, come what may, I believe that we shall go on making Christians (Cros, II, 159). That letter sufficiently explains the trust which Francis reposed in his two companions. Apparently the new Daimyô reissued the decrees of his predecessor in favour of the two Jesuits, but there is some confusion on the subject among writers (cf. Brou, II, 233, *n*. 2).

handful yet, perhaps two hundred at Kagoshima, thirty
at the fortress of Ichicu, a thousand at Yamaguchi, and a
few hundred at Hirado and Funai, not more than two
thousand in all, out of a population of some fifteen millions.[1] God, however, does not count by numbers, and
from this little flock at a later time came one of the grandest
regiments in the Church's white-robed army of martyrs.
As for Francis, looking back on his labours, he said that if
he could only make the universities of Europe understand
the joy and blessedness of work in the missions, then the
learned doctors would close their books and the canons
vacate their stalls in order to hurry to the heaven awaiting
them in Japan. "I crave your indulgence, Brothers," he
concludes, "for I have so much to say of Japan that I
would never end writing. I fear that the length of my
letter may have wearied you. . . . So I stop, without
being able to stop, because I am writing to my beloved
Fathers and Brothers and telling them of friends so true
and devoted as are the Christians of Japan."[2]

After tossing for a fortnight on the Tung Hai or Eastern
Sea, Francis was within swimming distance of his new
Canaan, China. The ship carrying him put in at the deso-

---

[1] The fifteen million is Murdoch's estimate, *A History of Japan*, Kobe,
1903, vol. II, p. 70. This very Protestant book is full of slighting references
to St. Francis and his brethren. "What really caused Xavier to be taken
seriously by the Japanese," says Murdoch, "was his knowledge of astronomy. This knowledge would now be regarded with an indulgent smile
of pity; the apostle no doubt plumed himself on being able to prove to the
benighted Japanese that the world was round," etc., etc. (p. 63). If the
astronomy of Francis dates him and merits an indulgent smile, so, by the
same token, does the prejudice of his History date Mr. Murdoch and merit
a disgusted grimace.

[2] *Monumenta Xaveriana*, vol. I, p. 696.

late St. John Island, otherwise known as Chang Chwen,[1] which lies about six miles off the Chinese coast, south-west of Hong Kong. China was then a closed land to foreigners, some of whom, even while Francis looked longingly to that *ripae ulteriori*, lay rotting in Chinese dungeons. Nevertheless, trade was carried on by the help of smugglers with whom the Portuguese merchants kept a rendezvous on this miserable island. Francis seems to have had no premonitions about the place at all. Indeed, he was happy there, for he met an old friend, Diogo Pereira, who had his ship, the *Santa Croce*, trimmed for the voyage to Malacca, whereas the other ship was bound for Siam. Francis transferred to the *Santa Croce*, and, while they sped through the South China Sea, disclosed to Pereira his great new ambition. For the sake of Japan, China must be evangelized. This was the plan. As only the ambassador of a foreign monarch would be permitted to set foot in China, the Viceroy at Goa must make Pereira ambassador of Portugal, charged to bring the Chinese Emperor the compliments and presents of his King. He, Francis, would accompany his friend, and then together they would secure a permit to preach the Gospel, the abrogation of the laws against foreigners, and the release of the unfortunate Portuguese prisoners at Canton. Francis had an eloquent way with him, and so com-pletely won the good merchant to his plan that he decided to finance it out of his own pocket. But Francis had also too much experience of life's *contretemps* to be over-confident. The plan promised so much for the cause of

---

[1] Or Chang-Tchouen or Sancian. When it comes to the spelling of Chinese place-names, one is offered a large choice by makers of maps and gazetteers.

God that the devil would surely try to cross it. Pereira waved away the devil. "You will see," said the author of the plan, and he certainly did see, before he was much older.[1]

At Malacca Francis found his beloved Father Perez waiting for him, with a letter from St. Ignatius. That letter has perished, except for one phrase in it which is immortal. "My true Father," replied Xavier, "I received a letter of your holy charity at Malacca when I returned from Japan. God Our Lord knows what a consolation it was for me to have news of a health and of a life so dear to me. Among other holy words and consolations of your letter, I read the concluding one, which ran: 'Entirely yours, without my being ever able to forget you, Ignatius.' I read them, my eyes full of tears, as they are now full of tears while I write them. The past comes back to me and I recall the great love that you bore and still bear me. I feel that my deliverance by God from the many perils and hardships of Japan was due to the intercession and holy prayers of your charity. Never would I be able to set down how much I owe to the people of Japan. . . . Your holy charity has written to me how greatly you long to see me again before your life closes. God Our Lord knows how these words of such great love have sunk into my soul, and what tears they draw from my eyes every time I think of them."[2]

At Cochin the returned wanderer attempted to catch up with his accumulated post, but was subjected to such a siege of visitors that he confessed himself unable to put his ideas in order. The ship was on the point of sailing,

[1] *Monumenta Xaveriana*, vol. II, p. 262. The story is from Pereira himself.
[2] *Monumenta Xaveriana*, vol. I, p. 668.

so the letters went off to Ignatius, to the Jesuits in Rome, and to Simon Rodriguez, as we now have them, a glorious jumble of odd sequences, original syntax, unorthodox spelling, rebellious punctuation, wearisome iterations, and thoughts that burn like flames. The new governor of the Indies, Dom Alonso de Noronha, was in Cochin then and gave the Chinese plan his fullest approbation. So much on the happy side of his ledger, but the debt of Francis to sorrow had piled up like the post in his absence. He found the missions gravely troubled by internal mismanagement, and it became almost his first duty to dismiss a priest and a lay-brother from the Society of Jesus. "It is a sore trial to me," he wrote to Micer Paul of Camerino, "to have reasons for dismissing them, and a still heavier distress to fear that they may not be the only ones. God Our Lord knows what it costs me to write you this letter. I had thought to find here some consolation after the many troubles I have borne. But instead I find other and grievous troubles to afflict me, such as law-suits and dissensions with the people, that cause small edification. Of obedience there seems to be little or none, judging by what I have seen since my return. May God be praised for everything."[1] Such is life, even on its heroic levels, for no history, however inspiring, will lack its Antonio Gomes. The Jesuits had opened a college in Cochin alongside the Church of Our Lady owned by the Confraternity of Mercy, a charitable organization of which the letters of St. Francis are full. All his life in the Indies Francis worked might and main to promote the interests of this excellent Confraternity. Its members, Portuguese merchants and other gentlemen, were not ungrateful and

[1] *Monumenta Xaveriana*, vol. I, p. 702.

put their church at the disposal of his brethren in Cochin. It is not known for certain who first conceived the idea of transforming the loan into a gift pure and simple, but it is known that Antonio Gomes brought this about through his great influence with the Governor-General and Bishop Albuquerque. It was a miserable manœuvre and, though, after a time, opposition to it calmed down and people seemed disposed to recognize for just what their Bishop, their Governor, and even their King had sanctioned, such was not the mind of Francis Xavier. The second day after his arrival in Cochin he invited the town council, the Brothers of Mercy, the Vicar-General and all the clergy, to meet him at the principal church of the city. There, with the keys of the other church in his hands, he declared that the aim of the Society of Jesus was to labour for the salvation of souls, not to raise conflicts whose clearest result must be a lessening of devotion to Our Lady. The donation of her church to his brethren had been a cause of dissension. Therefore, in the name of the Society of Jesus he renounced it, and, in the persons of its representatives, begged the pardon of the whole city for the scandal that had been caused. Then, he handed over the keys to the Brothers of Mercy.[1]

At Goa, where he arrived in February, 1552, more

[1] *Monumenta Xaveriana*, vol. I, pp. 144-5; Polanco, *Chronicon*, vol. V, pp. 670-1. Polanco mildly suggests that Francis may have been precipitate. By the strict letter of the law the church belonged to the Jesuits, so therefore, says the Secretary, "satis probabile videbatur quod P. Franciscus Xavier relinquere templum illud non poterat sine consensu majoris partis Societatis, si Litterarum Apostolicarum tenorem de bonis stabilibus alienandis consideraret." One would need to know more about the moneys with which the church had been built to decide that nice point. Were they private or diocesan? And if, as most likely, private, what right had Bishop, Governor, or King to transfer the ownership of the church?

trouble caused by the indiscretion and high-handedness of Gomes awaited Francis. Antonio had been spreading himself over India, laying bait for many suave rajahs whom he hoped to lure into the net of St. Peter. With all his genuine talents, he was a great innocent, and the rajahs, assessing him shrewdly, pretended to Christian leanings which they did not feel, purely to see what commercial advantages they might thus obtain. Far more damaging to Christian prospects than that absurd flutter of Antonio in high altitudes, was his mismanagement of the College of St. Paul. This institution, intended by its founders to give India a native clergy, he transformed into an ordinary boys' school, evicting all except one of the dusky-faced seminarists and replacing them with Portuguese young gentlemen. St. Francis, when he arrived, reconstituted the original delightful Babel. But what most offended the Saint was Antonio's contemptuous treatment of a man whom he loved, the gentle apostle of Goa's hospitals, Paul of Camerino. Saints are long-suffering people, but there are limits to their patience, and Francis had now reached his. By the sternest deed of his life, he first rusticated Gomes to the Portuguese station of Diu in the far north of India, six hundred miles from the plaudits of his admirers, and then, a little later, dismissed him altogether from the Society of Jesus.[1]

One of the keenest desires of Francis was that his men should always show proper respect and deference to the episcopal vicars of the various places where they laboured. Good and devoted Father Gonçalves Rodrigues, killing himself by inches on the Devil's Island of Ormuz, made some slip in this matter. At once he received an order

[1] *Monumenta Xaveriana*, vol. I, pp. 145, 744.

binding him under mortal sin to visit the vicar, and, on
his knees, ask pardon for whatever he had done to offend
him. Moreover, he must go to the vicar weekly for advice
and instructions. "This," said Francis, "is to confound
the devil, that lover of discord and disobedience. . . . I
write to you, not as to a poor coward in whom I had little
confidence, but as to a man strong in virtue who will
appreciate and understand. . . . I say no more except to
remember that this letter is written to you out of my
great love. . . ." At Meliapor Father Alfonso Cyprian
likewise quarrelled with the Bishop's representative. "It
is plain," wrote the Saint to him, "that little remains in
your memory of the conversation of our blessed Father
Ignatius. . . . You always let your violent nature have its
way, thus undoing with one hand what you do with the
other. Know that I have no stomach for the discontent
which you have caused. If the vicar does what he ought
not, he will not be cured by your reprehensions, especially
when given with so little prudence. . . . For the love of
Our Lord, I beg you to restrain your self-will. . . . To be
so passionate is not due to nature, but to your great carelessness of God, and of your conscience, and of your love
for the neighbour. I earnestly beseech you in the name of
our blessed Father Ignatius . . . to take yourself seriously
in hand and learn tolerance, meekness, patience, and
humility. . . . By the love and obedience which you owe
to Father Ignatius, I beg you when you have read this
letter to go to the vicar, cast yourself on your knees
before him, ask his pardon for all the past, kiss his hand
(I would be more comforted were you to kiss his feet),
and promise him that, as long as you remain there, you
will not again gainsay him in anything. Believe me, at

the hour of your death you won't be sorry for having done so. . . . I do beg you to have no more quarrels with the vicar, the Franciscan Fathers, the captains, and other persons holding authority in your parts, even though you may see things done badly. What you can remedy in a kindly way, remedy, and do not risk losing by dissensions all that you might well achieve through humility and meekness. O Cyprian, if you but knew the love with which I write you these things, you would remember me day and night, and maybe you would weep in remembering the great love I bear you. . . . Entirely yours, without my ever being able to forget you, Francisco."[1]

On his arrival in Goa Francis did not proceed at once to the Jesuit College, but, as was his custom, visited first the sick in the hospitals. His brethren had to wait, all drawn up at the door of their house, "filled," as one of them said, "with a mighty longing to see him." When he came, he embraced each and all "with his usual love, charity and genial good-humour" and asked immediately whether there were any sick in the house. "Being told there were, he went at once, before entering his own room, to visit them." This same witness describes what he looked like. He was a tall, dark-eyed man, with a high forehead and finely chiselled face. Once his hair and his beard had been black. What most impressed those who saw him was the gladness that seemed to shine out of him. "Alégre y de muy buena gracia," that was how he looked—joyful and gracious. The writer uses the word *alégre* or *alegría* five times in a few lines to describe him. "He went about with

---

[1] *Monumenta Xaveriana*, vol. I, pp. 708–10, 745–8. It will be noticed that Francis ends the second letter with the phrase of St. Ignatius which had so profoundly affected him at Malacca.

so joyful and ardent a look on his face that it caused much happiness to all who saw him, and sometimes when one or other of the brethren felt sad, the means he took to become cheerful again was to go and gaze at him."[1]

The last act of Francis in India was to constitute superior of the Jesuits there a man after his own heart, the Flemish Father Gaspard Berze, formerly master of arts of Louvain, soldier of fortune, and hermit at Montserrat. On becoming a Jesuit at Coimbra Gaspard made a declaration of his intentions: "I put myself completely in the hands of your Reverence[2] to be for ever the coadjutor of the professed Fathers of the Society of Jesus, to serve in the kitchen, to sweep the floors, to buy the provisions, to carry the Fathers' letters and messages over land and sea wherever they shall send me for the greater glory of God, whether in Christian lands or among Saracens, Turks or Pagans. I put myself in your Reverence's hands, not only to follow you personally, but the least members of our Society in the humblest offices. I shall serve my neighbour whoever he be, a leper or one stricken with the plague or other fearful disease, and all the sick in hospitals. . . . I offer myself for every sort of journey in the most distant countries. I shall go in coarse and tattered clothes, and expose myself to hunger, thirst, heat and cold, rain and snow, to all privations and all adversities, at the word of your Reverence." He did. His apostolate in the inferno of Ormuz is a minor epic by itself. To encourage his brethren in Europe and whet their appetites for the Indies, this is what he wrote to them: "Here you have no table, no bed, no roof over you. In Europe you take your meals at regular

[1] *Monumenta Xaveriana*, vol. II, pp. 881–2.
[2] Father Simon Rodriguez.

hours; here you have a right to absolutely nothing, neither companionship, nor books, nor food, nor clothes, nor sleep. There is no leisure whatever, no time to say Mass, not even liberty to exist. . . . O, my Brothers, come! . . ."[1] Describing his missionary methods to St. Ignatius, Father Gaspard said: "I employ all the tricks and stratagems which I learned as a layman, to see whether I cannot now do God as much service with them as I did Him disservice before. . . . Whether my zeal in this respect is good or bad, God knows, it being quite enough that I am a bad man myself. With those who laugh, I try to laugh; with those who sing, I sometimes sing; with those who make merry, I now and then make merry; with those who weep, I try to weep. . . . If I thought that by seeing me dance somebody might profit, I would dance for him. . . . Possibly, this way of acting is more a source of dissipation than of recollection, but I console myself sometimes on discovering similar traits in Father Francis, the strings of whose shoes I am unworthy to loosen."[2]

[1] Fragments of letters in Pagès, *Lettres de St. François Xavier*, 1855, t. II, appendice, pp. 437–49. This French translation of St. Francis was made from the highly oratorical Latin version of Poussines, and has been superseded by Père Thibaut's four volumes, based on the *Monumenta Xaveriana*, which appeared in 1922. The only approach to an English translation from the *Monumenta* will be found in Edith Anne Stewart's excellent *Life of St. Francis Xavier, Evangelist, Explorer, Mystic*, London, 1917. This book, except for occasional small ebullitions of Protestant sentiment, is more scholarly and satisfying than any English Catholic biography of the Saint.

[2] *Monumenta Xaveriana*, vol. I, p. 486, n. 2. The instructions which St. Francis left for the guidance of Father Gaspard in his office of superior make a little breviary of prudence and apostolic wisdom. There was no need to apply any spur to such a thoroughbred. Rather did Francis feel the necessity of reining him in, for he was so utterly self-sacrificial that, quite unconsciously, he tended to make holocausts of those under him too, not by his orders, but by his irresistible example. At Goa, after his return from

Having settled all the affairs of the missions in Goa, Ormuz, Bassein, Coulam, Cochin, Meliapor, Cape Comorin, Malacca, the Moluccas, and Japan, St. Francis delivered a last charge to his brethren at the College of St. Paul, embraced each one "many times with tears, as though to fix them in his heart,"[1] and set off for the third time into the unknown. It was Holy Thursday, the day if not the date on which he was born, in the year 1552. With him he took four Jesuit companions, two for China and two for Japan, and also a Chinese youth from the College to act as his interpreter. On his way to the ship, he called in to say good-bye to his friend, the Portuguese official, Cosmas Anes. "And when shall we see you

---

Ormuz completely shattered in health, he insisted on preaching as often as five or six times a day, and that though he could take no food but a few eggs beaten up with sugar. He even made a fuss about the expense of providing him with the eggs. "Add to this his confessions, his work in the house, his spiritual direction of lay people, and you can imagine what he will be up to if he gets his health back. I say nothing of his prayers, his vigils, his humility, his charm, his charity towards everybody, strangers and brethren, his mercilessness to himself." So spoke one who lived under Father Gaspard (*Selectæ Indiarum Epistolæ*, 151–2). At Ormuz he had formed a little noviceship, proposing to his recruits for ideal the lives of the Desert Fathers. The novices took to it with enthusiasm, and perished in a blaze of glorious fasting, etc., five out of eight. Francis deprecated such austerities, and advised instead that the novices be sent to care for the sick and to beg alms for the poor. In dealing with all his subjects, the new vice-Provincial will use "much love, charity and modesty, and not harshness and rigour, unless indeed they abuse your kindness." The whole attitude of Francis in government might be summed up in the phrase, *Societas Jesu societas amoris*. It was also the attitude of Gaspard, for, as Père Brou well put it, there existed between those two great men a sort of pre-established harmony. The instructions of St. Francis are in *Monumenta Xaveriana*, vol. I, pp. 900–23.

[1] "Com muitas lagrimas e abraços a todos dentro de sua alma metia" (*Selectæ Indiarum Epistolæ*, p. 159).

again?" asked Cosmas. "In the Valley of Josaphat", replied Francis.[1] He spent three days on board before a wind sang in the sails, and employed the time characteristically writing more counsels for Father Berze. Here are a few of these: "Visit women at their houses as seldom as possible. . . . If they are married, do your utmost to procure that their husbands may come near to God. Spend more time on cultivating the husbands than on the wives, for here more fruit may be reaped, men being more constant. . . . When discords arise between a wife and a husband which tend to separate them, be always for re-establishing concord. . . . Do not trust the devotion of wives who say that they will serve God better apart from their husbands, for such devotion does not last long, and is rarely practised without scandal. In public, guard against putting the blame on the husband, even though it may be he who is at fault. Counsel him privately to make a general confession, and in confession reprehend him with much modesty. . . . Incite him to accuse himself and then, on his accusation, condemn him with great love, charity, and meekness, for with these men of India much is accomplished by requests, and by force never a thing. . . . Be careful never to rebuke any one in anger, since such rebukes bear no fruit when you are dealing with lay people. . . . With friars and secular priests always act in a humble, deferential way, giving no place to anger and passion. I mean this, not only when you yourself have been in the wrong, but much more when you are innocent and they are the culprits. You will not desire a better vengeance than to be silent with reason on your side, when reason is neither listened to nor esteemed. . . .

[1] Anes himself, in *Monumenta Xaveriana*, vol. II, p. 260.

Go on always praying to God for them. . . . Seek no other vengeance than that. . . ."[1]

At last a breeze stirred, and the ship carrying Francis to his rendezvous with Pereira glided away into the southern storms. Malacca was reached after much tribulation, and then began martyrdom. The good Pedro da Gama no longer controlled the coming and going of ships, but his mean, ambitious brother Alvaro, who bitterly resented the appointment of a mere merchant like Pereira to a post so full of the promise of gain as ambassador to the grandest empire of Asia. When Pereira appeared from Singapore on the *Santa Croce* to take Francis away, the bully had the rudder of the ship detached and impounded. Francis might go to China, or to the devil, if he liked, but Pereira would not accompany him while he, Alvaro, remained "Captain-general of the Sea."[2] Pedro da Gama, da Sousa, governor of the Moluccas, and Alvarez, controller of the King's revenue, all interceded with the man in vain. When Alvarez threatened to charge him with high treason if he further resisted the King's instructions which Francis carried, the *Capitão mor* spat on the floor, wiped out the blot with his foot, and shouted: "That's what I care for your King's instructions!" Francis, thinking that as a Catholic Alvaro might respect the Papal *Decretals*, had the Vicar of Malacca read to him one denouncing excommunication against those who hindered Apostolic Nuncios in the prosecution of their duties.[3] But the Captain metaphorically spat on that

[1] *Monumenta Xaveriana*, vol. I, pp. 924–7.

[2] A few years later this miserable creature was arrested, taken back to Portugal and condemned to life imprisonment for his injustices and thieveries.

[3] *Monumenta Xaveriana*, vol. I, pp. 928–30.

too, and burst into a furious tirade against the Nuncio, calling him a depraved and vicious hypocrite who had forged his so-called credentials. The man's lackeys and boon companions then organized a definite persecution of Francis who could not stir from his place of residence without being abominably insulted. Soon he dared not appear in the streets at all. His nights he spent in the church, prostrate on the ground at the foot of Our Lady's statue, and each morning he said Mass for Alvaro as a measure of revenge.[1]

Not with Francis, however, but with his friend Pereira was Alvaro's contention, and when he had satisfied his jealousy by holding the merchant in Malacca, he permitted his ship to sail and take the Saint out of his sight. The embassy, so hopefully conceived, was over, but there remained those poor prisoners in Canton to rescue, and for their sake the Saint departed.[2] He blamed himself for the great expense to which Pereira had been put unavailingly. "I beseech you, Senhor," he wrote to him before he left, "to remember that my intention was always to serve you, as God Our Lord and your Excellency know. If this were not so I would die of pain. And I beg you also not to come to me here, for the pain would be renewed and intensified into a greater heartbreak by my seeing you and remembering that I had ruined you. Your sad and disconsolate friend, Francis."[3]

From Singapore he wrote to Father Berze, saving in

[1] *Monumenta Xaveriana*, vol. II, pp. 325–6, 341.

[2] *Monumenta Xaveriana*, vol. II, pp. 325, 352.

[3] *Monumenta Xaveriana*, vol. I, pp. 757–8. The Saint wrote to the King of Portugal begging him to recoup Pereira whose losses had been incurred in His Majesty's service. Pereira, who knew well that Francis was in no way to blame, behaved nobly throughout the whole miserable business.

nautical language that, though now "unmoored from all human help," he was hoping some good heathen would land him on the coast of China. In that hour of bitter disappointment he is as mindful as ever of his brethren and their labours. Gallant Father Beira, fighting like an old crusader to save natives of the Malay Archipelago from Moslem domination, needed reinforcements, and Father Berze is instructed to provide them. If he has no priests to spare let him send lay-brothers who in those parts can do as much as priests and are often more suitable, "because of their humility and peaceableness." He is to write to Francis all the news of India and Portugal, of the Bishop, of the Franciscan and Dominican Fathers, and to give the latter his "most particular good wishes" and earnest petition for a remembrance in their holy Sacrifices and prayers. But the chief obsession of the voyager is Japan: "Master Gaspard, let the alms which you have to send to the Brethren in Japan be in gold only and that the best you can procure, such as the Venetian. The Japanese have a liking for the best gold which they employ only in working and gilding their weapons. Anyone going to Japan in '53 will need nothing so much as to be prepared for many trials, both at sea getting there and on reaching his destination. Let him go well equipped against the cold, and take Portuguese cloth for himself and for those already there. Your Brother in Christ, who loves you much, Francisco."[1] Pereira, too, had letters from "this Strait of Sincapure," letters of such love and gratitude and sweet encouragement that the good merchant might have considered his four or five thousand lost *pardãos* a small price to pay for them. "If, as I hope,

[1] *Monumenta Xaveriana*, vol. I, pp. 768, 774.

God brings me to China," says Francis, "I shall tell the Portuguese captives how much they owe to you. I shall salute them all in your name, and give them an account of the great expenses that you went to in order to redeem them. I'll encourage them with hope of their freedom, God willing, being next year. I beg you as a favour, Senhor, to visit often the Fathers of the College and to console yourself in their company. *Vosso muito grande amigo, Francisco.*"[1]

On the ship, ploughing its way north through the tropical seas, were many sick folk, Christians and Moslems. "The Father," reported one of the passengers, "took no repose except in prayer, the rest of his time being devoted to the sick. If they needed chicken, he bought the birds for them with money which I gave him, at two *cruzados* apiece. Of his own dinner he reserved the greater part for the sick, and begged for them whatever else they required, taking it to them with his own hands. That was how he occupied himself all the time of the voyage."[2] At length in the late summer of 1552, the *Santa Croce* reached the smugglers' Paradise of Chang Chwen where several other Portuguese ships already lay at anchor. There were no houses on the island, only some temporary huts which the merchants took care to destroy each time before leaving. They kept to their ships at night, always on the alert for government junks, and during the day did traffic with the Chinese smugglers. Among the Europeans on the island was a man who by some incredible luck had escaped from the gaols in Canton. Francis became this man's friend, as he did everybody's, and, no doubt, learned from him some

---

[1] *Monumenta Xaveriana*, vol. I, p. 780.
[2] *Monumenta Xaveriana*, vol. II, p. 278.

of the amenities of the gaols where the unhappy foreigners who had dared to violate the Celestial soil lay chained flat to the ground in long noisome galleries, worms and no men for the rest of their mortal existence. Far happier was the fate of those who, after some brief torture, had been executed.[1] The effect of such revelations on Francis was not to frighten but to stimulate him. He might not be able to secure those poor captives their liberty but he could at least bring them the consolations of their faith. So from one merchant to another he went, and from one Chinese skipper to another, praying them, beseeching them, to take him over. All had the same story: it was far too dangerous. Heavy with hope deferred the weeks went by, while the watching, waiting Saint catechized the children and the slaves of the Portuguese, acted umpire in disputes between the merchants, attended day and night to the sick and dying, and begged alms for the miscellaneous rag-tag of commerce who had no resources except his charity.[2]

At length, on October 22nd, Francis announced to his two friends in Malacca, Diogo Pereira and Father Perez, the joyful news that he had found a Chinese trader, "an honourable man of Canton," who was willing to smuggle him with his "books and little bundle of clothes" as far as the gates of that city for a reward of twenty *picos* of pepper or two hundred *cruzados* in cash. Once in Canton, he would proceed straight to the house of the Governor, present Bishop Albuquerque's letter, and say that he had been sent by the authorities of Portugal to "declare the Law of God." The divine *insolence* of the programme

[1] *Monumenta Xaveriana*, vol. I, p. 791.; Brou, II, 340–1.
[2] *Monumenta Xaveriana*, vol. I, p. 786.

takes one's breath away, but supposing he had been common-sensical, supposing he had not thrown his cap over the topmost pagoda of the Celestial Empire, would we love him better, would we admire him more, would we find in his example a finer inspiration? "Had he returned sadly but tranquilly to the Indies, others might have felt authorized by the example of so great a man not to attempt the impossible. As for him, after human dreams were exhausted, he did not think himself yet arrived at his *consummatum est.* It remained to go on, all the same, leaning on God alone. When the wisdom of this world has said its last word, divine folly takes up the story."[1] It was not as if Francis had not counted the cost. "According to the natives of the Country," he told Father Perez, "the risks which we run are two. The first is that, having received his two hundred *cruzados,* our transporter may abandon us on some desert island or cast us into the sea to avoid discovery by the Governor of Canton, and the second, that, if we are taken to Canton and reach the Governor, he will order us to be tortured or thrown into prison. . . . Besides these two risks there are many other more serious ones, not connected with the Chinese, . . . for instance, the danger of losing trust in the mercy and power of God because of the perils we may run into on His service. That is a much greater danger than the mischief which all the enemies of God could do to us. . . . Considering those dangers of the soul, . . . we find that it is safer and surer to pass through the physical ones, . . . and so, by whatever way, we are determined to go to China. . . . Pray much to God for us because we run the very greatest risk of being made prisoners, but we

[1] Brou, *Saint François Xavier,* vol. II, p. 347.

178

comfort ourselves with the thought that it is far better to be a captive for the love of God alone than to be free by fleeing the toils and pain of the Cross."[1] When Francis writes "we," he means himself and the young Chinese interpreter, Antonio, whom he had taken from Goa. Just then he had no other helper or friend near him. One by one the Portuguese ships had sailed away, until only the *Santa Croce* was left, with its crew composed chiefly of partisans of the hostile Captain-general at Malacca. The most that those men did for the Saint was to build him a little log chapel and to put at his disposal one of the improvised huts on the island which afforded very poor protection from the biting sea-winds of November. We hear also of his receiving from them a handful of almonds. Otherwise he was left to fend for himself, and the faithful Antonio relates that often he was both hungry and half-frozen. Still, he remained undefeated and fixed another string to his bow of resolution, which however much bent would never break. If he could not get to China the direct way he had planned, he would go to Siam and enter the forbidden land by a back door. Then Father Perez and another designated by Father Berze would join him. The letters to both men are full of his gratitude to Diogo Pereira, the donor of the *cruzados* for that Chinese trader on whom he was pinning his immediate hopes. Diogo receives letters too, in which he is told that Francis will in due course await a visit from him, "either as a prisoner in the stocks of Canton, or at Pekin, where they say the King of China has his residence." Fever, hunger and cold slowly sapped his vitality. On November 13th he wearily wrote the last of his letters, addressed to

[1] *Monumenta Xaveriana*, vol. I, pp. 784-5, 800-1.

Perez and containing a message for Berze. "It is a long while," he said, "since I felt less inclined to go on living than I do now."

At last, November 19th, the day of his assignation with the Chinese smuggler, dawned. His books and his little bundle of clothes beside him, Francis waited, watching the shore. Hour after hour till dark he waited. There was nothing to see, not a sign of the brown sail he had hoped for. Then he knew that China had beaten him, and the poor body, so long driven by the dauntless spirit, took its revenge. "It was at that moment," wrote his one faithful follower, Antonio, "that he fell ill."[1] A fortnight later, the night of December 2nd, 1552, he was dead, forty-six years and seven months old. Nothing has been said here about his famous miracles, in the first place because a small book cannot be expected to include everything, and secondly, because his faith, hope and charity attested God more eloquently than the most stupendous miracle.[2]

[1] Cros, *Saint François de Xavier, sa vie et ses lettres*, vol. II, p. 346. The relation of Antonio given here contains a very touching day by day account of the Saint's last illness.

[2] The miracles are a matter of evidence which people interested have a full opportunity now of judging for themselves in the second vast volume of the *Monumenta Xaveriana*. A few things seem clear. Many of the cases mentioned in the processes of canonization were based on misunderstandings, exaggerations, and faulty identifications. Many other cases almost certainly happened, e.g., the story of the crab retrieving the lost crucifix of Francis, but are susceptible of a natural explanation. St. Francis himself, far from laying claim to miraculous powers, invariably denied that he possessed them. On the other hand, he was the kind of man who made it easy and excusable for people to regard him as a thaumaturge. Finally, it is quite certain that he did work some miracles. How the well-known hymn, "O Deus, ego amo te," one of the most perfect expressions of the pure love of God, came to be attributed to St. Francis is not yet

decided. The hymn is the translation of a Spanish sonnet which appeared first in 1628 in a work entitled *Vida del Espiritu*, by A. de Rojas. No name of an author was supplied by Rojas, but twenty-nine years later the Hungarian Jesuit, John Nadasi, attributed the original Spanish sonnet to St. Francis or St. Ignatius. After that, writers generally gave Francis the honour and so the hymn became specially associated with his name. He certainly did not compose the Latin version and the probability that he wrote the original Spanish is exceedingly small, but the sentiments of the sonnet so well suit him that those who made him the author had some excuse for their mistake. As the Spanish text is so much more beautiful and less known than the Latin translation, it may be given here:

No me mueve, Señor, para quererte
El Cielo que me tienes prometido;
Ni me mueve el Infierno tan temido
A no dexar por eso de temerte.

Tu me mueves, Señor, mueveme el verte
Clavado en essa Cruz, y escarnecido;
Mueveme el ver tu cuerpo tan herido,
Mueveme tus afrentas, y tu muerte.

Mueveme en fin tu amor, en tal manera
Que aunque no hubiera Cielo, yo te amara,
Y no hubiera Infierno, te temiera.
No me tienes que dar porque et quiera,
Porque aunque lo que espero no esperara
Lo mismo que te quiero, te quisiera.

CHAPTER VI

TEACHERS OF GOOD THINGS

THE early Jesuits had a passion for universities, those greatest creations of the medieval Catholic genius. Ignatius himself had tried his fortunes at three of them, Alcalá, Salamanca, and Paris. Paris, "the common mother of all northern universities, the recognized fountain-head of the streams of knowledge which watered the whole Christian world,"[1] indelibly impressed him, and thither in 1540, before there existed a Society of Jesus, he sent his first colony of Jesuits-to-be. From their number he detached three men in 1542 to start that remarkable college in Coimbra, Portugal's famous centre of learning, which immediately became a nursery of great missionaries and in the short span of six years gave St. Francis Xavier thirty-two of his fellow labourers. In April of the same year four others, including the later illustrious Juan Polanco, set up house in a modest way at the celebrated University of Padua. Owing to the outbreak of war between France and the Empire in 1542, the eight Spanish Jesuits studying in Paris had to separate from their French or neutral companions and fly for their lives. As by instinct they hurried north and settled at the University of Louvain. In 1544 it became the turn of Spain to receive

[1] Rashdall, *The Universities of Europe in the Middle Ages*, Oxford, 1895, vol. I, p. 546.

its first Jesuit foundation which, as usual, was planted in the shade of a university at Valencia.[1] Then followed, two years later, a settlement at Alcalá, begun by one of the most attractive figures in early Jesuit history, Francisco de Villanueva. This Francis was born in 1509 into the family of a poor labourer of Estremadura, so poor that he had not a surname to give his child. Villanueva is simply the name of Francisco's native town. As a boy he managed somehow to learn to read and write, and there his education ended. He obtained the post of sacristan to a local parish priest and was sent by him on a mission to Rome in 1541. At Rome he came upon the Jesuits, one of whom, the novice, Ribadeneira, has left a description of him: "A penniless rustic, under-sized, swarthy of complexion, entirely uneducated, vile and despicable in the eyes of men."[2] But not in the eyes of one man, for when he applied to St. Ignatius to be received into the Society of Jesus he was promptly accepted, though at the time the Order had its numbers restricted to sixty, and only the one grade of professed Fathers. After his novitiate Ignatius sent him to Coimbra to study. On the way there, through a bitter winter, he claimed the right as the oldest of the party to carry the knapsacks of his four companions as well as his own, a charity that nearly cost

[1] As higher authorities were slow to grant Valencia a university, the worthy burghers hired a solitary Bachelor of Arts to begin teaching in the place. But a local Bishop excommunicated them for this arrogance and imprisoned the poor B.A. It was not till 1500 A.D. that the city obtained its university, by a bull of its own Pope, Alexander VI (Rashdall, II, part I, 100–101).

[2] Quoted in Astrain, *Historia de la Compañía de Jesús en la Asistencia de España*, vol. I, Madrid, 1902, p. 259. The other details about Villanueva given in the text are from this admirable work.

him his life. Father Simon Rodriguez did not much appreciate this new addition to his family. "I am quite unable to understand how you can accept people so little suitable for our great labours," wrote he to Ignatius,[1] who replied that if twenty out of the sixty students then vowed to the Order proved to be men of Francisco's stamp he would be perfectly contented. As the climate of Portugal did not suit his bad health Ignatius transferred him soon to Alcalá, where, all alone and dependent on alms for his subsistence, he began the study of Latin grammar at the age of thirty-four. But that was not the only way in which he re-lived the early life of the Founder of the Jesuits. Though entirely uneducated, he showed so rare an understanding of spiritual things that doctors of theology put themselves to school with him. All that he ever acquired of book-knowledge was "a little grammar badly learned," but he grew so well in wisdom that, after eight years of humble, unremitting effort to make God loved, he was ordained on the title of his sanctity. In 1545 he had the joy of a visit from Pierre Favre to whom he unfolded his hopes of a fine harvest of vocations, if only the Society of Jesus could secure a permanent foothold in Alcalá. Pierre promised him a few men from Coimbra with whom to start a little college, and at the same time appointed him its superior. Then began a valiant adventure in hope, for Francisco had not a *peso* of funds nor other home for his men than some crumbling rooms in a derelict house. The spring-cleaning of those rooms to render them habitable nearly killed the pioneers. But their superior kept them in good heart, and under his inspiration the college of Alcalá became in a few years the principal

[1] M.H.S.J., *Epistolæ Broëti*, p. 533.

well-spring of the Society of Jesus in Spain. This result
was not obtained without much suffering, caused by various
zealous men who conceived the new Order to be a deadly
menace to the Church. One learned professor of Salamanca had come to the conclusion from his studies and
observation of life that the end of the world was at hand
and Antichrist already born. Further reflection convinced him that Ignatius and his Jesuits must undoubtedly
be the precursors of the Man of Sin, which theory he
preached from the pulpit and tirelessly diffused in the
University, until he had everybody shaking their heads
over the Jesuits.[1] Another earnest priest named Barberá
or Barbaran campaigned far and wide against those dangerous people, specifying exactly what ought to be done
with them. Please God he meant well, but anyhow we
owe him a debt of gratitude because he was responsible
for the following letter of St. Ignatius to a friend in
Spain, dated August 10th, 1546: "M. Doime, Tell the
Father, Friar Barbaran, that, as he says all of our men discovered between Perpignan and Seville[2] ought to be
burnt, I say and desire that he and all his friends and
acquaintances, not only between Perpignan and Seville
but in the whole world, may be set on fire and consumed
by the Holy Ghost, so that all of them, coming to great
perfection, may be deeply stamped with the glory of His
Divine Majesty. Also, will you tell him that our affairs
are now being dealt with before the Governor and the
Vicar of His Holiness, who are about to pronounce sentence, and that, if he has anything against us, I invite him
to make a deposition and prove it before the above-

[1] M.H.S.J., Polanco, *Chronicon*, vol. I, pp. 298–9.
[2] This corresponds roughly to our own John O'Groats and Land's End.

mentioned judges. If I am guilty, I would be happier to pay the penalty and suffer alone, rather than that all those from Perpignan to Seville should have to be burnt."[1]

Father Villanueva's most redoubtable foe was, curiously enough, another rustic from Estremadura who bore the name of Guijero, Latinized into Siliceo, meaning flinty or full of pebbles. By all accounts the name suited him to perfection. He had a hard, brilliant head and a forceful nature which brought him eventually to the highest peak of ecclesiastical eminence in Spain, the archbishopric of Toledo. From that commanding position, he launched, like a Jove enthroned, thunderbolts against the Jesuits of Alcalá. Edicts forbidding them to preach or administer the Sacraments were promulgated throughout the diocese, and any priests who allowed them to officiate in their churches or made a retreat under their direction found themselves excommunicated and sentenced to a money fine of five thousand *maravedis*. For abettor, the fierce Archbishop had the brightest star of theological learning in Spain, the famous Melchior Cano, who from his own high professorial post at Salamanca tirelessly denounced as heretical the *Spiritual Exercises* of St. Ignatius. Both men appear to have been sincerely convinced that they were fighting the battles of the Lord, but the weapons which they wielded hardly suited their role of crusaders. Of Cano and his coterie Ignatius wrote to his friend, Blessed John of Avila: "What I believe is that good zeal rather than due knowledge inspires their opposition."[2]

---

[1] M.H.S.J., *Epistolæ et instructiones*, vol. I, pp. 408–9.

[2] M.H.S.J., *Epistolæ et instructiones*, vol. II, p. 317. Referring to Cano after his death, Fr. Jerome Nadal, Ignatius's right-hand man, wrote as follows: "This good Father has extracted many Masses and prayers from

It was the fairest thing ever said about a campaign which achieved nothing except to darken counsel and hamper the humble, inoffensive apostolate of men like Francisco de Villanueva.

The year after that unpretentious hero was born in a labourer's cottage, another Francis came into the world in the ducal palace of Gandia on the Valencian coast who had for great-grandfathers Pope Alexander VI and King Ferdinand the Catholic.[1] He bore the ill-omened name of Borgia, and, as far as man could, redeemed it from infamy. Not in all the famous annals of Spain was there another such nobleman, one who consorted familiarly with his Emperor and walked more humbly with his God than the least of his dependents. The phenomenon of holiness so near the grandest of European thrones dazzled the biographers of Francis Borgia. They made him a saint from his cradle, whereas he won his spiritual spurs in battle, like a soldier. They turned him into a dull legend, a stiff, thin-lipped, brocaded saint, viceregal even when he scourged himself, whereas, in fact, the only evidence of high, if crooked, lineage that clung to him was an exquisite

---

me and several other Fathers. . . . He exercised us in patience and charity . . . by his zeal for religion and his piety" (*Epistolæ Nadal*, vol. II, p. 47). Father Astrain remarks drily that Nadal's opinion was dictated by his heart, not by his head! Cano's campaign against the Jesuits ended only with his life in 1560. Anyone interested in the wretched controversy will find a long account of it in Astrain's *Historia*.

[1] Before his simoniacal election to the Papacy Rodrigo Borgia had four illegitimate children, the second of whom, Juan, left a son with his own name before dying by the hand of an assassin. This Juan married Doña Juana of Aragon, illegitimate daughter of an archbishop of Toledo who was himself the illegitimate son of King Ferdinand. Juan and Juana were the parents of St. Francis Borgia.

courtesy of demeanour. They drained him of humanity, to hang on him, as on a flat robot, a whole basketful of abstract virtues when, in truth, he was a very tender-hearted man who adored his wife and kept green to his dying day the memory of his friends. Indeed not only was he human but a humanist, a saint in the line of Assisi's Francis, who loved music and everything else beautiful that had kept its innocence. It is pleasant to know too that the bag of bones which he is represented as being in pictures has no authenticity. Though always very austere and a great faster, he was till late in life exceedingly stout, "the biggest man in Valencia," whose belt, according to one of his servants, would go round three normally proportioned people. The tables at which he sat in his palace of Gandia had to have large half-moons cut out of them to accommodate his frontal superabundance.[1]

When Viceroy of Catalonia in 1541, Francis came to know his first Jesuits. They were a contrasted pair whom he met, the intense and vehement Antonio Araoz and the gentle, companionable Pierre Favre. Both impressed him deeply, and his first letter to St. Ignatius was an urgent petition that Araoz should not be removed from Barcelona, which city had been stirred to its murky depths by his sermons. That letter inaugurated a wonderful, life-long friendship, for with the two men it was, so to say, a matter of love at first reading. Francis soon learned to confide all his worries to his Jesuit friends. One of the

[1] Suau, *Histoire de S. François de Borgia*, Paris, 1910, p. 138. This critical and measured study re-discovered the Saint buried under the dreary rubbish-heap of pious writers. Dr. Otto Karrer's biographical essay (Freiburg 1921) carried the good work a stage further. The best way of all to appreciate the sweetness and lovableness of St. Francis is to read his own letters, now available in the *Monumenta Historica Societatis Jesu*.

things that troubled him most was the religious condition of his Duchy where in more than a thousand families only eighty could boast Spanish blood and Spanish traditions. The rest, 947 to be exact, went by the name of "New Christians," Jews and Moors whose great-grandparents had been given the option of baptism or exile by the Duke's own great-grandfather, King Ferdinand. They had chosen baptism but remained true to Moses and Mohammed at heart, even unto the third and fourth generation. One measure which the Duke contemplated for turning these nominal Christians into real ones was the foundation of a sort of catechetical school to provide their children with thorough instruction in the faith. He appealed to St. Ignatius and Ignatius immediately promised him assistance, but suggested a school open to all applicants, no doubt in the belief that full-blooded young Spaniards needed Catholic instruction quite as much as did the baptized sprigs of Israel or Islam.

On November 16th, 1545, seven Jesuits, headed by Father Andrew Oviedo, arrived in Gandia. The sight of them kindled in Francis a new ambition. He was not a grandee for nothing. Even his spirituality took some of its colour from his social position, God appealing to his mind and heart chiefly under the aspect of His *infinita grandeza*, a noun used technically to mean the pre-eminence and dignity of a grandee of Spain. It was natural for such people to be grandiose in their planning, so Francis determined to found, not an ordinary college, but a university. Father Araoz winced on hearing the news and confided his misgivings to Ignatius. However, saintly dukes were too uncommon to be gainsaid, especially one who had already, as Oviedo expressed it, "become lost in the affairs of the Society." Little Gandia must have its university, even though only forty miles up the coast great Valencia already boasted such an institution. The death of his wife Eleonora in March, 1546, brought Francis closer than ever to the Society of Jesus. In May the first stone of the new Jesuit house was ceremoniously laid by Father Favre, the second by the Duke himself, the third by Father Oviedo, and then five more by the Duke's sons, Carlo, Juan, Alvaro, Ferdinand and Alfonso. Twenty-six years later when he lay dying those were the last names on the lips of Francis. His college erected, he set to work building his University, and, in 1547, obtained from the Pope, who could refuse so good a man nothing, a lordly bull conferring on it all the privileges of the venerable and famous institutions in Paris and Salamanca. Paris and Salamanca had no reason to be jealous, for the new creation was in fact a mere toy university which could never hope to compete even with its relatively unimportant neighbour at Valencia. The Jesuits knew that very well, but nevertheless, to please the good Duke, they took and kept charge of his venture until the suppression of their Order in the eighteenth century. The solemn inauguration ceremony was held on March 7th, 1549, at which Father Andrew Oviedo received his letters patent appointing him first rector and chancellor of the University. Poor Father Andrew desired nothing less, except, perhaps, the dignity which Providence still held in reserve for him.

Meantime, Francis had pronounced before that priest a vow to enter the Society of Jesus as soon as he had settled the affairs of his Duchy. He was on intimate terms for years with the Franciscans and Dominicans, and among the latter numbered as his friend the great St. Luis Bertrand, who was to be canonized in his company. But he passed over the older orders with their glorious records for one without a history. The Jesuits themselves could scarcely believe the report, and we may almost feel the tremor of emotion in the letter which Ignatius addressed to the Duke on October 9th, 1546. He tells of the joy which his Lordship's resolution has given him, and calls upon all the holy angels and saints of heaven to render God "infinite thanks for the great mercy with which He has refreshed the Society of Jesus." The Duke's entrance into the Society will be an example profitable to countless souls and will animate those who are already Jesuits "to begin anew to serve the divine Father of families who gives us such a brother and has chosen such a labourer for the cultivation of this His newly planted vine." Coming to practical considerations, Ignatius advises his illustrious new son to keep his determination a secret until a more favourable occasion, because as yet "el mundo no tiene orejas para oir tal estampido"—the world has not the ears to hear such an explosion. Francis must see that his three daughters and his eldest son are "very honourably" married. The remaining four sons ought to be given separate allowances to enable them to pursue their studies, not at Gandia, but in one of the great universities. Gandia, however, would suffice for their Father. "If it were possible," says Ignatius, "I should like you to take the degree of doctor of theology in the University of Gandia." Francis accordingly became one of the first pupils of his own foundation.[1]

Though that foundation had little significance from a cultural point of view, it yet made scholastic history by

[1] M.H.S.J., *Epistolæ et instructiones*, vol. I, pp. 442–4.

directing the activities of the young Jesuit Order into educational channels. In its most primitive form the Society of Jesus was intended exclusively for men bound by solemn vow to go at a moment's notice wherever the Pope might direct them. Men so bound obviously could not engage in regular educational work entailing a fixed place of residence. Consequently, in the earliest sketches of the Jesuit Constitutions provision is made only for the teaching of Christian doctrine to children, and for colleges in which young aspirants to the Order might be trained. In the draft signed on March 4th, 1541, by Ignatius and five of his first companions ordinary teaching and university lecturing are definitely excluded from the scope of Jesuit undertakings—"No estudios ni lectiones en la Compañia."[1] The houses opened subsequently in Paris, Lisbon, Padua, Coimbra, Louvain, Goa, Valencia and Alcalá were purely private hostels for Jesuit students. Gandia marked a fateful change, inasmuch as the Jesuits there embarked on the education of lay pupils side by side with their own young brethren. The credit for the innovation belongs to Father Oviedo, acting under the inspiration of St. Francis who desired to extend the benefits of his foundations to all students, and not only to his favourites, the Jesuits. It is good to know that the step was taken in the presence of two saints, for Francis invited his friend the Archbishop of Valencia to preside at the academic display inaugurating open lectures, and that Archbishop

[1] M.H.S.J., *Constitutiones*, vol. I, p. 47. Older books such as Hughes' *Loyola and the Educational System of the Jesuits* (1892), and Schwickerath's *Jesuit Education* (1904) are quite astray on this point. The learned authors, both Jesuits, had not the *Monumenta* to bar such erroneous statements as that "Ignatius had founded a religious order which made the education of youth one of its primary objects."

was the famous friend of the poor, St. Thomas of Villa-
nova. A few months earlier, in June 1546, St. Ignatius
had been empowered by the Pope to establish two new
grades in his Order, those of spiritual coadjutors or priests
not bound by the fourth vow, and of temporal coadjutors
or lay-brothers. With their coming the original reason
for eschewing education as a Jesuit activity disappeared,
and Oviedo's action at Gandia, a mere nothing in itself,
proved to be like the pebble which decides the course of a
great river. Gandia, we might say, was in some sense the
mother of all the imposing colleges, the Louis le Grands
and the Stonyhursts, of the future. It providentially
opened a sluice and the flood poured through, so that when
St. Ignatius died ten years after its foundation his sons
were already conducting thirty-three colleges for others
besides their own brethren in seven European countries.

The domestic history of Gandia's College is an unusually
interesting mixture of bizarrerie and high spiritual aspira-
tion, controlled by the wisdom and winning charity of
St. Francis and St. Ignatius. The zeal of the young
superior, Father Oviedo, knew no bounds, but his discretion was limited. He had a passion for solitude and
would retire at times to a hermitage outside the town to
spend there a fortnight in unbroken contemplation. He
expressed the view that all professed Fathers of the Society
of Jesus should spend a month annually in a figurative
desert. St. Francis, who loved him, notified St. Ignatius
that he used to get up at midnight and pray for seven
hours on end. In February, 1548, "Andrew the Publican," as he liked to sign himself, humbly petitioned St.
Ignatius for leave to go into the wilderness for seven

years.[1] Out of his intense devotion to the Holy Sacrifice, he also yearned to say three Masses every day, which prompted St. Ignatius to reply that if Andrew were in Rome he would soon cure him of his longing by forbidding him to say Mass at all.[2] St. Francis, austere by nature, became infected with the penitential fervours of his Jesuits, and went in for excessive fasting and other imprudent mortifications, until the ever-vigilant Ignatius put a stop to the mischief. His letter to the Duke, dated September 20th, 1548, is worth giving somewhat fully: "Your way of proceeding with regard to both spiritual and corporal things for the progress of your soul has given me fresh cause to rejoice greatly in Our Lord and to give Him eternal thanks. . . . But feeling as I do in the same Lord that spiritual and corporal exercises, . . . salutary for us under some circumstances are not so under others, I shall tell your Lordship . . . my views on the matter, since you ask me for them. First of all, as to the time devoted to interior and exterior exercises, I would be for cutting it in half. . . . From what I know of your Lordship, I feel that it would be better to give the other half to study, . . . to the government of your estates, and to spiritual conversations, always striving to keep your soul calm, at peace, and disposed for whatever Our Lord may desire to bring about in it. It is undoubtedly a greater virtue and grace to be able to enjoy your Lord in various occupations and places than in one alone. . . . Secondly, as to fasting and abstinence, I would advise you for Our Lord's sake to look after and fortify the stomach and other natural organs, rather than to weaken them. When a man

[1] M.H.S.J., *Epistolæ Mixtæ*, vol. I, pp. 467–72.
[2] M.H.S.J., *Epistolæ et instructiones*, vol. II, pp. 11–13.

is so disposed that he would choose to die rather than commit even the least offence against the Divine Majesty, and when moreover he is not troubled by any special assaults of the devil, the world or the flesh, as I am sure is your Lordship's case, . . . then, and it is a point I would most earnestly impress on you, since both body and soul belong to their Creator and Lord who will demand an account of them, you must not allow your natural powers to become weakened. If the body is ailing the soul cannot properly function. . . . We ought to love and cherish the body in so far as it is obedient and helpful to the soul, for with such obedience and assistance the soul can the better dispose itself to serve and praise our Creator and Lord. Thirdly, with regard to castigation of the body, I would be for avoiding altogether any form of it that could cause a single drop of blood to appear. . . . Instead of seeking to shed our blood, it is much better to seek directly the Lord of us all and His holy gifts, such as tears for our sins, . . . an intensification of our faith, hope, and charity, joy in God, and spiritual peace, . . . all with humility and reverence to our holy Mother, the Church, and her appointed guides. Each of these holy gifts ought to be greatly preferred to all corporal actions, which are good only in so far as they tend to obtain the gifts for us. I do not mean to say that they ought to be sought for the contentment which they bring. But, since we know that without them all our thoughts, words and works are muddled, cold, and troubled, we desire them in order that the same may be rendered ardent, lucid, and righteous for the greater service of God."[1]

For Francis to hear that calm, quiet voice was to obey.

[1] M.H.S.J., *Epistolæ et instructiones*, vol. II, pp. 233–6.

Not only did he moderate his own austerities but he took in hand Andrew the Publican also and completely weaned the dear man from his desire of the desert. In His own good time God would give him desert enough to satisfy his wildest expectations.[1] Writing about him to Ignatius on November 30th, 1549, the Duke said: "I love him. . . . I have changed him. He is now quite comforted and immersed in his studies, so I beg your Reverence as a favour to write and cheer him up, congratulating him about what I have told you. All said and done, he is a true son of the Society, even if he desired in his innocence to be *ut passer solitarius in tecto*."[2] Ignatius wrote, and his letter, reported Francis, gave new life to Father Andrew: "He goes kissing your Reverence's name and sign-manual, and speaks another language. *Bendito Dios por todo*." Towards Father Araoz, too, a much less tractable or likeable man, St. Francis showed a winning, genial charity. In July, 1546, he writes to him: "I am sending your Reverence some juice of the sugar-cane grown in these parts to assuage your thirst when you are feverish. I beg of you for the love of the Lord who gives the fever to accept His remedy. . . . As for me, do not regard what I send but rather what I would send if I could and there were any need, my heart itself. Let us take up our abode in the Heart of the Lord by His great charity, and may He ever increase in the hearts of all men living.

[1] The Pope appointed him Bishop and subsequently, in 1567, Patriarch of Ethiopia, the reputed dominion of Prester John. But the fascinating, heroic story of his sufferings and solitude there are outside the scope of this book. All the materials for it are grandly edited in C. Beccari's magnificent collection, *Rerum Aethiopicarum Scriptores Occidentales*, vol. X, Rome, 1910.

[2] M.H.S.J., *Borgiæ Epistolæ*, vol. II, p. 566.

Amen." A year later Araoz receives a letter full of anxiety about his health: "The mere news that your Reverence had arrived at Valladolid made my soul melt away within me. I am full of envy of Vega because he will see your Reverence before I do. I long for your coming that I may know in detail how your health fares. . . . For myself, *Padre mio*, I am quite well physically. Spiritually, since I am not in Hell I flatter myself I am not doing too badly. That consideration makes everything abound for me, everything smile for me, everything have a savour for me."[1] When Araoz arrived at the College, the Duke went over and spent the entire day with him. At dinner time he boiled the ailing Father two eggs with his own hands and said that he must eat them because they were the first eggs he had ever boiled in his life. This half-playful, almost whimsical humour lightened both the conversation and the correspondence of Francis, and made it easy for people to love him. He had the habit of command but so exercised it that to obey him seemed a sort of privilege. In seven years he gave away in charity more than fifty thousand ducats. Each morning a doctor brought him a list of the sick poor, for all of whom he provided with lavish generosity. His fortune had come to him from Alexander VI, and it seemed to be his great anxiety that as much as possible of it should go back to the poor before he died. When his beloved Father Ignatius dissuaded him from scourging himself to blood, he did not perhaps remember that it was Borgia blood, tainted blood, that cried out to be shed in expiation. That is the clue to the life-long and terrible austerities of Francis.

[1] *Borgiæ Epistolæ*, vol. III, pp. 16–9.

To save his friend from an uncoveted dignity which the
Emperor seemed about to force upon him, St. Ignatius
obtained from the Pope early in 1548 faculty for an
anonymous layman to make his solemn religious profession while still in the world and engaged in the settlement of his affairs. So discreetly was this managed that
the Pope had not the slightest suspicion of the magnificent
Duke of Gandia being the beneficiary. On February 1st,
Francis, "pecador abominable," as he described himself
in the formula, took the vows which made him irrevocably
a Jesuit. One of the first things he did in that new disguise
was to appeal to the Pope above the hot heads of Melchior
Cano and his allies on behalf of the *Spiritual Exercises*. Let
the Pope decide between them and Ignatius. Francis
petitioned that the Holy Father should submit the manuscript of the *Exercises* to his official theologian, the
Dominican Master of the Sacred Palace, and other outstanding men, for examination. This was done, and then,
on their report, the Pope issued the Apostolic Letter,
Pastoralis Officii, dated July 31st, 1548, which gave the
Spiritual Exercises for all time rights of citizenship among
the classics of Catholic asceticism. At last they could be
printed, and the costs of that first edition were borne by
the Duke of Gandia.[1] Thereafter Catholics remained free
to say, if it so pleased them, that the *Exercises* were un-
liturgical, mechanical, anti-mystical, but never again could
they say, as some had done, that they were diabolical or
heretical.

In 1550 St. Francis came to Rome in all the panoply
of his *grandeza* to visit St. Ignatius. It was to be their first

[1] *Borgiæ Epistolæ*, vol. III, pp. 24-5, 28-9; Polanco, *Chronicon*, vol. I,
p. 267; *Epistolæ Mixtæ*, vol. II, p. 67.

and last meeting in this world. At the time, Ignatius had his heart set on establishing in Rome a seminary for the education of an élite clergy. But he was penniless, he was always penniless. Francis gave him 4,532 gold ducats to start the work, which made the grateful Saint want to call the institution Borgia College. This, however, the Duke would not allow, so it became known as the Collegio Romano until, in recognition of Pope Gregory XIII's benefactions, it was rechristened the Gregorian University. No other university still in existence can boast of having had two canonized saints for its founders. After that and other generous deeds, Francis hurried back to Spain, fearful lest his closely guarded secret might leak out prematurely. As it was, the tassels of a red hat threatened to entangle him, for Paul III who had received the cardinalate from his great-grandfather desired to include him in the sacred college. Francis personally seemed to like the idea as something that would enable him to be of even greater service to his Jesuits. But it horrified the more experienced Ignatius, who, to exorcize the menacing hat, bade his great son take the special vow whereby Jesuits bind themselves not to accept honorific ecclesiastical dignities unless in obedience to a solemn command of the Pope. Francis took the vow with the best will in the world. In Spain he settled out of devotion and affection on the native heath of Ignatius. His regard for Ignatius is a beautiful and touching thing which does honour to both saints. There was a small Jesuit house in those parts, one of whose men, Father Miguel Ochoa, wrote as follows to Rome on January 8th, 1552, after Francis had abdicated all his titles and become a simple priest in the Society of Jesus: "We have been to the Hospital of St. Mary Magdalen where your Paternity liked to lodge when you were here. We all rejoiced to be in the same house, especially Father Francis, who desired to have his meals at the same little table that served your Paternity and to sleep in the room in which you used to sleep. We also came across the pony which your Paternity left at the Hospital sixteen years ago. He is very fat and very good, and still extremely useful to the institution. He is a privileged animal in Azpeitia, and even when he breaks into corn-fields people wink at it. Father Francis says about him: *respexit Dominus ad Abel et ad munera ejus.*"[1] The Saint, who never used his family name again, carried on an active apostolate in Guipúzcoa and other places until 1554 when Ignatius divided the rapidly multiplying Spanish Jesuits into four provinces and gave him a general charge of them all.

In that position of commissary-general for Spain, the Duke turned Jesuit came into close contact, and sometimes mild conflict, with the Majorcan, Jerome Nadal, who, while a student at Paris, had firmly declined the hand of friendship proffered to him by St. Ignatius. Previously in Alcalá he had witnessed the arrest of Ignatius by the Inquisition and conceived a deep distrust of him. He tells how he met the advances of the Saint in Paris: "I said to him, holding out the New Testament which I carried, 'This is the book for me. . . . Leave me alone.'" After taking a brilliant arts degree, he went to Avignon to study Hebrew under some Jewish rabbis, with whom he had

---

[1] M.H.S.J., *Litteræ quadrimestres*, vol. I, p. 494. These letters were so called because, in accordance with a Jesuit law, they had to be addressed to the General of the Order every four months by all superiors of houses outside Italy and inside Europe. Italian superiors were obliged to write once a month, and superiors in missionary lands beyond Europe once a year.

lively contests. He became seriously ill and confesses that never in his life did he feel less inclined to piety than then when he needed it most. Well again, he was arrested as a Spanish spy and about to be hanged when a lucky revolt in the French camp saved him. In the course of his flight, hugging a precious copy of the Pentateuch in Hebrew under his arm, he was intercepted by a soldier who seized him by the beard and despoiled him, calling him a dog of a Jew. He was always running into such trouble and he had no health to speak of, yet before leaving Avignon he won the biretta of a doctor of theology. Then he sailed home to his family in Palma, to meet with even greater tribulation. "For seven years," he says, "I was not a day, not an hour, not a moment even, without pain in my head and stomach. My friends marvelled to see me always so melancholy and feared I would become a misanthrope. I was always in the hands of doctors and swallowing their medicines." Everything went wrong with him. His sermons made no impression. When he tried to lecture, his audience faded away. He quarrelled with his uncle over a horse and with his brother over a wife. His mother whom he worshipped died. He took to a hermit's life but that in no way diminished his melancholy. "Why, when you have everything heart could desire, are you always so sad?" a friend asked him. "Ah," he replied, "if you could tell me that you would fulfil my dearest longing." One who knew him intimately relates that in his trouble he knocked at the door of the local Charter-house. "Father," said he to the Prior, "for seven years now I have been leading the life you know of and in all that time have been unable to find peace. It seems to me that something is wanting to me. What would you advise me to do?" The Prior replied: "If you were an assassin or a robber I would say to you, *Declina a malo et fac bonum.* But leading the life you do, I am certain that God requires some greater service from you. What it is and how you are to render it you must persistently beg Him to reveal, offering your Masses, prayers, and other good works for that intention." Jerome did as he was told and reports the sequel himself: "I sought peace but it fled from me because I fled from God who was calling me. And yet my God drew me back by a sweet and merciful stratagem, as I then began to understand. A friend sent me from Rome a copy of a letter of Master Francis Xavier in which that eminent Father relates the abundant and wonderful fruit of souls given by the Lord, and thanks God for the confirmation of the Society of Jesus by the Holy See. At those words I began to wake up as it were from a long sleep, and found myself stirred to the depths of my soul, remembering what had occurred between myself and Father Ignatius. I banged the table with my hand, exclaiming, 'Nunc hoc aliquid'—now this is something!" Lost in his studies and his troubles, Jerome had until then been entirely ignorant of the subsequent history of Ignatius. And now the quondam prisoner of the Inquisition whom he had repulsed in Paris was the head of a new religious order fully approved by the Church. It almost beat belief, so he decided that he must at once proceed to Rome to investigate the phenomenon.

In Rome, where he arrived riding a mule on October 10th, 1545, he did not immediately throw himself at the feet of Ignatius. Far from it, he declined the invitation of Father Domenech, whom he had known in the old Parisian days, to lodge at the Jesuit house, and took up quarters with a fellow-Majorcan, an auditor of the Rota. "Thus," says he, "the fish escaped the hook that time." He remained a whole month guest of the auditor who treated him with great honour and consideration, even to the extent of hanging his room with tapestries. "During all this time," he continues, "I was completely distracted and dissipated in soul. While at home I hardly ever missed saying daily Mass, I did not once offer the Holy Sacrifice during those thirty days. I wandered a great deal about the City, studiously investigating the monuments of antiquity. From time to time, I went, led by the spirit of God, to visit Father Ignatius, but the evil spirit did all in his power to keep me away. Fathers Laynez and Domenech often spoke to me about the Spiritual Exercises, but I paid no attention to them. Sometimes Ignatius used to invite me to dinner when he would converse with me mildly and sweetly, as was his manner. Since he had said nothing to me plainly about changing my way of life, I constrained him once at dinner, after asking him to send the other Fathers away. 'These Fathers,' said I, 'are stuffing me[1] with much talk of the Exercises, and I know perfectly well what their game is, namely, to get me to change my method of life and come to you. Now in this matter I want you to hear from my own lips many things which seem to indicate that I am not suited to your institute.' Then I told him pretty well all the troubles of my past except my sins. He listened to me attentively, and, if I remember, smiling. When I had done, he replied in his pleasant way: 'That's all right. If the Lord calls you to the Society, you won't want for occupation.' After that I began to think seriously of the Exercises, but Peter

---

[1] *Infarciunt.*

Santini, whom Ignatius, fearing my fits of melancholy, had charged to procure me a spacious room with a pleasant garden in which to make them, experienced difficulty in finding such amenities. I chafed at the delay . . . and, moreover, I was afraid of the auditor and the other Majorcans in his family, to whom I explained that I wished to retire for twenty-five or thirty days to try certain meditations of Father Ignatius . . . for the good of my soul, before I went on to the Council of Trent. . . . The auditor, an upright man of whom I stood not a little in awe, did not gainsay me, so with Father Domenech for instructor I went into retreat on November 5th. I was in good heart, though vexed with bad health and depression. In the first stages, I was all on fire for something out of the ordinary to happen to me, a vision, a revelation, a sign of some sort. I got fruit from the First Week and made a general confession to Father Ignatius. In the Second Week I experienced even greater fruit, . . . but when I reached the election I became so perturbed and distracted that I could not keep either my mind or my body still. My mind was in darkness, my will sterile and obstinate, my body afflicted in head and stomach, and with a fever. I wrote down a great number of *pros* and *cons*, but I could reach no decision and remained so suspended that Father Domenech was visibly depressed. On the seventeenth day, he said that we must go ahead, as I had already wasted days on the election without result. I replied that I would like to devote one night more to it, and then I had a singular grace from God. I seized my pen and wrote as the Spirit of Christ moved me, with the utmost joy in my heart. . . . : 'In the Name of the Most Blessed Trinity, Father, Son and Holy Ghost, I determine and propose to follow the evangelical counsels, with vows in the Society of Jesus.' "

That was done on November 23rd at half-past twelve in the afternoon, but Father Jerome had still some way to go before attaining his ultimate peace. St. Ignatius played a waiting game with him, most delicately refraining from bringing any pressure to bear. A sort of inertia of the will seemed to come over Nadal. He wanted to pronounce the vows of a Jesuit, yet all he could do was to vow again and again that he *would* pronounce them, as long as hope remained of the Society being ready to receive him "in any capacity." Ignatius took him into his community and put him to work helping the cook and the gardener. "He told me to read a chapter of Gerson[1] every day and to meditate on it. It was wonderful how he praised that little book, saying to me that wherever I opened it at random I would find something suited to the need of the moment, as he had himself experienced." Jerome gives us little vivid pictures of his life in the novitiate, sweeping the kitchen with a worn-out broom, "which tested me," digging in the garden in a heavy coat while Ignatius walked up and down talking to Dr. Torres, suffering from "an extraordinary hunger" but too scrupulous to seek the remedy until Ignatius said to him with a smile, "Eat, my poor man, eat," visiting the Seven Churches with another novice who "on the whole journey could not get a single word out of me." Ignatius treated his difficult, moody guest with exquisite tact. "Most pleasant and intimate he was in his dealings, very often having me at his table, visiting me frequently in my room, and taking me for walks. . . . He forbade me to fast in Lent and when

---

[1] *The Imitation of Christ*, attributed in those times to Chancellor Gerson.

205

I stammered that some in the house might be scandalized, he replied warmly, 'Show me them and I shall at once show them out of the Society.' . . . After being four months in the house, Ignatius desired me to be its minister, an office whose functions I carried out honestly, indeed, according to my lights, but with too much severity, and so I displeased the brethren."[1] Jerome had no illusions about himself.

For two years Ignatius patiently and lovingly moulded his clever, delicate, moody Majorcan. His uncanny power of assessing men appears at its best in the training of Nadal. Jerome's wretched health, his vacillation, his suspiciousness, must have appeared as unpromising to common sense as the rusticity and illiterateness of Villanueva, but the Saint had a kind of X-ray eye for the core of spiritual genius that lay hidden under such external infirmities. Nadal's genius was for loyalty, for perfect devotion. Once surrendered to Ignatius, he became Ignatian through and through, a second self by whom the Saint, fast bound in Rome, could send his spirit on the widest travels. None of his first companions who had been with him so many years understood Ignatius as well as this eleventh-hour recruit. In January, 1548, Nadal received his first big commission which was to open at Messina in Sicily a mixed college for the education of young Jesuits and non-Jesuits. This venture had great significance, as it marked a definite change or development in the attitude of St. Ignatius to the question of studies in his Order. With the exception of

---

[1] All these details are from a little Latin autobiography left by Father Nadal, or from an Italian commentary on his life written by his intimate, Father Diego Ximenes (M.H.S.J., *Epistolæ Nadal*, vol. I, pp. 1–46). Father Jerome's Latin as printed is a thing fearful and wonderful to behold. He

Gandia which had been more or less forced on him as a *fait accompli*, he was unwilling to assume the charge of external pupils. In the fourth part of his Constitutions where he legislates about colleges and studies his thought is entirely of private Jesuit seminaries to which others besides members of the Order might not be admitted, except in rare cases to meet the wishes of founders. From this attitude of opposition to teaching as a Jesuit activity, the Saint was dislodged by the pressure of events. When first approached by the authorities in Messina he hesitated and made difficulties, but when the Viceroy of Spain in Sicily, the Spanish Ambassador in Rome, and the Pope himself, all united their voices in support of the appeal, he recognized the will of God for his Order. From his men in Rome he chose an international team of ten, four priests and six not yet ordained, by origin French, German, Spanish, Italian, Belgian, Dutch, Tirolese and Majorcan. These he allowed the unusual privilege of settling by ballot who should be their superior. Probably he felt sure of the result, as, in the event, all votes except his own were cast for Father Nadal.

The nine internationals quite obviously knew their Majorcan. It is related that on the journey to their ship at Naples Nadal "showed the deepest anxiety for the health and comfort of his brethren, striving patiently and indefatigably with paternal care to help and relieve the hardships of those who were unaccustomed to horseback, and

---

and Laynez held the record for undecipherable handwriting among the early Jesuits. The Count de Feria who was very partial to their Society remarked that the first undoubtedly bad thing he had seen in it was a specimen of Nadal's handwriting.

using infinite pains to get them good lodging at the public inns." At the end of each day's ride he took charge of all the horses and groomed and fed them himself.[1] The voyage from Naples, which can now be done easily in a day, dragged on for nearly a fortnight owing to continuous' storms and the necessity of keeping inshore to avoid pirates. During the whole time Nadal and his fellow-Majorcan, Father Benedict Palmio, were violently seasick. We lay there, reported Jerome to Ignatius afterwards, looking half dead—*medio muertos*.[2] A few weeks later, and this candidate for sea-burial who had not had a day without pain for nine years was astounding all the good people of Messina, and his own brethren too with their exacting standards of self-sacrifice, by his inexhaustible energy. Like Stromboli near by, he was always active, always on fire. In the new college he taught theology, Hebrew and mathematics, and controlled the lives of 238 students. On Sundays he lectured by the hour at the Cathedral, taking St. Paul's Epistles for his subject. With his brethren he laboured among the poor and the sick in slums and hospitals, and for Sicily, threatened by the Turks, organized a great island-wide campaign of prayer. Watching him, Father Palmio, himself no shirker, was lost in astonishment. "All of us," he wrote to Ignatius, "are fed and nourished on his spirit. How much he means to us we discover when he is away.

[1] Aquilera, *Provinciæ Siculæ S.J. ortus et res gestæ*, pars prima (Palermo, 1737), p. 12.

[2] M.H.S.J., *Litteræ quadrimestres*, vol. I, p. 95. The other two priests on board were the first Belgian Jesuit, Father Cornelius Wischaven, a man as full of oddities as of zeal and charm, and the first German Jesuit, Father Peter Canisius, now St. Peter Canisius, Doctor of the Church.

Who more diligent or fervent than he? When does he ever rest? What toil does he ever spare himself?"[1]

From Messina he extended his activities to Palermo, Trapani, and other places, established a second college and a convent of nuns, and organized the first separate house for novices in Jesuit history. He had the fortitude of an ancient Stoic combined with the candour and humility of a child. In 1551, when the Viceroy fitted out a fleet to defend Spain's precarious hold on the African coast, he immediately volunteered to be chaplain to the sailors and soldiers. Eight of the ships were lost in a storm and that on which Father Jerome sailed foundered off the island of Lampedusa, near Tunis, drowning his one Jesuit companion. Of this lost son he says that "he died valiantly like a brave man, and holily, like a martyr." Himself, he scrambled somehow on to a rock, and reports that at the time of writing he is well enough, "though somewhat battered by the sea."[2] Then in the Spanish encampment he devoted himself heart and soul to the fighting men who daily expected battle with the Turks. Some kind of hospital had been put up, and in it he spent his happiest hours, nursing the sick. Thinking wistfully of Africa's unbaptized millions, he sighs in a letter to St. Ignatius: "I wish I had time to learn Moorish, but there isn't any." No, there wasn't any, for he gave every moment of it to his fellow-men, and so his "grandissima compasión" for the brown or black natives could not find even such assuagement as his noble fellow-Majorcan, Ramón Lull, had derived from the study of Arabic. Four months, the vacation months of the College, he

[1] M.H.S.J., *Litteræ quadrimestres*, vol. I, p. 425.
[2] M.H.S.J., *Epistolæ Nadal*, vol. I, p. 110.

remained blistering under the African sun, upheld in his hard life by that "spirito claro della Compagnia" of which he spoke so tenderly to his brethren at Messina. "Keep it and cherish it always," he said, "in the centre of your souls, and grieve it never. The Lord gives me much consolation in the thought of you. I have you all more deeply engraved than I can express *in visceribus cordis mei in Christo et spiritu Societatis ejus.*"[1]

Nadal went to Africa, not in obedience to an express order nor still less out of any love of adventure for its own sake, but simply because he felt that it was what St. Ignatius would want him to do. His loyalty was so sensitive that it acted with a kind of child-like precipitation on a mere hint of his superior's desire. Polanco noticed in him "a wonderful solicitude to understand and carry out, even to the last detail, the wishes of Father Ignatius."[2] He deferred his solemn religious profession for four years so that he might have the joy of making his vows before Ignatius. He genuinely thought himself unfit to be professed, and, given the choice, would gladly have belonged to the spiritual coadjutors of his Order, that Order which honours him as its second founder. The roots of the famous *Ratio Studiorum* which, after half a century of experiment, gave Jesuit education its uniform charter, sprang out of his work at Messina. Steeped in the new learning of Paris, he experimented boldly, and worked out a plan of studies which respected the past but definitely faced towards the future. Hoary Donatus and ultra-modern Erasmus both taught in Jerome's school, and while he lectured in traditional form out of the scholastics on week-

---

[1] *Epistolæ Nadal*, vol. I, p. 114.
[2] *Chronicon*, vol. I, p. 286.

days, he expounded the Hebrew and Greek text of the
Scriptures on Sundays. His educational writings show
him as concerned for the little boys chanting *mensa,
mensae, mensam*, as for the grown men to whom he
taught the wisdom of Aristotle or Durandus. Those
writings had influence beyond Messina, for they were
adopted by the Roman College as the basis of its system of
study and so led on to the reform of the organizing genius,
Ledesma, which issued eventually in the *Ratio Studiorum*.[1]

After 1552, when St. Ignatius recalled him to Rome to
discuss the Jesuit Constitutions, Father Nadal became the
greatest rover that his Order has probably ever known.
Others covered far more of the earth's surface, but not
even St. Francis Xavier nor St. Peter Canisius was such a
perpetuum mobile as Father Jerome. One almost gets dizzy
in trying to keep pace with him as he tramps or rides or
sails from one end of Europe to the other, carrying to the
far-flung Society of Jesus the spirit and the comfort of
its Founder. That was his mission in life, to mould the
growing Society *secundum cor Ignatii*, just as he had
moulded the little Sicilian boys *secundum Cor Christi*.
It was the same task on a grander scale because those two
hearts were as one. He began with Portugal in 1553,
and then traversed the whole of Spain to give each of its
138 Jesuits the whole of his burning devotion. Sometimes
in a college he would deliver as many as twenty-one
exhortations on the Constitutions before moving to
another place. He had a perfect genius as a peace-maker,

---

[1] M.H.S.J., *Paedagogica*, pp. 89–107. At the Roman College, however,
St. Thomas Aquinas had pride of place, with two professors lecturing on
his *Summa*.

and wherever he passed discord died at the sight of him. In Valencia on his first arrival in Spain, he encountered a young swashbuckler named Pedro Martinez, and so strangely affected the dashing, magnificently-plumed fellow that he literally stormed his way into the Society of Jesus. Appearing at the college with his possessions in a bundle on his back, he demanded to be allowed to dig in the garden. Nadal and the other Fathers argued with him to no purpose. He would not budge. When they objected that the house was too poor to support him, he retorted that he had not come to eat but to work. "There is nowhere for you to sleep," they pursued. "I did not come here to sleep," answered the hero. Willy-nilly they kept him that night, and next day Nadal, having heard something of his story, decided to risk receiving him as a novice, however unorthodox his application. Pedro justified that trust by turning his *galanteria* heavenwards, and, thirteen years later, laying down his young life for the faith on the coast of Florida, the first Jesuit martyr of the North American continent.[1]

Twice again before he died Father Nadal was to go the weary round of Portugal and Spain, and what he did for his Order and for the Church in those countries, he repeated in Italy, in France, in Belgium, and in Germany. As the years passed, he loomed ever larger in the policy of the Popes as well as of the Jesuits. St. Ignatius and his successor both took him into partnership in the government of the Order, and Julius III and St. Pius V sent him on their business to historic Diets of the Empire. Germany, he knew well, was of all countries the one most in the thoughts of St. Ignatius. To help it in its desolation,

[1] Astrain, *Historia*, vol. I, pp. 392–3; vol. II, pp. 286–9.

the Saint had founded at Rome in 1552 the most cherished of his life's works, the German College, whose red-robed alumni still advertise when they walk abroad the immortality of his zeal and patience. United as he was heart and soul to Ignatius, Nadal constituted himself beggarman all over Europe for the Roman and German Colleges. Without the help which he procured Ignatius could never have kept those two great power-houses of the Counter-Reformation going, so he may well be considered their second founder, just as he was of the Society of Jesus. Twice in his life he had the entire charge of the Roman College committed to him, and it owes him more than to any man except Ignatius and Pope Gregory XIII. Germany at the time of his first visit in 1555 was a country to daunt the most courageous. Even that rock of a man, St. Peter Canisius, whom Favre had won for the Jesuits, used sometimes to despond as he watched the Protestant flood with its silt of moral corruption rise everywhere higher. Poland and Austria seemed doomed to be lost to the Church; Bavaria was hard pressed on every side; even the Rhineland wavered. Without, the Turks had ravaged Hungary and were hammering at the gates of Christendom. It seemed like the Day of Judgment. To Nadal, great soul, it seemed like the day for which he had been born. From Augsburg where the fatal Diet of "Cujus regio ejus religio" was in progress, he wrote to tell Ignatius of the "mighty compassion, zeal and longing" that devoured him when he contemplated the condition of Germany. Joyfully would he give his blood and his life to save her. It was no fault of his that they were not required of him, for he staked them cheerfully on land and sea a score of times in his wanderings. In Vienna by

the grave of the beloved Claude Le Jay,[1] he wrote again
to Ignatius: "Padre mio, since my coming to Germany
I have had a feeling of well-being and alertness springing
from hope of the great good which Our Lord could bring
about in these nations by means of the Society. The
thought of staying here to help gives me great consolation.
Certainly, I think that nowhere else is the Society more
needed, or more likely to do good. It is not only a
question of helping the heretics, with the divine favour:
if the Catholics are not helped, there is the greatest danger
that two years from now not one of them will be found
in Germany. . . . What stimulates me most is the fact
that everybody has practically despaired of it being possible
to help Germany. . . . The Catholic princes and bishops,
not knowing what to do, tolerate priests who are married
or living in open concubinage, and preachers who are
half Lutherans, because they can find no others. . . . Not
a Catholic in the country but reads the books of the
heretics. . . . Practically no other books are sold. . . .
We found all the inns full of the works of Luther and
other heretics, which even in so-called Catholic parts are
read by children and women. It fills me with the greatest
pity and compassion in the world, and inflames me with
the most intense desire to remain here and help by every
means in my power. . . . In truth, Father, I have felt

[1] He died on August 5th, 1552, aged fifty, worn out by hard work and
suffering. Once, in a German town the Lutherans threatened to throw him
into the river, whereupon he smiled at them and said: "It is as easy to go to
Heaven by water as by land." He was a most lovable, gentle soul, and left
behind him, as St. Peter Canisius testified, "in all places where he had been
the sweetest memory." Another Father, the one in whose arms he died,
confessed to Polanco that he could not help "weeping for him day and
night" (*Epistolæ Broëti*, 402).

strongly impelled to remain. Were I not by the grace
of God free in obedience, I would never write to you in
this fashion. But by God's grace nothing weighs with
me so much as resignation of the will and understanding
to obedience. However your Paternity may freely dispose
of me, I shall find consolation in everything. At this
moment I feel happy, as always, in the thought of any
imaginable command you might lay upon me."[1] Such
a one was the meek and mighty Jerome Nadal who, if all
could be told, would be seen to have done more perhaps
than any of the standard heroes to keep the faith by which
it lives burning bright in Europe. He loved to be hidden,
and it must please him now above the stars that he is not
known, even to the *Catholic Encyclopedia*.

In 1546, while Jerome was still a novice full of headache
and indecision, Pierre Favre returned wearily to Rome,
Laynez and Salmeron went to the Council of Trent, and
Bobadilla, but for his big hat, had lain dead by a bridge
in Landshut.[2] Favre was only forty then, and at the
end of his journeyings. Six years of intolerable hardship
in Germany, France and Spain had broken everything in
him except his spirit, which retained its strength and sweetness to the last. Only five months before he died he wrote
as follows from Madrid to impetuous Laynez who had
asked him for some counsel on the subject of converting
heretics: "Dearest Brother in Jesus Christ. May the grace
and peace of our Redeemer be always in our souls. My

---

[1] *Epistolæ Nadal*, vol. I, pp. 301-2.
[2] *Bobadillæ Monumenta*, pp. 103-104. A Protestant soldier struck him a
fierce blow on the head with a halberd. He followed the Catholic forces
on a mule which he describes as "fortis et furiosa." The beast frequently
threw him off.

excuse for not replying sooner to your letter is that I had not time to attend to it. There was no peace for me in the house. I could plead too that my hand is not so strong and steady as is necessary. But the best excuse of all is to say that I do not know whether what I have to offer you will meet your questions. However, I shall tell you some things which have now occurred to me. The first is, that whoever desires to become useful to the heretics of this age must be solicitous to bear them much charity and to love them truly, excluding from his mind all thoughts which tend to cool his esteem for them. Secondly, it is necessary to gain their good-will, so that they may love us and keep a place for us in their hearts. This we can achieve by familiar intercourse with them, speaking of the things which we have in common and avoiding all contentious argument. . . . When we meet a man, not only perverse in his opinions but evil in his life, we must go round about to persuade him to abandon his vices before speaking to him of his errors in belief. It has happened to myself, for instance, that a man came wanting me to satisfy him about some erroneous views which he held, especially concerning the celibacy of the clergy. I dealt with him in such a way that he unburdened his conscience to me, on which lay the mortal sin of many years' concubinage. I persuaded him to abandon that life, . . . and no sooner had he done so and found himself by God's grace able to live without a woman, than he also renounced his errors, without saying another word about them.[1] . . .

---

[1] Speaking of the parish priest with whom Favre had lodged in Mainz, St. Peter Canisius said: "He turned him from a *concubinarius* into a Carthusian so that I believe he ended his days in the Cologne Charterhouse" (*Fabri Monumenta*, 485).

Such people have need of admonitions and exhortations
on morals, on the fear and love of God, on good
works, to counter their frailties, distractions, tepidities
and other afflictions, which are not principally or in
the first place from the understanding, but from the
hands and feet of the body and soul. ..."[1] The proofs of
the way in which Favre was loved and revered are legion.
Here is one Carthusian Prior writing about him to another
Carthusian Prior in 1543: "With the Cardinal of Mainz
is a man of great sanctity called Master Peter Favre, a
theologian of Paris. To men of good will who come to
him he gives certain spiritual exercises whereby in a few
days they obtain true self-knowledge, the grace of tears,
genuine, hearty conversion from created things to their
Creator, progress in virtue and a secret intimacy with
God in love and friendship. How I wish that I had a
chance of going to Mainz! Indeed, such treasure a man
might well go hunting for even in the Indies. I hope that
God will give me to see this man of God, His singular
friend, before I die, and that I may be directed by him
to interior reformation and union with His Divine
Majesty."[2] The dear Prior, himself as like a saint as makes
no difference, had his wish and went through the Exercises
under Favre's guidance. In 1544, that devoted, selfless man
had to leave his German friends to answer an urgent appeal
from Portugal. On his way to the port of Veere in
Walcheren from which he sailed, he was accompanied by
a new recruit, the saintly priest Cornelius Wischaven,
Father in God of all Belgian Jesuits. Cornelius lost his big
heart altogether to Favre. He begged for a keepsake and

[1] *Fabri Monumenta*, pp. 399–402.
[2] *Fabri Monumenta*, p. 448.

Pierre gave him two little knives he had. As the ship moved away, Cornelius stood bareheaded following it with his eyes as long as it could be seen, while Pierre, standing on the poop, raised his hand again and again in blessing. When Favre died, the other man put a new invocation into his prayers: "Sancte Pater Petre, ora Deum pro me Cornelio peccatore."[1] In this he did but anticipate the Church's judgment, for Pierre was long ago beatified.

[1] *Fabri Monumenta*, p. 467.

CHAPTER VII

ENTREATING AND COMFORTING, AS A
FATHER DOTH HIS CHILDREN

FAVRE had been called home from Spain to go with his brethren Laynez and Salmeron to the recently opened Council of Trent, at which Le Jay, in solitary grandeur, was acting as procurator, or deputy with vote, of Otto von Truchsess, Cardinal Archbishop of Augsburg. The three in Rome had been chosen by Ignatius at the Pope's command to be the special theologians of the Holy See. As Favre was bound for Heaven, the others had to go without him and arrived in Trent on May 16th, 1546. There Laynez received Pierre's last letter, written a week before he died, reminding him not to fail in the press of his new duties to write and console his mother in Spain on the recent death of his father, Juan Laynez. It was a tender, last worry, but its addressee did not need it, as he had a nature deeply if undemonstratively affectionate. On August 10th, 1546, he sent his mother a letter that fills seven solid pages of print and breathes the very spirit of Christian love and consolation. Gently and sweetly he deprecates her too great eagerness to see him: "Since I have promised God Our Lord obedience, and desire by His grace to keep my promise during the few days that remain to me,[1] I am unable to do more than

---

[1] He was thirty-four!

write to Rome what you wish, and what my father wished, God rest him. So I shall leave it to my superior to decide, and judge best whatever he may ordain. If I am offered the choice of going, I shall gladly avail myself of it. If I am prevented, I shall never cease as long as I live to be with you by my prayers and letters. Besides, I matter so little that I am sure anyone who really knew me would not care very much to see me in the flesh, and so for the love of Our Lord I beseech you, too, to hold that best which God shall arrange, and to discount whatever comfort I might be able to give you by going against my profession and vow of obedience. . . ."[1]

Why the Pope who had all the Christian world to choose from should have turned to the Benjamin of religious orders for his Tridentine theologians is a matter that need not here be discussed, beyond absolving St. Ignatius from any ambition to see his sons in the Council. Ignatius kept a very free heart in such questions, his only ambition being to place his sons where they could serve God most fruitfully. Laynez had not been six months at Trent when the Saint ordered him to Florence, a move frustrated only by the direct intervention of Cardinal Cervini, one of the three Presidents of the Council. "You may perhaps be wondering," wrote that eminent man, afterwards Pope Marcellus II, to Ignatius, "why I have kept Master Laynez here longer than you or he would have wished. I did so for a good purpose and in the public interest, as I have entrusted him with the lengthy task of drawing up a list of all the dogmatic errors of the heretics which are to be condemned by the Coun-

[1] M.H.S.J., *Lainii Monumenta*, vol. I, p. 44.

cil."[1] Luckily for the two Spanish Jesuits who did not know a word of that crabbed and forbidding German in which the Protestants usually enshrined their opinions, their young brother from the North, Peter Canisius, came to the Council in January, 1547, to assist Father Le Jay. Peter was only twenty-five, but he had already published new editions, learned enough for their time, of the great Church Fathers, St. Leo and St. Cyril of Alexandria, thus gaining for himself whatever glory may be attached to the position of pioneer author of the Society of Jesus. He was attracted to those Fathers in particular by the governing conviction of his entire career that the Church must be mainly what her Popes and bishops make her. Never in the Church's history was there a more ardent 'bishops'-man' than he.

For his men at Trent St. Ignatius drafted the following suggestions: "I should be slow to speak, and would do so in a thoughtful, friendly fashion. . . . I would help myself by listening quietly, so as to appreciate and understand the point of view and disposition of the speakers, that I might the better reply, or keep silent. When speaking about matters in debate or other questions, the reasons on both sides ought to be given that you may not appear prejudiced, and you should be careful to displease nobody. . . . If the matters discussed are so plainly right that one ought not to keep silent, you should give your opinion with the greatest possible composure and modesty, concluding with deference to better judgment. . . . The greater glory of God is the purpose of our Fathers at Trent, and this will be procured by preaching, hearing

[1] *Lainii Monumenta*, vol. I, p. 53, n. 1.

confessions, lecturing, teaching children, visiting the poor in hospitals, and exhorting the neighbour, according to each one's talent for moving people to devotion and prayer, so that we may all pray and beg God to pour forth His Divine Spirit on all those who are engaged with the business of the Council. . . . In preaching I would not touch at all on the differences between Protestants and Catholics, but simply exhort to good habits and devotion, stirring people up to know themselves truly and to acquire a greater knowledge and love of their Creator and Lord. I would constantly harp on the Council in my sermons and end each of them with prayers for it. So, too, when lecturing, my desire would be to inflame souls with the love of their Creator and Lord, and I would conclude with prayers for the Council. In hearing confessions I would speak in such a way that what I said might be repeated in public, and for penance I would give some prayers for the Council. . . . The hospitals ought to be visited at the hours best suited to health, and you should shrive and comfort the poor people, and also bring them something whenever you can, not forgetting to obtain their prayers for the Council. . . ."[1]

The four Jesuits at Trent had plenty of scope for the charitable activities suggested by their Father, for the Council had attracted to Trent an extraordinary collection of Europe's most enterprising vagrants. These tough knights of the road slept in the open until some compassionate cardinals found them a shelter. The Jesuits took charge of them, and by dint of begging were in a short time able to report to Ignatius that they had "provided

---

[1] *Epistolæ et instructiones*, vol. I, pp. 386–9. Ignatius repeats his instruction about obtaining prayers for the Council nine times.

clothes for seventy-six poor people, giving each a shirt, a smock, leggings and boots."[1] Most of the work done by the four men at the Council was of a humdrum, inglorious kind, except now and then when circumstances thrust Laynez or Salmeron involuntarily into the lime-light. As Papal theologians they had been exempted from the ruling of the Legates that precluded members of the Council from preaching in public, so Laynez was to be heard every Sunday and feast-day in the Church of Santa Maria Maggiore, the meeting-place of the Fathers. Once Salmeron preached before them with such fire and felicity that they required him to have the sermon printed and published,[2] but Laynez beat that achievement by securing a place for one of his discourses in the official records of the Council. He delivered it after no less than sixty-one general congregations and forty-four partial ones had been devoted to the most difficult and vital of all the questions of the day, the doctrine of Justification.[3] Tempers sometimes ran very high in the discussions, and on one dreadful occasion the debate turned into a fight in which the Bishop of La Cava played havoc with the Bishop of Crete's beard.[4] On October 8th, 1546, Girolamo Seripando, one of the most learned and devout of the

[1] *Lainii Monumenta*, vol. I, p. 49.

[2] Polanco, *Chronicon*, vol. I, p. 181.

[3] It has become a vital question of our day, too, as the Barthian "theology of crisis" is no more than a twentieth-century edition of Luther's doctrine of Justification by faith alone.

[4] Merkle, *Concilii Tridentini diariorum II et III*, pp, 444, 561. This splendid volume is one of the great collection of Tridentine documents which the Görres-Gesellschaft began to publish in 1901. Several volumes have appeared but the series is not yet completed. It may satisfy the reader's sense of the proprieties to know that the Bishop of La Cava was lodged in prison for his hair-pulling exploit.

Fathers, who afterwards became a President of the Council, put forward a theory of Justification which had certain points of resemblance to the Lutheran view. It was an effort towards reconciliation and was expounded with equal skill and modesty. Then Laynez rose in his place and delivered a tremendous three-hour speech in refutation of Seripando which not only destroyed his theory but so greatly impressed the Fathers that they desired to have the discourse in the form of a written treatise. Thus elaborated it was included in the Acts of the Council, the one and only document from any Father's or theologian's pen to achieve such permanent fame.[1]

When Laynez spoke on that occasion and turned the scales against a seductive doctrine which made a dangerous appeal to learned Catholics, he was thirty-four years of age, "a little white-faced man, somewhat emaciated, cheerful-looking and having a modest, pleasant laugh in his mouth, with a large aquiline nose and big, lively, very bright eyes."[2] Those big, bright eyes must often have

[1] The discourse has been edited separately by the great Reformation scholar, Hartmann Grisar, in his *Jacobi Lainez Disputationes Tridentinæ*, Innsbruck, 1886, vol. II, pp. 153–92. Among other interesting writings of Laynez which Grisar includes in these volumes is a splendid little treatise on the art of preaching which lays down that the first requirement of the Christian orator must be "mucho amor á nuestro Señor Dios." Laynez wrote an enormous amount on every sort of topic, theology, metaphysics, prayer, pedagogy, economics, but unfortunately his interminable travels and ministerial occupations prevented him from revising and polishing his manuscripts, which needed such attention all the more because his handwriting was so atrocious. The sad result has been that only a fraction of his work, including 2,230 letters in the eight volumes of his *Monumenta*, is available in print. But even that fraction, that foot of print, shows him to have been a theological Hercules, one of the giants of his generation.

[2] *Las Obras del P. Pedro de Ribadeneyra*, 1595, p. 287. Ribadeneira was closely associated with Laynez for twenty-five years.

gleamed at Trent, as their owner shared with Salmeron the sentinel's duty of watching for erroneous or venturesome opinions in the theologians' discussions and challenging them at the end of the debate.[1]

Early in 1547 an outbreak of the plague at Trent and of temper at the Court of Charles V compelled the Fathers to remove the seat of the Council to Bologna. On his way thither Salmeron collapsed from overwork and undernourishment. Le Jay, who had tried in vain to persuade him and Laynez to take a few days' rest from their studies and discussions, found him at death's door in Padua, but "resigned with full joy and contentment to the most holy will of God." Alfonso, then thirty-one, was, however, a man to take some killing. Soon he stood on his feet again and attributed his recovery to the prayers of St. Ignatius, knowing, as he told him, "the affection and paternal love with which your Reverence has us written on your heart." That was very true of all Ignatius's sons. His Boswell, Father Luis Gonzales, relates that he used to question him again and again about the brethren, particularly those who were farthest away, and want to know what they ate, how they slept, how they were clothed. Once he exclaimed to Father Luis: "*Cierto*, I'd love to know if I could how many fleas bite them each night!"[2] The Jesuit quartette did not remain long at Bologna, as, owing to the opposition and intrigue of Charles V, who at the same time heard two Masses every morning, the Legates were obliged to prorogue the Council indefinitely. Nearly four years went by before it met again under a

[1] *Salmeronis Epistolæ*, vol. I, pp. 26–7.

[2] M.H.S.J., *Scripta de Sancto Ignatio*, vol. I, p. 196: "Cierto, yo me holgara de saber, si posible fuera, quantas pulgas le muerden cada noche."

new President and a new Pope. In the interval Le Jay had to fight a long action with his good weapon of absolute self-abasement to escape the bishopric of Trieste which Ferdinand, King of the Romans, greatly desired him to assume. Canisius went school-mastering to Sicily, and Salmeron made the provinces of Venezia and Emilia the theatre of a great preaching campaign. All three met at Bologna in October 1549 to take the degree of doctor of theology there, and then journeyed north to teach that subject in the Bavarian university of Ingolstadt. Laynez occupied his time preaching, lecturing, catechizing, "slumming," and acting as army chaplain in Florence, Perugia, Siena, Padua, Venice, Bologna, Naples, Palermo, Monreale, Rome, Trapani, and a "campo sobre Africa." The African expedition which he accompanied as chaplain was directed against the formidable corsair Dragut, terror of the Mediterranean. Conditions on board ship in those days usually resulted in more casualties than ten Draguts could have caused, so, in the camp near Tunis where he found himself, Father Diego had from fifty to two hundred and forty sick soldiers and sailors on his hands, all of whom he daily doctored and fed with indomitable devotion. It is touching to find him mentioning to St. Ignatius in apology for the shortness of his letters that he could hardly find a moment to snatch a bite of food or take a little sleep.[1] Before they went into battle the soldiers deposited with him their pay and other little worldly possessions, a mark of confidence that affected him deeply. As he was high in the favour of the Viceroy of Sicily who directed the expedition, ducats would have rained about him for the mere wishing, but he accepted

[1] *Lainii Monumenta*, vol. I, pp. 166, 168.

nothing beyond his daily rations, and went about, even at Trent, in a gown that shocked grandee bishops and captains by its many patches.[1]

On February 7th, 1551, after an exciting and disedifying conclave of ten weeks, Cardinal Giovan del Monte was "acclaimed" Pope in succession to Paul III. He took the title of Julius III. While, to the sorrow of earnest-minded Catholics, he brought with him to St. Peter's throne many of the bad habits of the Renaissance Popes, Julius yet cherished a sincere desire to remedy the evils that afflicted the Church. His first move in this direction was to begin preparations for the re-opening of the General Council, to which, in its first phase, four years earlier, he had been a wise and capable pilot. This time the Emperor gave no trouble, but the King of France, just to be different, openly threatened schism and set about mobilizing troops for a descent on Northern Italy. What prompted his hostility to the Council was a fear that it might win over the German Protestants, and so secure peace for the Empire to the peril of the House of Valois. Despite his hectoring, the Council resumed its sessions on May 1st, 1551, but not a single French bishop dared show himself at Trent. On July 21st the Pope addressed a warm protest to the King of France, challenging him to a meeting before the judgment-seat of God. "Yes," replied Henry insolently, "I am quite ready to appear before God's judgment-seat. I know well that I shall not find your Holiness there."

That was the state of affairs when on July 27th Laynez and Salmeron, accompanied by a lay-brother, once more entered the Council in their former capacity of Papal

[1] *Salmeronis Epistolæ*, vol. I, p. 19; Ribadeneira, *Obras*, p. 230.

theologians. According to Polanco, as soon as the handful of Fathers then in Trent heard of the Jesuits' arrival, some of them exclaimed: "Now that those two have come, we believe that there really is going to be a Council."[1] Despite their reputation, the pair were not very honourably accommodated by the authorities. Cardinal Crescenzi, the President, received them with every mark of affection, but Angelo Massarelli, to whose care they were committed, proved himself a better secretary to the Council than guest-master to the Jesuits. The good Angelo's ideas of hospitality amused Laynez, as appears in the following lines to St. Ignatius: "He took us to his own house . . . and gave all three of us for apartment a very small, smoky oven of a room, furnished with one ordinary bed and one truckle-bed which, when pulled out, made it impossible to walk two free paces in the room. There was no table to study or write a letter at, and just one solitary foot-stool. But there were any number of boots about, belonging to the Secretary and his valet, and also a big portmanteau, an ancient harp, and a sword of the valet's. . . . I said to Master Salmeron, 'Look here, this promises to be more than we bargained for. Let us go lodge at the inn.' . . . But Salmeron thought it better to remain in the *oven*, stifling though it was, in order not to appear dissatisfied or disgusted with our accommodation. So he slept that night upon a chest, and John and I in the two beds. The following night, he betook himself to the contiguous house of the Bishop of Verona to sleep. I was offered the same comfort, but that we might not all seem to be abandoning the apartment, John and myself went on sleeping in that *oven*. On one occasion the Legate's

[1] *Chronicon*, vol. II, p. 249.

secretary came and asked if we lacked anything, and I answered with my usual freedom or folly, 'You can see for yourself; we lack everything'. And he said, 'True enough, but at the moment what do you require?' I answered, 'At least we need a candle to go to bed by.' Then, quoth he, 'What else?' And I, laughing heartily, said, 'A candle-stick to put it in.'" They spent nearly a fortnight in the *oven*, unable to study or receive the many visitors who wanted to speak with them, until Laynez was at last roused into protesting to the Cardinal and seeking other quarters on his own account. "The Cardinal excused Master Angelo, saying that as we preached patience to others, it would be a good thing to practise it ourselves. I told him truthfully that I had not protested in order to escape suffering, because the previous year I had spent three months in Africa, lying in the open under a sheet, tormented by the heat during the day and by the cold at night, and that in the *oven* I could laugh and be content. I had spoken out because it was not fitting that we should be without the means to prepare our sermons, lectures or anything else. . . . And I told him with all sincerity that if I had done wrong in any way, he should give me a penance, which I would perform very gladly on condition that he bore no grudge against the Society or ourselves. . . . And so, being frank with one another, we have remained good friends. . . . We have wanted to write this to your Reverence, not to lodge a complaint against any one, for we certainly have none, . . . but because I am so made that I could not be at peace if I had not advised you of my fault, with a view to your correcting it."[1]

Among those who knew Laynez best was Pedro

[1] *Lainii Monumenta*, vol. I, pp. 192–3.

Ribadeneira. Pedro used to ply the Father with questions about his reading and methods of study. One thing he learned was that at Trent Laynez never cited in his speeches any ancient doctor or theologian whose works he had not read from beginning to end. And, says Pedro, "he cited thirty-five or thirty-six doctors who are the masters and luminaries of the world, . . . including one, the author of so many books that a life-time seems too short for anybody to get through them."[1] While preaching daily and visiting the sick during Lent in Bassano, continues the same authority, Laynez went right through all the tomes containing the acts and decrees of the Church's councils. He used to make copious extracts from the books he read, the purpose of which was not always plain to Salmeron when he borrowed the notes. What had you in mind when you made this, that, the other entry? asked Alfonso. Diego replied: "With this sentence or these words one confutes such and such a heresy, or confirms what was determined by such and such a Council, or answers such and such a difficulty."[2] Ribadeneira tells a pleasant story to illustrate the contemporary fame of Laynez as a great scholar and theologian. In those days the Jesuits had the good fortune to attract to their Order one of the most accomplished scholars and charming characters, "semper subridens, semper subtristis," it has ever known, the Spaniard, Diego Ledesma, who when he came to them

---

[1] Father Astrain will have none of this story, and suggests that Ribadeneira imagined it. But it cannot be denied, for we have the treatises in Grisar's two volumes to prove it, that Laynez had a vast acquaintance with patristic literature, and, being a tremendous student all his life, may well have read all such works of the Fathers whom he cites as were then published.

[2] Ribadeneira, *Obras*, pp. 232, 287.

was a doctor three times over, of Alcalá, of Paris, and of Louvain.[1] Once, when they were on a journey together from Flanders to Rome, Ledesma and Ribadeneira fell to talking about their secret longings. "He told me," relates Pedro, "that he had cherished a desire to have lived in the time of St. Augustine or some other of the great saints and famous doctors who were wells of learning, in order to speak with them and profit by the light of their teaching. Afterwards, when he had become intimate in Rome with Father Laynez, he informed me that God had now granted that desire of his, and that he no longer hankered for the times of St. Augustine."[2] However, learning is all very well, but there are better things. St. Francis Borgia used to say that he envied St. Ignatius for his prudence, and Father Laynez for "the gentleness and sweetness of his heart."[3] It was the kindest heart, "quick to forgive injuries and to sympathize with the sorrowing, always wide open to receive the necessitous and the disconsolate." That again is Ribadeneira speaking, who bears out his words with the following story: "Once, at a little place eight miles from Florence he saw an unfortunate Spanish soldier, a captive of the war with Siena, led out to be hanged. Recognizing the poor fellow as a man who had formerly been to confession to him, he stopped the pro-

[1] M.H.S.J., *Monumenta Paedagogica*, pp. 859–63; Ribadeneira, *Obras*, pp. 235–8. By his great work in the organization of studies at the Roman College Ledesma laid the foundations of the *Ratio Studiorum*, which he did not live to see appear. With all his immense learning, he had the piety of a little child and people from all parts, including his fellow-Jesuits, used to tumble over one another to get to confession to him. He died "ex nimio labore" in 1575.

[2] *Obras*, p. 238.

[3] Astrain, *Historia*, vol. II, p. 211.

cession, and with his persuasive way prevailed upon those in charge to hold up the execution until he had sent a messenger with a letter to the Duke of Florence about the case. This he did, and waited in the village for the reply. So by his authority and intercession he saved that poor man from death, and bestowed on him the few copper coins which remained of his journey-money after he had paid the messenger. . . . He used to show the same compassion and tenderness to everybody he met."[1]

At Trent, during the second assembly of the Council, Laynez who was quick-tempered, impulsive and utterly devoted to his Society of Jesus, had a famous brush with the great destroyer of Jesuits, Melchior Cano. In the innocence of their hearts he and Salmeron thought it would be a nice idea to pay Melchior a friendly call and explain what Jesuits were really for. They received a very chilly welcome, which nettled our Diego. "Father," said he, after two hours of fruitless argument, "why do you take upon yourself the office of the Bishops and of the Supreme Pastor, the Vicar of Christ, to condemn and reprobate those whom they have approved and now approve?" It was a fair question, but Melchior evaded it with the smiling exclamation: "O Lord, would your Honour not have the dogs bark when the shepherds sleep!" To that Laynez answered, "O, yes, let them bark, but at the wolves and not at other dogs." So far the story is from Ribadeneira who evidently blushed to go on with it. Not so Jerome Nadal from whose notebooks we learn that both men lost their tempers, and that, on a further insult from Cano, Laynez hurled at him an epithet

[1] *Obras*, p. 291.

not heard in polite society nor to be found in dictionaries, and fled the room. "But before he reached the street," continues Father Nadal, "he repented of that liberty, and returning, threw himself upon his knees before Cano and begged his pardon. Cano, however, reckoned the offence atrocious and used to refer to and complain about it hyperbolically, by aposiopesis."[1] Poor Melchior, it was hard on him not to be able to tell his audiences the exact word used by Laynez!

After the second enforced prorogation of the Council of Trent in April 1552, St. Ignatius nominated Laynez superior of the Jesuits in Italy, most of whose houses he had had some hand in establishing. One day Ignatius told Ribadeneira that "to nobody in its ranks was the whole Society more indebted than to Master Laynez, not even excepting Francis Xavier."[2] Yet nobody did Ignatius treat with greater rigour than he did Laynez, coming down on him heavily for the most trifling inadvertencies, due to nothing more wicked than his natural impulsiveness. While exercising his office of provincial at Venice in the late summer of 1552, Laynez, out of sheer kindness, suggested to the prior of the Holy Trinity in the city that he should ask Ignatius for another Father in place of the poetical André des Freux who had been withdrawn from his service. He also admitted to Salmeron and another Jesuit that he was not happy about the with-

---

[1] Ribadeneira apud Astrain, *Historia*, vol. II, p. 562; M.H.S.J., *Epistolæ Nadal*, vol. II, p. 45. This was not the only time that Laynez used unparliamentary language. He had a very explosive temper which tended to go off when his two great loyalties were affronted, to the Catholic Church and to the Society of Jesus.

[2] Ribadeneira, *Obras*, p. 292.

drawal of Father des Freux. Then to crown his offences, he sent a candidate for the Order to Rome, without letting Ignatius know first what sort of a candidate he might be. Poor Polanco, who with Nadal shared the unhappy lot of Laynez as a target for the Ignatian lightning, was ordered to tell Laynez exactly what Ignatius thought about him. It is typical of the Saint that he delayed the letter until November 2nd to give the erring Provincial time to recover from one of his constant bouts of the quartan ague—*mi quartana*, as he called it almost affectionately. Polanco, who loved and revered Laynez, began his letter thus: "Padre mio, This letter comes, not from your Reverence's son which in my quality of Polanco I am, but from the organ or the pen of our Father who has ordered me to write what it contains. . . . Our Father is not a little vexed with your Reverence, and so much the more in proportion as the faults of those who are greatly loved weigh more heavily on those who love them. He bids me tell you some of your defects that your Reverence may know yourself . . . and amend, which will be easy with such good will as God Our Lord has given you." The much embarrassed Polanco then describes with a good deal of dictated asperity the aforesaid peccadilloes of Laynez, and continues: "Our Father bids me tell you to attend to your office which, if you fulfil as you ought, will be no small achievement, and not to tire yourself by giving your views about matters that belong to *his* office. He does not want your Reverence's advice except when he asks for it, and less now than before you took up your present charge, because in the administration of it you have not gained much credit with him." Polanco concludes by instructing Laynez

that he is to write to St. Ignatius and tell him what penance
he thinks he deserves.[1]

Such was the letter of Ignatius to the most loyal and
deeply loved of his sons except Francis Xavier. Laynez
answered from Florence on November 15th, 1552, as
follows: "May the grace and peace of Christ Our Lord
be with us all. Amen. I have received the letter which
your Reverence addressed to me personally and have read
it again and again. By the grace of Our Lord I have seen
in it, to my confusion and misery, nothing but reason
for great praise of His mercy and for an increase of the
love and respect which by many titles I owe to your
Reverence. I beg of you that as often as it may be necessary—and would that it might not be!—you will correct
me, without the slightest regard to my being ill of the
quartan ague or any other circumstance. . . . I accept
lovingly all that you say to me lovingly, and feel as if my
hungry soul was waxing fat on a dainty feast. . . . As to
my choice of penance, Father, for some days now I have
been filled with a special longing to die to myself and all
my peculiarities and to live only for God Our Lord. . . .
It is now, I reflected, about twenty years since I first proposed to serve the Lord according to the evangelical
counsels, and, though I have had such great help to this
end, I have borne so little fruit, while the close of this
brief life approaches, that, I told myself, if I were to be
treated openly as I deserve, namely, as dung and nothing-
ness, it would help me to live interiorly with my God, . . .
dead to the whole world and the world dead to me.
Accordingly, when your Reverence's letter reached me I
commended myself to God and made my choice with

[1] M.H.S.J., *Epistolæ et instructiones*, vol. IV, pp. 498–500.

many tears—a rare thing to happen to me. Now, shedding a few more, I choose for those faults and for the root from which they spring . . . that your Reverence should, for the love of Our Lord, deprive me of the charge of others which I hold, stop my preaching and studying, and, leaving me only my Breviary, order me to beg my way to Rome and there exercise me in the kitchen, or in waiting at table, or in the garden, or in everything: if, however, I am found no good for such tasks, then in the lowest class of grammar in the school. All this to be until death, without any more external care of me than if, as I say, I were the remains of an old broom. That is the penance which I choose by preference. Alternatively, I elect for the same, limiting the time to one, two, or three years, or more, as your Reverence may decree. My third choice is to go without supper this Advent, and every Friday to take the discipline in my room, to be deprived of my office, and hereafter, when I write to your Reverence, first to commit myself to God, to weigh what I am going to put down, and to read the letter over when finished, being watchful to see that I have made no mistake nor written in a way to give your Reverence pain either in matter or in manner, but rather so as to ease your burdens and console you. I know well the magnitude of my obligation to do this, were it only because your Reverence so acts by me. Besides, I know an infinite number of other reasons. And I intend to take this same care not to offend you in word or deed, whether absent or present, nor in my heart, though, thanks be to God, I have had little difficulty *there* all my life. . . . Since, as your Reverence writes, some persons may have been disedified by my conduct, I think that you might show them this letter, in

which I testify with all truth that I recognize my errors
and repent of them and resolve to amend. I beg them for
the love of Our Lord to forgive me and to help me with
their prayers. One of these three is the penance that I
ask for and desire, in the order mentioned, but, finally,
what will please me more than these or other penances
will be whatever your Reverence may deign to impose
upon me. For, as I have said, I do not want to follow my
will but God's and that of your Reverence who holds
His place. All I beg is that in your soul before God you
will not reject or vomit out my soul, but rather hug and
help it, as you began and have continued to do for so
many years now. As for the exterior, I do not mind if
you have no care of me, provided you make me go
straight ahead, carrying Our Lord's cross in all lowliness
and simplicity, and desiring only His glory. May He
preserve your Reverence to us and increase in you His
gifts and mercies, as we all desire and need."[1]

In contrast with the severity of Ignatius towards Laynez
was his treatment of two other old companions, Bobadilla
and Rodriguez. Bobadilla went to Germany in 1542 as
theologian to the apostolic nuncio at the Diet of Speyer.
His peregrinations during the subsequent six years are
indicated by the places from which he wrote letters,
Innsbruck, Vienna, Nuremberg, Passau, Speyer, Prague,
Worms, Brussels, Cologne, Liége, Ratisbon, Landshut,
Ingoldstadt, Breslau, Eichstätt and Augsburg. Some of
those places received several visits from him. He certainly did not spare himself, and gallantly sustained the
harassed Catholics by sermons, lectures, disputations,
writings, and charitable avocations. Ferdinand, King of

---

[1] *Lainii Monumenta*, vol. I, pp. 216–19.

the Romans, brother of Charles V, esteemed him immensely, a fact which gave him considerable satisfaction. Indeed, the trouble with Bobadilla was that he tended to be too self-satisfied, to rub in his record, lest his brethren might overlook it. His name suits him well, for he was always bobbing up in this fashion. From Vienna on June 24th, 1542, he wrote as follows to Codacio and Laynez: "I have been to converse with His Majesty two or three times and we have arranged together for longer talks. To his great satisfaction and joy, and that of his entire Court, I have taken a room in a hospital, . . . not that the Señor Nuncio would not have given me the best room in his house, indeed the whole of his house, but because the hospital is near a church and the Palace, and I shall thus be able to converse with everybody and work more conveniently. . . . I do not know whether you are dead or alive. To this very day neither I nor the other brethren in Germany have received a letter from you. . . . I do not understand it, . . . not that I cannot serve those whom I serve without letters from anybody . . . I ask you again, as I have already done more than thirty times, to write. . . . Their Serene Majesties, the King and Queen, show me great favour in public and private, by the grace of Christ." Four days later he sends a chit to keep his memory green with all the brethren in Rome: "Though I could have many houses and palaces at my disposal, I am lodging in a hospital, and the Court has the same good opinion of me as is held of you, namely that I neither desire nor accept anything, though I am many ways pressed to do so." In September he dashed off a few more lines to the Roman brethren: "As far as I can see, I am having better fruit in these parts than any of our men in

Germany. All and sundry, King, Court, and Nuncio, are pleased with me, though I tell them plainly that I am not so with them. . . . The King summons me every day for converse about spiritual things and the affairs of religion. I am on intimate terms with the Venetian Ambassador, with Señor Don Sancho de Alarcón, and with many other noblemen." From Passau on January 6th, 1544, the same fifty or sixty Roman Jesuits are addressed: "I am engaged on various negotiations in this diocese. By the grace of God there is not much business transacted by the King which he does not make me privy to. . . . He carries out every good work which I recommend, and the esteem and authority which I have with him would appear to be the doing of God." So it goes on and on, not exactly bragging, but a naive determination that Nicholas Bobadilla shall have his due meed of credit from his beloved brethren. He tells St. Ignatius how much he is loved by the King and the bishops, and lets Cardinal Cervini know that he is wanted everywhere, by the princes, by the Emperor, by the King, by the Bishop of Passau, etc. When he hears confessions, everybody turns up, and he proves to Pope Paul III by the examples of Moses, Our Lord, the Apostle of the Gentiles, and the Patriarch Jacob, that he ought to be granted sixteen different kinds of faculties.[1] There is something comic about all this, but it is also true that there was something genuinely great in Father Nicholas. He had the energy of a whirlwind and the courage of an Andalusian bull. All that he related of himself was perfectly true. He won esteem and affection wherever he went, and the most likely explanation of that fact is that, despite his eccentricities, or maybe partly on

[1] M.H.S.J., *Bobadillæ Monumenta*, pp. 36, 38, 39, 43, 45-6, 48, 63.

account of them, he was an estimable and lovable man. The first historian of the German Jesuits summed him up in one good sentence—*ubique sibi semper, id est, indefatigabili in vinea Domini operario, similis*. He was the first Jesuit army chaplain, anticipating Nadal and Laynez in that post by four years. While accompanying the hosts of Charles V in the War of Schmalkald, he caught the plague and recovered, was made a prisoner and escaped, and received the full force of a Protestant halberd on his head and lived to tell the tale, thanks to the thickness of his hat.[1] His respect for King Ferdinand did not deter him from speaking very plainly on occasion: "Certainly, I could desire that Your Majesty had more authority over your courtiers. I hope in God that soon we shall free Germany from servitude and captivity. Then we shall go on to rescue your Majesty from your vassals and counsellors and officials who covet monasteries, make themselves friars and then elect themselves abbots. But God will confound those who seek to conquer and corrupt the property of the Church."[2]

As he stood up to the King, so did the fearless Nicholas beard the Emperor in all his omnipotence after the great victory of Mühlberg. Seeking to ease the religious situation in his dominions until such time as a council more amenable to his wishes than Trent met on German soil, this devoutly Catholic monarch who ended his days in a monastery issued on June 30th, 1548, the famous eirenicon which, on account of its provisional character, came to be known as the *Interim*. In this he allowed the Protestant clergy to have wives and made it legal for them to adminis-

[1] *Bobadillæ Monumenta*, pp. 103–5, 109.
[2] *Bobadillæ Monumenta*, p. 107.

ter the Sacrament in two kinds. The results were most disappointing, for the Protestants did not need his concessions, and the Catholics rightly judged that by making them he was usurping the functions of the Pope. Without consulting St. Ignatius or pausing to consider the possible effect of his action on his brethren in the Emperor's dominions, Bobadilla hurled himself into the fray. At top speed he drafted two vigorous criticisms of the *Interim* which he then had the imprudence or effrontery to circulate among the Court officials, under the Emperor's nose. Of course Charles at once ordered him to quit the country, a sentence that by no means saddened its victim, as he had already been urging St. Ignatius to let him go elsewhere. "Just think what I have suffered from poverty," he said. "In seven years they have sent me only a hundred *scudi*, which were not enough for the expenses of my journeys, to say nothing of hiring a servant or of buying clothes and books. *Sit Deus' benedictus.*" To his patron, Cardinal Cervini, he wrote still more explicitly: "In the midst of all my anxieties and labours nobody spares me a thought. Any horse in a stable costs more than I do, yet there is care for the horse but none for me. *Sit Christus benedictus.* I shall not for that reason desist from the toils which duty imposes, and some fine day I shall give your reverend Lordship a good account of myself. You will see then that I have not wasted my time in Germany. With this a hearty farewell to you."[1] Bobadilla's action seriously embarrassed St. Ignatius, but the *enfant terrible* of the early Jesuits was not required to excogitate a suitable penance, nor addressed as though he had been a small boy caught robbing an orchard. The Saint sent him to work accord-

[1] *Bobadillæ Monumenta*, pp. 133, 135.

ing to his fancy in Naples, and when a college was opened there three years later appointed him its superintendent.

Another born cloud-gatherer was Father Simon Rodriguez, who, like Bobadilla, enjoyed the enervating patronage of royalty. There was nothing that King John of Portugal would not have done for his Simon, and so brethren to Simon sprang out of the soil like mushrooms in the morning. Twelve years after the foundation of the Society of Jesus, they numbered 318, or a good third of all the Jesuits then in existence.[1] As we know from the way in which they flocked enthusiastically to India, they were eager and fervent souls, but as we know, too, from the history of Antonio Gomes, some of them hardly understood the meaning of obedience. Though as early as 1545 St. Ignatius had heard disquieting reports about Father Simon's happy-go-lucky methods of government, he nevertheless confirmed him in his post the following year, with the title of Provincial. He had tried to bring the good man to Rome at the time to discuss the situation, but the King who doted on him interposed his veto. Four years went by during which Simon gave increasing proofs of waywardness and instability. In October, 1548, he conceived a sudden desire to go to India or Ethiopia, and expressed himself as ready to defy the King if he tried to prevent him. Then he as suddenly changed his mind and yearned for the forests of Brazil. But Brazil, too, faded into the light that gleams through palace windows, and Father Simon went on being the big man at court and the adored man at Coimbra. His Jesuit subjects loved

---

[1] M.H.S.J., *Epistolæ Mixtae*, vol. III, p. 25.

him intensely, partly because he deserved to be loved, and partly for the less noble reason that he allowed them to do pretty well as they listed. It all went to his head, never a very wise head, and he gradually came to think and act almost in independence of St. Ignatius. St. Francis Xavier longed to have his old friend Simon whose zeal he appreciated with him in India, but, knowing his man, warned him that this must be entirely at the discretion of Ignatius. "He is our Father," he wrote from Cochin, "and we must not budge without his counsel and command."[1]

Simon visited Rome early in 1551 and so plainly showed his contrariness that Ignatius felt it essential for the well-being of the whole Order to remove him from his post in Portugal. By this time even King John had come round to that opinion, which made the Saint's course easier. But he bore a peculiar affection to Rodriguez and was miserable at the prospect of wounding him. To ease the blow, he went the length of dividing the Spanish Jesuits, who were not nearly so numerous as the Portuguese ones, into two provinces, Castile and Aragon, and nominated Father Simon provincial of Aragon. Tact could scarcely have gone further, but it was wasted on the wayward man who sulked and kept to his room when the news reached him.[2] He made things as difficult as he could for his successor in Portugal, Father Diego Miron, and only left the country to assume his new post under pressure of a stringent order from Rome. Sad to say, he even stooped to the miserable revenge of spreading defamatory stories about St. Ignatius, as that he had used the wealth of the Duke

[1] M.H.S.J., *Monumenta Xaveriana*, vol. I, p. 373.
[2] M.H.S.J., *Epistolæ Mixtæ*, vol. III, p. 33.

of Gandia to enrich his own relatives.[1] Things became so bad that before the year 1552 was out the Portuguese Province of the Society of Jesus saw half its members renounce their allegiance and become enemies. It was in these tragic circumstances that St. Ignatius addressed to the Jesuits in Portugal what has since become one of the most celebrated documents in the literature of Catholic asceticism, the *Letter on Obedience*.[2]

At first Rodriguez displayed satisfaction with his new position as Provincial of Aragon. "I am very well contented in this country," he informed St. Ignatius from Barcelona in September, 1552, "and if I go on being so, I am thinking of asking your Reverence to let me stay here for good, unless you send me to Prester John. Not to Brazil, though, for I would not like to go there, the people being very barbarous and of small intelligence. All the same, if you order me, I am ready, so have no hesitation in telling me what to do, because though I may be a bad son, I am notwithstanding your son."[3] Barely a month had passed before he was writing again, this time a querulous, lachrymose letter full of his ailments, on account of which he demands permission to return to Portugal. Ignatius granted his request in a letter of charming friendliness and solicitude, bidding him "sepultar todo lo pasado," but before the leave arrived Simon had already set off on the return journey to his native land

---

[1] Letter of Father Luis Gonzales, M.H.S.J., *Epistolæ Mixtæ*, vol. II, p. 808. Poor Simon made a feeble attempt to stir up national animosities also by alleging that Ignatius, a Spaniard, was sending his riff-raff to Portugal and removing elsewhere that country's most valuable sons.

[2] The original Spanish text of the letter is given in *Monumenta Ignatiana: Epistolæ et instructiones*, vol. IV, pp. 669–81.

[3] *Epistolæ Broëti*, p. 636.

where for a few months he lived in state as the guest of
his great champion, the Duke of Aveiro. While there, he
received a long letter from Father Villanueva, the same
labourer's son whom ten years before he had blamed
St. Ignatius for receiving into the Order: "Very Reverend
Father in Christ. The grace and consolation of the Holy
Ghost be always in your soul. Amen. Our Lord knows
how I long to console your Reverence. For this reason I
left my house in Alcalá . . . and came so many leagues . . .
to give you the opinion which you asked from me. . . .
I came by Coimbra and met the brethren there, who, as
far as I can see, yield to nobody in the affectionate desire
and love which they entertain for the spiritual and corporal
welfare of your Reverence. They would seek these for you
even at the price of their blood, were it possible. And I
found the same dispositions among all our Fathers at
Lisbon. . . ." Villanueva next tells Father Simon the
rumours that are current about him. People declare him
to be self-willed and disobedient, ambitious and "unable
to live without the palaces and pomp of the world," one
who went seeking the views of physicians and theologians
as to whether he might not lawfully ignore his superior.
To kill all such rumours Father Villanueva can see only
one good weapon, that his Reverence should go to Rome
and throw himself at the feet of Ignatius.[1]

His presence in Portugal caused such widespread scandal
that in May, 1553, Ignatius felt obliged to summon him
peremptorily to Rome, but, as usual, sweetened the order
by a covering letter full of the most exquisite charity.
"As for your reputation," says the Saint, "I can only tell
you that I shall care for it no less jealously than you would

[1] Astrain, *Historia*, vol. I, pp. 619–21.

do yourself. . . . By ways which you would not now easily guess, you will be completely contented. Do trust me in this for the love of Christ Our Lord, and lovingly enter on this journey. Verily, if it be the pleasure of His Divine Majesty, I would be greatly consoled to see you again before I leave this world. . . . If I ought to have this longing to see all my brethren, much greater should it be for the first of them whom God Our Lord deigned to unite in our Society, and especially for you who know that I have always borne you a particular love in Our Lord. Do not be afraid of illness, because He Who is eternal salvation will give you all the health you need. . . . Again I say, you may trust me, for, whatever may be the case, I shall strive, as is only right, for your consolation and good reputation, to the divine glory." That letter was written on May 20th. The days, the weeks, nearly two months went by, while Ignatius watched the road from the "far country" for a sign of his prodigal. Then on July 12th he wrote again: "Master Simon, my son. Do trust me that your coming here will be a refreshment to my soul and to yours in Our Lord, and that, as you and I both desire, everything will end happily, to the greater glory of God. . . . Master Simon, put yourself at once on the road, and doubt not at all but that we here shall have cause to rejoice over your good health, corporal as well as spiritual. . . . Only trust me in everything, and keep your soul in great content in Our Lord." Truly might Ignatius have said, What more could I have done for my vine that I have not done? Before taking the final sad step which the good of the whole order demanded, he appealed to the King of Portugal to help him, but meantime the Provincial of the Jesuits there, appalled by the damage that the contumacy of Rodriguez was causing, held over Simon's head a threat of excommunication.[1]

That at last brought the unhappy man to his senses, whereupon his local superiors, once sure of his obedience, treated him with the greatest honour and consideration. He spent his last days in Portugal maligning them. In Rome where he arrived on November 11th, 1553, St. Ignatius received him with a charity that amazed some of the other Fathers. He gave him the best room in the house as a substitute for the fatted calf, and paid him every sort of delicate attention, desiring nothing more than to bury the unhappy past.[2] But Simon was more in the mood for post-mortems than for burials. He demanded a set trial, and in that too Ignatius humoured him, even allowing him the main say in the choice of his four judges. The process began with all solemnity on December 1st, two representatives of the Portuguese Province acting as accusers. Those men, Simon and the judges were all put on their oath to present and assess the evidence according to their consciences. The accusers drew up an indictment which they read, at the same time placing before the judges all the letters and reports received from their country during the previous years. Father Simon then laboured for twenty days on his defence which he likewise read. This was answered by the Portuguese Fathers, whereupon Rodriguez had the privilege of the last word. Before giving their judgment, the four Fathers charged with the task were ordered by Ignatius to spend three days in prayer and to offer Mass for the divine assistance in its execution,

[1] All religious orders have this power as a final resort with recalcitrant members.

[2] *Epistolæ Mixtæ*, vol. IV, p. 185.

and the others had to bind themselves to abide by the findings.

The judgment, pronounced on February 7th, 1544, went against Rodriguez on almost every count, and he was forthwith sentenced to write to the Duke of Aveiro and other notables, as well as to the Jesuits of Portugal, asking pardon for the disedification he had given, to keep away from Portugal for the rest of his life, to say daily a Pater Noster and Ave Maria in recognition of his faults, to offer Mass once a week for seven years on behalf of the Society of Jesus in Portugal, to take the discipline once a week for seven years, and for two years to speak only with persons named on a list presented to him.[1] Rodriguez made a great show of humility when the sentence was read to him, and even tried to kiss the feet of the judges, saying that they had not been nearly so severe as his behaviour merited. With his letters to Portugal went one from Ignatius declaring that, though "carisimo Hermano Maéstro Simon" had erred in some respects, it was always with a good intention, and that from his conversation and company he, Ignatius, "daily received more and more satisfaction." The letters brought his sentence to an end, as Ignatius immediately cancelled the rest of it, except the prohibition to return to Portugal.[2]

But this amnesty did not satisfy the disgruntled Simon, and soon he was intriguing behind the back of Ignatius to have his cause tried by a Papal tribunal. He said the most outrageous things about the judges whom he had himself chosen, and, desiring to retain the privileges of his religious status while setting aside its obligations,

[1] M.H.S.J., *Scripta de Sancto Ignatio*, vol. I, pp. 677-9.
[2] *L.c.*, p. 680.

endeavoured to extract from the Penitentiary a licence to lead a hermit's life, independent of his Jesuit superiors. In great distress Ignatius brought Salmeron and Bobadilla to Rome, hoping that those old friends might prevail where he had failed. At the cost of some scratches from his claws, they did so far succeed in pacifying Simon that he expressed a desire to go on pilgrimage to Jerusalem. Ignatius jumped at the forlorn hope and at once provided him with a companion and funds for the journey. But Simon hung about in Venice nearly a whole year, alleging that the sea was too dangerous with Turks and his health too insecure with indigestion for him to embark. Also his Jesuit companion, Sebastian, failed to give satisfaction. "It is I who must look after him instead of him looking after me," complained the hero. Ignatius wrote to the worried superior at Venice, instructing him to assure Simon of his enduring, undiminished affection, and to tell him that if he tired of being there he might care to spend the summer at Monreale in Sicily, "for its air the finest and for its situation the most beautiful of any place on earth where the Society has a residence."[1] At Christmas of 1554, the undecided pilgrim wrote to inform Ignatius that his expressions of affection were all very well, but that, as the proverb ran, love is proved by deeds, and he had yet to be convinced by such an argument.[2] What he really wanted was permission to return to the flesh-pots of Portugal, and that in the circumstances Ignatius could not conscientiously have granted. In the summer of 1555 he went off to live as a hermit at Bassano, where he had been taken seriously ill eighteen years earlier. It was

[1] M.H.S.J., *Scripta de Sancto Ignatio*, vol. I, pp. 699–700.
[2] M.H.S.J., *Epistolæ Broëti*, 652–5.

his Damascus road, for he remembered how on that occasion Ignatius who was suffering from fever at Vicenza had jumped up from the straw on which he lay and rushed the eighteen miles to Bassano to nurse him.[1] At that moment of recollected grace, Nadal providentially arrived on the scene and completed his conversion. "Father Nadal is here at this hermitage," he told St. Ignatius in September 1555, "and greatly gladdens me with his presence and his conversation. I am sorry for the trouble I have caused him, and also for those letters of mine which he tells me displeased your Reverence.... I desire to examine into the case no further than to confess my fault, and to express my readiness to obey and do whatever your Reverence may order me, and as you may order it. Since you are my Father and I am your son, I beg you for a plenary indulgence with remission of guilt and temporal punishment, so that the devil and many others may be frustrated by seeing that I am your son and you my father. From Rome, issue me a blessing so big that it may reach as far as these mountains of Bassano, whither, now exactly eighteen years ago, your Reverence came to see me when I was dying, as you know. As God on that occasion gave me the life of the body, so do you now, Father, bring it to pass with your prayers that He may give me the life of the soul."[2] Notwithstanding his many ailments about which he made such a song to the last, Father Simon lived yet another generation and did his Order and the Church good service. For twenty years he worked in Italy and Spain, and then, in 1574, was permitted to return home to Portugal where by his advice and example he helped greatly to put the Society of Jesus

[1] See above, p. 59.   [2] *Epistolæ Broëti*, pp. 663–4.

on its feet once more. He died in 1579, bequeathing to
that Society in atonement for the great trouble he had
brought upon it the precious gift of a little history of its
origins. Much may be forgiven him for the love which
shines in the simple story, written in suffering old age to
meet the desires of his superiors.

The case of poor Father Simon revealed the reserves of
tenderness and pity in the heart of St. Ignatius. Ignatius
was indeed far from being the cold monolith which he is
sometimes represented. He had like everybody else, sinners included, his limitations, and nursed a few pet aversions such as an absolute intolerance of avoidable dirt.
But in the realms of feeling, his difficulty was to restrain
rather than to stimulate the movements of his heart. He
used, say those who knew him, to be so thrilled by the
sight of any of his sons that he could not refrain from
laughing out loud in sheer happiness. "Perceiving, therefore, that this excessive laughter flowed from his interior
joy, he took to inflicting on himself daily as many lashes
of the discipline as times he had laughed. He did this that
he might moderate his laughter and rejoice those whom he
met by the merriment of his countenance alone. . . . He
radiated such kindness towards any passer on whom his
eyes rested that it seemed as though he wanted somehow
to hide him away in his heart."[1] A charming instance of
his consideration for the feelings of the newest novice was
given when the Fathers of the Roman College invited a
certain abbot of Ferrara to a domestic feast. This abbot
had three young relatives in the novitiate, and all three
were by Ignatius's orders issued a similar invitation. Then,
fearing that the other novices might be grieved at not

[1] M.H.S.J., *Scripta de Sancto Ignatio*, vol. I, pp. 490–1.

being invited also, the Saint caused them to be informed immediately that their turn would come the following day when they would dine in style at the Roman College.[1] He liked his young men to enjoy themselves and encouraged them to play two games, a sort of primitive croquet and a table-game resembling the modern squails. A hearty appetite in his men gave him "wonderful pleasure", and he used to invite Benedict Palmio to sit near him in the refectory because he was fat and a fine trencherman.[2]

Perhaps the most marked of the Saint's traits as a superior was his minute care for the health of all under him. When Lent came round he used to summon a doctor and have him examine every member of the community before he gave permission for fasting. Only those on a list prepared by the doctor received the permission, and Ignatius, they tell us, would spend hours going anxiously through the list to see whether some names ought not to be removed. He caused the same to be done in the Roman and German Colleges, and in general took such precautions for health that there was hardly ever a sick man in those establishments. "Whenever he noticed any of the younger brethren, particularly juniors or novices, looking paler or more listless than usual, he used diligently to inquire into the cause, prescribe them longer sleep, and instruct the minister of the house to have a particular care of them as regards their food and work. For the same reason, he laid a special injunction on ministers to treat those who were making the Spiritual Exercises as though they were invalids, and to refresh them with better food in the refectory."[3] Ignatius kept a wary eye

[1] *Scripta de Sancto Ignatio*, vol. I, pp. 492–3.
[2] *L.c.*, vol. I, pp. 240, 496.   [3] *L.c.*, vol. I, p. 495.

on his ministers and procurators to see that in their zeal for economy they did not stint the brethren. At one time in Rome the procurator was a capable, hard-headed, parsimonious Provençal named Ponce Cogordan. The Saint heard that Père Ponce had been out to dine with a cardinal who feasted him on lampreys. When he returned well pleased with life, Ignatius sent for him. "So you dine on lampreys, do you?" he said. "I have nothing against that, but you do not buy the brethren even decent sardines. Go now, and in future buy them lampreys." The idea struck horror to the thrifty soul of Ponce, who protested that there was not money enough for such an outrageous expense. Ignatius remained inexorable. "Find the money and buy the lampreys," he ordered, and left the man in financial misery for long enough to cure him of his stinginess.[1] He also kept the cook under observation, and, being something of an expert himself in preparing a savoury dish, laid down minute rules for his guidance. For instance, he prescribed that food when cooking must not be salted once and for all, lest too much or too little should go in. No: the operation had to be performed in three separate stages, half the salt when the water in which the meat was stewed began to bubble, a quarter a while later, and the remaining quarter at the end. Another rule of Ignatius required the minister or sub-minister of the house to visit the kitchen before dinner and supper and "taste two or three times the food in each pot to see whether it was well cooked and appetizing."[2] Heaven

[1] *Scripta de Sancto Ignatio*, vol. I, pp. 249, 497–8. Lest we be shocked, the good Father who tells the story comments that "the holy Father did not so act because he desired us to be fed on lampreys, but because he wanted to take a few chips off the Procurator and incline him to charity."

[2] *L.c.*, vol. I, pp. 498–9.

help them otherwise, for though the Saint himself lived
on next to nothing, as often as not "a small morsel of
bread" being his dinner, he was determined that the
natural virtues of the steaks and cabbages served to
the brethren should not be utterly corrupted in the
kitchen.

This preoccupation with the health of his sons showed
itself most beautifully in his absolute devotion to the sick.
For the sick he seemed prepared to do and dare anything,
even to dismiss from the Order valuable men who had
been found guilty of neglecting them. Each day, he used
to summon the buyer of the house and inquire whether
he had provided everything needed in the infirmary. If
money was lacking for this purpose, he gave orders that
various objects in the house were to be sold and the
proceeds used, and he also established a little lottery to
raise funds, in the following manner. Ignatius, the buyer
and the procurator each staked a blanket from his bed.
Then they had a draw, and the loser's blanket was promptly
sold. "In a word," says Ribadeneira who tells the story,
"there was not a mother who had so much care for her
children as our Blessed Father had for his sons, particularly
those who were delicate or infirm." When, in 1554,
Ignatius at the urgent entreaty of his doctor and his
brethren took a little rest from the labours of government
and resigned his burden temporarily to Nadal, he still
reserved one province for his exclusive oversight, the care
of the sick. The last of the rules which he composed as a
guide to infirmarians would considerably brighten our
modern nursing-homes if they adopted it: "Let him
diligently inquire from the sick man which members of
the community he likes best and would wish to have visit

254

him, and let him admit these only, and not any others, to cheer up his patient."[1]

The Saint's general dealings with those under him were marked by a delightful freedom and *bonhomie*. He used to tease and chaff them genially, and employ all sorts of little affectionate tricks to put them in good humour. On one occasion, portly young Benedict Palmio met an old lady as he was going to some church to preach and unblushingly invited her to come along if she wanted to hear a fine sermon. Ignatius laughed when told the story, and a little later gave its hero some commission or other to discharge. "Benedetto," he called after him, "if you perform this task well I shall myself bring another old lady to your next sermon."[2] A novice came to him one night to say that he desired to leave the Society. When asked for his reason he answered sulkily that it was because he, Father Ignatius, had declared him unfitted for the life. "No," answered Ignatius, "what I said to you was that if you did not wish to be obedient you were not suitable for us." They argued the whole night through till at last the novice, vanquished by kindness, fell on his knees and asked the Saint's pardon. "And now," said Ignatius, "what penance would you like?" to which the blushing novice replied, "Whatever penance pleases your Reverence." Ignatius then said: "Your penance will be not to be tempted any more, and I shall do penance for you every time I have a stomach-ache."[3] With another novice who wanted to go he spent two hours, trying to learn the cause of the young man's trouble. Suspecting that it had something to do with sins of the past which the poor fellow

---

[1] *Scripta de Sancto Ignatio*, vol. I, pp. 451–2, 500–1.
[2] *L.c.*, vol. I, p. 495.   [3] *L.c.*, vol. I, pp. 294–5.

feared to avow, Ignatius began to tell him part of his own history, including the evil things he had done, "to take away his confusion." The novice then blurted out his trouble, "a very little thing," and all was well. Parallel with his loving anxiety to dig out the roots of unhappiness went a most tender regard for the good repute of all his sons. Those who knew Ignatius well regarded it as extremely dangerous, as the equivalent of asking for a heavy penance, to utter the slightest criticism of other people in his hearing. He was most sensitive on the point, and himself so habitually put a good construction on the doings of others that the "interpretationes Patris" became a byword with the Roman Jesuits for lenient judgments. "He showed his love marvellously," says Ribadeneira, "by the way he used to cover up and bury in perpetual oblivion the faults of those who trustfully opened their hearts to him. . . . They could be sure that never in any word or deed of his, in his attitude towards them or in his heart, would there remain a trace or memory of those faults, no more than if he had never been told of them."[1]

Father Oliver Manare relates that while in the novitiate Ignatius used to invite him and the other young men individually to sit and chat with him in the garden, or at his private table, when he would peel an apple or a pear and present it to his guest of the moment. Years later the same Manare was sent by Ignatius to take charge of the college in Loreto. "I asked him," reports Father Oliver, "what rules I should observe, as but few of the rules of the Roman College would suit the circumstances of Loreto with its crowds of pilgrims, nor would it be possible to apply those of the professed house for the same

[1] *Scripta de Sancto Ignatio*, vol. I, p. 451.

reason. To this he replied: 'Oliver, do as you consider best, and as your spirit of fervour will teach you. Adapt the rules to the place as best you can.' When I inquired as to how I should distribute offices in my community, he answered again in a few words: 'Oliver, cut your coat according to your cloth, but tell me what you do and how you settle the question of the offices.' Once it happened that I acted contrary to an order which I had received from him by letter. I explained that I had done so only after imagining that he was present before my eyes and saying to me: Do as you propose, for were I with you that is what I would order. He wrote to tell me that I had been perfectly right. 'Man,' said he, 'assigns the office but God gives the discretion. I want you, for the rest, to act without any scruple, as you judge from the circumstances ought to be done, notwithstanding rules and ordinances.' "[1] To say the least, that is not the portrait of a dictator.

Another conspicuous trait in the character of Ignatius was an imperturbable trust in God. At a time when the Roman College possessed only a sort of rented bungalow and twenty-eight students, he ordered Father Manare to make the place ready for a hundred students. "Now," says Manare, "there was not a penny in the coffers of the College or the professed house at the time beyond five gold crowns. Even these, which Father Polanco, our treasurer, hoarded for building purposes, were under the legal weight. He wished to give them to me, saying that they were all he had in the world, but I was ashamed to take them. . . . We both set to work to obey our instructions, he by collecting funds, and I by borrowing whatever furniture and provisions I could for the College. Mean-

[1] *Scripta de Sancto Ignatio*, vol. I, p. 519.

time, our Blessed Father came along to see how the
College was being made ready for the future brethren,
and found a large dormitory full of beds, chairs and tables.
Taking stock of these, he turned to Father Polanco and
said: 'So, Master Polanco, *this* is where our brothers are
to lay their heads, is it? So they will be exposed to the
rigours of the coming winter, will they? . . . So they are
to live and work immediately under the tiles, are they?'
Father Polanco replied: 'But, Reverend Father, there is
no money, and we cannot borrow any more.' And then
he said: 'My Polanco, have another storey added, and do
not let the brethren sleep in this place. God will provide
for His servants.' . . . . Father Polanco obeyed, . . . and,
lo and behold, the following day when he was out trying
to borrow money or obtain a loan at interest from friends
and bankers, he met a certain Spanish archdeacon, well
known to me, who requested him to accept a sum of
five hundred gold pieces, to be paid back in instalments.
Then, on top of that, the procurator of the Order of St.
Jerome brought a much larger sum. . . . Not long afterwards, both loans were repaid out of alms given to us by
devout people, and so, as we felt certain, through the merits
and prayers of our Blessed Father, we discharged all our
debts and provided for every need of the moment."[1]
That story is typical of many that are told. One Christmas, there was so much debt and poverty at the German
College that the Rector, Père Guy Roillet, felt constrained to appeal to Ignatius for help, though he knew the
Saint to be equally insolvent at his own house. Having
heard the Rector's story, Ignatius asked him with a smile:
"Master Guido, will your young men have any celebra-

[1] *Scripta de Sancto Ignatio*, vol. I, pp. 521-2.

tion on Christmas Day?" Poor Guy replied: "Oh, Father, they will scarcely have a crust of bread to eat, for the baker refuses to send us any more." Then said Ignatius: "Be of good heart. God will come to your assistance. Meantime, buy some kids for the students' dinner, and something else as a treat for the young men, leaving God to act in the matter." And so, concludes the story, "he sent the man away comforted, with his head in the air, and, two days later, what should Pope Julius III do but make our Father a present of five hundred gold pieces, which he divided between the Roman and German Colleges."[1]

At this point it may be objected that the harsh letter which Ignatius addressed to Laynez ill agrees with the portrait of him as the loving, considerate father exhibited in the foregoing stories. Let us see how the difficulty appeared to Ribadeneira. "The love of our Father," he writes, "was neither soft nor remiss, but wide-awake and efficacious. It was both sweet and strong, tender as the love of a mother, and stern and bracing as the love of a father who strives that his sons may grow and progress daily in honour and virtue. . . . He helped each one to advance according to his strength and capacity. To those who were children in virtue he gave milk, but the more advanced received from him plain bread, and that he handed to them roughly. As for the perfect, he treated them with even greater rigour that they might run the more swiftly to their goal. Thus, he hardly ever said a kind word to Father Juan Polanco, who was his secretary and his hands and feet for nine years, . . . and sometimes admonished Father Nadal so severely that he wept many tears. . . . What most astonished me, however, was his

[1] *Scripta de Sancto Ignatio*, vol. I, pp. 521–3.

treatment of Father Laynez. Our Blessed Father assured
me that there was not a man in the Society to whom it
owed more than to Father Laynez, . . . and he had told
the Father himself that he designed him to be his successor.
Yet during the year before he died he showed so much
severity towards this Father that at times it made him
completely miserable. I had this from Father Laynez
himself. So miserable used he to feel, he said, that he
turned to Our Lord and asked: 'Lord, what have I done
against the Society that this Saint treats me as he does?'
The reason for it was that the Blessed Father desired to
make Father Laynez into a saint, and to inure him to hardship with a view to his being General, so that from what
he had himself gone through he might learn how to govern
others."[1] That was how the problem appeared to Ribadeneira who was intimate with all concerned, and nobody
can deny the reasonableness of his explanation. But, as a
modern writer has suggested, there may well have been
another motive at work also, and "this harshness towards
men in whom he had perfect confidence may have been
self-defence against a heart that feared its own tenderness
because his will was bent to keep faithful, even in the
affections, to a superhuman ideal that would not give up
to his old comrades what God wished given to all the
Company."[2]

[1] *Scripta de Sancto Ignatio*, vol. I, pp. 454-5.
[2] Van Dyke, *Ignatius Loyola*, pp. 349-50. It may be added that sometimes
the "old comrades" asked for the trouble that came on them by a too
obstinate adherence to their opinions. The severest reprehension which
Nadal received was due to his urging that, if not all Jesuits, at least those in
Spain should be given more than an hour for their prayer in the morning.
Ignatius, who was in bed ill at the time, knew well where his beloved
Vicar had imbibed this notion, knew in fact that some of the Spanish

For eighteen years Ignatius remained tied to his desk in Rome, hardly ever going beyond the walls of that Casa Professa whose poverty and discomfort we may guess at from the few narrow, low-ceilinged rooms of it still in existence. From those rooms he sent out thousand upon thousand of letters and instructions to guide or check or cheer his sons in their wanderings all over the world. One of the last things he did on earth was, as his Boswell, Gonzales, puts it, to "arrange Prester John's business," meaning, to organize a mission to Ethiopia at the desire of the Pope and the King of Portugal. So eager was he about this strange and hazardous undertaking that he made Father Gonzales himself call at the Portuguese embassy in Rome every third day for three months on end to keep the ambassador alive to its importance. He also addressed a long letter to the Emperor of Ethiopia, which is in the nature of a small treatise *De Primatu Romani Pontificis*.[1] Already in 1548 he had sent four of his sons to the Congo where they achieved nothing lasting except personal sanctification through suffering. The following year they entered Brazil and had such success that Ignatius was able in 1553 to establish a separate province of his Society in the country. Two years more and the first Jesuit to set foot in China, the first Christian missionary since the

---

Fathers would turn the Society of Jesus into a purely contemplative order if they had their way. He was extremely indignant, as well he might be, and, after telling Nadal just what he thought about him, ended the interview by saying: "A truly mortified man would find a quarter of an hour ample to unite himself with God in prayer, . . . and his quarter of an hour would be better than another man's two hours" (*Scripta*, I, 250, 278).

[1] The letter is published in the collection, *Cartas de San Ignacio* (6 vols., Madrid, 1874–89), vol. I, pp. 68–81.

Middle Ages, arrived at Canton. Ignatius had begun with ten companions and a little loaned house in Rome. At the time of his death his Order possessed a hundred houses and a thousand members divided into the eleven provinces of Italy, Sicily, Portugal, Aragon, Castile, Andalusia, Upper Germany, Lower Germany, France, India and Brazil. He could with a good heart sing his *Nunc Dimittis*.

In fifteen years the Saint had been seriously ill fifteen times. The doctors had in fact become so used to his being ill that they paid no special attention when they found him constantly prostrated during the spring and summer of the year 1556. There were other sick men in the house and to these Ignatius directed the worthy physicians. At eight in the evening of July 30th he called for his faithful Polanco, told him death was near, and asked him to go and obtain the benediction of the Pope, that same unfriendly Paul IV whose election, says Gonzalez, had caused him "to shake in every bone of his body."[1] The doctors came again, examined the invalid, and assured the troubled Secretary, who had urgent letters to write, that there was no immediate cause for anxiety. The visit to the Pope would be time enough next day. Polanco and another Father sat with Ignatius while he took his supper. Everything seemed normal, even the conversation, which turned on the purchase of a new house in Rome. Ignatius asked many questions about this affair. Then the Fathers retired, and when they next came to him at dawn of July 31st he was in his agony. Polanco rushed to the Vatican but was too late. Ignatius died in character, almost alone, without Viaticum or Extreme Unction,

[1] *Scripta de Sancto Ignatio*, vol. I, p. 198.

and his last coherent words were not of God, but of a prosaic matter of business. Death for such as he to whom God meant everything was just part of the day's work, on the same footing as the purchase of that new house in the Piazza Margana.

INDEX

al. = allusion to. *quo.* = quoted as authority or otherwise.
ef. – given as a reference. L. = St. Ignatius Loyola.
X. = St. Francis Xavier.